The Core Knowledge™ Series

Resource Books for Children from Year 1 to Year 6

PRAISE FOR THE CORE KNOWLEDGE UK SERIES

'The Core Knowledge Sequence puts knowledge back into primary education. Rich in content, challenging and with clear progression and continuity, it offers an excellent framework to ensure that pupils leave primary school with solid foundations for future learning.'

– Peter Lawson, Head of Primary, Grindon Hall Christian School

'Our recent Core Knowledge lessons on the Arctic have provided our children with a wealth of understanding. The lessons give children the facts, then we are free to create an enjoyable and engaging learning experience. Core Knowledge fuels our pupils' desire to learn more about the world around them.'

– Emma Greaves, Reception Teacher, West London Free School Primary

'It is vital that children receive a solid body of knowledge when they are at primary school because it allows them to expand their comprehension and access a wider field of learning. The Core Knowledge approach does just that. I cannot recommend it enough.'

– Matthew Laban, Headteacher, Kingfisher Hall Primary Academy, London

'Creativity, the arts and design are crucial to the environment and life of every citizen. They should occupy a central place in the curriculum at both primary and secondary levels. The new series published by Civitas, giving examples of how the arts and creativity can play a part in the education of every child, is a real contribution to the teaching of these subjects in all our schools.'

– Sir Nicholas Serota, Director of Tate

'A strong foundation of knowledge gained in the earliest years of education is such an important asset for children, sparking their imagination and providing the cornerstone for their future learning. I welcome the aim of the Core Knowledge books to do just that and I am sure that they will be valued by many parents wishing to help their children to do well at school.'

– Munira Mirza, Deputy Mayor for Education and Culture of London

What Your Year 1 Child Needs to Know

PREPARING YOUR CHILD
FOR A LIFETIME OF LEARNING

Edited by E. D. HIRSCH, JR. *and* JOHN HOLDREN

General Editors for the Civitas UK edition ANNALIESE BRIGGS *and* ROBERT WHELAN

Published by

Civitas
55 Tufton Street
London SW1P 3QL

Independence: Civitas: Institute for the Study of Civil Society is a registered educational charity (No. 1085494) and a company limited by guarantee (No. 04023541). Civitas is financed from a variety of private sources to avoid over-reliance on any single or small group of donors.

ISBN: 978-1-906837-23-5

Book Design and Layout by Luke Jefford

First edition published in the USA and Canada September 1997 as *What Your Kindergartner Needs to Know*
UK edition published June 2011
Reprinted April 2015

Printed in Great Britain by Berforts Group Ltd, Stevenage, SG1 2BH

Editor-in-Chief of the Core Knowledge Series: E. D. Hirsch, Jr.

Editor: John Holdren

Project Manager and Art Editor: Tricia Emlet

Writers: Curriculum Concepts, Inc. (Mathematics, Music); Diane Darst (Visual Arts); Susan Hitchcock (Science); John Holdren (Literature and Language, History and Geography, Music, Mathematics, Science); Mary Beth Klee (History and Geography)

Artists: Special thanks to Gail Mcintosh for exceptional colour art and other fine pieces; Leslie Evans, Julie Grant, Steve Henry, Bob Kirchman, Giuseppe Trogu

Art and Photo Research and Permissions: Martha Clay Sullivan

Research Assistant: Deborah Hyland

Acknowledgments: US edition

This series has depended on the help, advice, and encouragement of two thousand people. Some of those singled out here already know the depth of our gratitude; others may be surprised to find themselves thanked publicly for help they gave quietly and freely for the sake of the enterprise alone. To helpers named and unnamed we are deeply grateful.

Advisers on Multiculturalism: Minerva Allen, Barbara Carey, Frank de Varona, Mick Fedullo, Dorothy Fields, Elizabeth Fox-Genovese, Marcia Galli, Dan Garner, Henry Louis Gates, Cheryl Kulas, Joseph C. Miller, Gerry Raining Bird, Connie Rocha, Dorothy Small, Sharon Stewart-Peregoy, Sterling Stuckey, Marlene Walking Bear, Lucille Watahomigie, Ramona Wilson

Advisers on Elementary Education: Joseph Adelson, Isobel Beck, Paul Bell, Carl Bereiter, David Bjorklund, Constance Jones, Elizabeth LaFuze, J. P. Lutz, Sandra Scarr, Nancy Stein, Phyllis Wilkin

Advisers on Technical Subject Matter: Marilyn Jager Adams, Diane Alavi, Richard Anderson, Judith Birsh, Cheryl Cannard, Paul Gagnon, David Geary, Andrew Gleason, Blair Jones, Connie Juel, Eric Karell, Joseph Kerr, Mary Beth Klee, Michael Lynch, Joseph C. Miller, Jean Osborne, Margaret Redd, Nancy Royal, Mark Rush, Janet Smith, Ralph Smith, Nancy Strother, Nancy Summers, James Trefil, Nancy Wayne, Linda Williams, Lois Williams

Conferees, March 1990: Nola Bacci, Joan Baratz-Snowden, Thomasyne Beverley, Thomas Blackton, Angela Burkhalter, Monty Caldwell, Thomas M. Carroll, Laura Chapman, Carol Anne Collins, Lou Corsaro, Henry Cotton, Anne Coughlin, Arletta Dimberg, Debra P.

Douglas, Patricia Edwards, Janet Elenbogen, Mick Fedullo, Michele Fomalont, Mamon Gibson, Jean Haines, Barbara Hayes, Stephen Herzog, Helen Kelley, Brenda King, John King, Elizabeth LaFuze, Diana Lam, Nancy Lambert, Doris Langaster, Richard LaPointe, Lloyd Leverton, Madeline Long, Allen Luster, Joseph McGeehan, Janet McLin, Gloria McPhee, Marcia Mallard, William J. Maloney, Judith Matz, John Morabito, Robert Morrill, Roberta Morse, Karen Nathan, Dawn Nichols, Valeta Paige, Mary Perrin, Joseph Piazza, Jeanne Price, Marilyn Rauth, Judith Raybern, Mary Reese, Richard Rice, Wallace Saval, John Saxon, Jan Schwab, Ted Sharp, Diana Smith, Richard Smith, Trevanian Smith, Carol Stevens, Nancy Summers, Michael Terry, Robert Todd, Elois Veltman, Sharon Walker, Mary Ann Ward, Penny Williams, Charles Whiten, Clarke Worthington, Jane York

Schools: Special thanks to Three Oaks Elementary for piloting the original Core Knowledge Sequence in 1990. And thanks to the schools that have offered their advice and suggestions for improving the Core Knowledge Sequence, including (in alphabetical order): Academy Charter School (CO); Coleman Elementary (TX); Coral Reef Elementary (FL); Coronado Village Elementary (TX); Crooksville Elementary (OH); Crossroads Academy (NH); Gesher Jewish Day School (VA); Hawthorne Elementary (TX); Highland Heights Elementary (IN); Joella Good Elementary (FL); Mohegan School-CS 67 (NY); The Morse School (MA); Nichols Hills Elementary (OK); Ridge View Elementary (WA); R. N. Harris Elementary (NC); Southside Elementary (FL); Three Oaks Elementary (FL); Washington Core Knowledge School (CO). And to the many other schools teaching Core Knowledge – too many to name here, and some of whom we have yet to discover – our heartfelt thanks for 'sharing the knowledge'!

Benefactors: The Brown Foundation, The Challenge Foundation, Mrs. E. D. Hirsch, Sr., The Walton Family Foundation.

Our grateful acknowledgment to these persons does not imply that we have taken their (sometimes conflicting) advice in every case, or that each of them endorses all aspects of this project. Responsibility for final decisions must rest with the editors alone. Suggestions for improvements are very welcome, and we wish to thank in advance those who send advice for revising and improving this series.

Acknowledgements: UK edition

General Editors of the UK edition: Annaliese Briggs and Robert Whelan

Assistant Editor of the UK edition: Aoife O'Donnell

Editor and author of the British History and Geography section for the UK edition: Robert Whelan

Editor and author of the Visual Arts section for the UK edition: Jo Saxton

Design and typesetting of the UK edition: Luke Jefford

Owl illustrations: Mark Otton

Compiling the UK edition of a book that has already become an established classic in the USA has been both a privilege and a challenge. Our first thanks must go to E.D. Hirsh, Jr., Linda Bevilacqua and the team at the Core Knowledge Foundation for sharing with us the fruits of their labours over many years. Their co-operation at every stage of the process has been invaluable and has made our task much easier. We fully share their view that all children deserve access to a first-class education, and we hope that the Civitas edition of the Core Knowledge texts will do as much for children in the UK as the US edition has done for thousands of children in America and elsewhere.

Many people have helped us with both advice and practical assistance. Jason Stainer made important suggestions that helped to make the US Kindergarten English and maths suitable for Year 1 children in the UK. Jo Saxton wrote the Visual Arts chapter using paintings and sculptures that children can see in the UK, whilst following the US volume's approach. Chris McGovern, Sean Lang and Margaret Lenton offered valuable suggestions for British History. Jenny Grant advised us on the choice of songs and vocal exercises in the Music chapter and David Blackwell advised us on the accompanying lists of online resources. We were grateful for help and advice from Emma Mulvey, Rowena Gammon, Sonia Gomez, Anne Robertson, Sarah Knollys, Helen Powell and Irina Tyk. We were also grateful for support from Paula Rollo, Susan Porter and Michael McBrien at TASIS: The American School in England. Marilyn Brocklehurst of the Norfolk Children's Book Centre and Adam Lancaster at the Federation of Children's Book Groups shared their passion for good children's books by advising us on the lists of recommended resources. We are indebted to Nick Oulton and his team at Galore Park Publishing for help with the illustrations. We were privileged to be able to use the fine illustrations prepared for the US edition by Gail McIntosh, Bob Kirchman and Steve Henry, who also created new work for the UK edition. Finally, our thanks are due to Anastasia de Waal, head of education at Civitas, and our colleagues in the Civitas office who contributed so much time and so many suggestions to develop the concept and fine-tune the text.

A Note to Teachers

Throughout the book, we have addressed the suggested activities and explanations to 'parents', since you as teachers know your students and will have ideas about how to use the content of this book in relation to the lessons and activities you plan. To discuss using Core Knowledge materials in your school, please contact Civitas at 55 Tufton Street, London SW1P 3QL, 020 7799 6677.

Email: coreknowledge@civitas.org.uk.

Website: www.coreknowledge.org.uk

About the Authors

E.D. Hirsch, Jr. is a professor at the University of Virginia and the author of *The Schools We Need* and the bestselling *Cultural Literacy* and *The Dictionary of Cultural Literacy*. He and his wife, Polly, live in Charlottesville, Virginia, where they raised their three children.

John Holdren has been a teacher of writing and literature at the University of Virginia and Harvard University, and is now Director of Research and Communications at the Core Knowledge Foundation. He lives with his wife and two daughters in Greenwood, Virginia.

Contents

I. Language and Literature

II. History and Geography

III. Visual Arts

IV. Music

V. Mathematics

VI. Science

Foreword to the UK Edition of the Core Knowledge Series

This is the first in a series of books for parents who want to help their children do well at school. It describes what every child should aim to have learnt by the end of the school year. It is not a description of everything that could be known but rather a guide to the knowledge that children will need to advance to the next stage of their education. Nor is it primarily a textbook, although it could be used as such – along with other teaching resources – if schools wish.

The Core Knowledge series gives parents the tools to judge how effectively their children are being taught. And it provides teachers with clear aims that can be shared with parents, thereby enlisting them in the common cause of getting the best from every child.

Why publish a British version of a book originally designed for American children? For the last 50 years in both Britain and America there has been no consensus about how and what children should be taught. Sometimes knowledge was dismissed as mere 'rote learning', which was contrasted unfavourably with 'critical thinking skills'. Others argued that education should be 'child centred' not 'subject centred'. Professor Hirsch, who inspired the Core Knowledge series, was among the first to see that the retreat from knowledge was misguided. Above all, he showed that to compare 'knowledge' with 'thinking skills' was to make a false contrast. They are not mutually exclusive alternatives. Thinking skills can be 'knowledge-rich' or 'knowledge-lite'. The purpose of a good education is to teach children how to think clearly – to see through dubious reasoning, to avoid being conned, to learn how to question their own assumptions, to discover how to be objective, or to argue a case with clarity. Knowledge does not get in the way of reasoning: it's what we reason with.

The Core Knowledge approach has six main strengths.

● It helps parents to bring out the best in their children. It provides a guide to what young people should be learning and helps parents decide on the school best suited to their child.

- It helps teachers. By providing clear expectations that are shared with parents teachers are better able to benefit every child. Schools are always at their best when parents and teachers work together.

- It helps children to learn on their own initiative. The books are written in language suitable for each year group, so that children can read alone or with their parents.

- It provides more equal opportunities for everyone. Some children do not receive effective support at home, perhaps because some of us did not ourselves get the best education. A good school can do much to make up for lost ground and the Core Knowledge curriculum is designed for this very task. The books describe what every child can learn if given the chance. What's more, many parents find that they learn as much as their children!

- It encourages social cohesion. Britain today has more cultures, ethnic groups and religions than 50 years ago. If we all share in a common stock of knowledge, social solidarity based on mutual respect for our legitimate differences is more likely.

- It strengthens democracy. A free and democratic society depends on the mass of people being well-informed. We often say that modern societies are 'knowledge based'. It's true. People who do not share in the knowledge that is regularly used by television news programmes or in our newspapers are at risk of being misled.

We are keen to work with teachers who share our ideals and who hope to play a leading part in developing this new curriculum in Britain. In co-operation with teachers, we will be evolving model lesson plans and resource guides, and if any teachers would like their school to be one of the pioneers, please contact Civitas at coreknowledge@civitas.org.uk

David G. Green
Director of Civitas

Introduction to the UK Edition of the Core Knowledge Curriculum for Year 1

The concerns which led Professor Hirsch and others to set up the Core Knowledge Foundation in the USA in 1986 are shared by many in Britain. Civitas has acquired direct experience of the problem through its network of supplementary schools. Beginning with a group of children in the East End of London in 2005, Civitas now runs 20 supplementary schools for over 500 children in different parts of the country. The children attend once a week, either on Saturdays or after school, for help with English and maths. The children are, for the most part, attending full-time schools in areas with higher-than-average indicators of social deprivation, where academic outcomes are not the best in the country. Some children join supplementary schools at the age of seven, eight or even older, unable to read properly and unable to handle simple addition and subtraction. Our approach in the Civitas schools has been to employ dedicated teachers with high expectations and a commitment to providing solid learning foundations. Children are assessed annually and it has become quite usual to see them make two or three years of progress in their reading and maths ages over the course of one calendar year.

The concepts that Professor Hirsch mentions in his General Introduction such as 'critical thinking' and 'learning to learn' have been just as prevalent in the UK's schools, where the curriculum has become less knowledge-based and more focused on attaining 'skills', as if the two things can be separated. The acquisition of skills requires knowledge, and a knowledge-poor curriculum is one that condemns pupils – especially children from less advantaged backgrounds – to remain outside the mainstream of attainment and fulfilment. The Core Knowledge Foundation believes that all children should be able to unlock the library of the world's literature; to comprehend the world around them; to understand where they stand (literally) on the globe; and to realise the heritage that the history of their country has bestowed on them.

Making a reality of this ideal has been the outstanding achievement of the Core Knowledge Foundation in the hundreds of schools across the USA where its curriculum is being taught, and it is why we so admire the work of Professor Hirsch and his colleagues at the Core Knowledge Foundation.

As Professor Hirsch explains in his General Introduction, the project operates within the overarching framework of the Core Knowledge Sequence, produced by dozens of educators over a gestational period of several years. To bring this sequence into the classroom or the home, the Sequence is fleshed out by a book for each year group. We at Civitas were honoured and delighted to be entrusted by the Core Knowledge Foundation with the task of adapting the books for teachers, parents and pupils in the UK. This has entailed some changes to reflect differences between our cultures, for example, replacing two uniquely American Tall Tales from the US edition – Johnny Appleseed and Casey Jones – with selections that are more relevant to British students – St. George and the Dragon and King Arthur. For the most part, the US text has been left intact – because knowledge is universal! The most significant change is the replacement of American history and geography with British history and geography; American history will be incorporated into the world history chapters in the UK edition. In addition, we have revised resource references for books and other educational materials so that they include titles and publications readily available in the UK.

We share the view of the Core Knowledge Foundation that knowledge is best conveyed through subjects, and so we have followed their division of each book into chapters covering Language and Literature, History and Geography, Visual Arts, Music, Mathematics and Science. We will be producing volumes for each year group up to Year 6, and these will tie in with our UK version of the Core Knowledge Sequence that can be accessed online at: www.coreknowledge.org.uk

As Professor Hirsch explains, the first book in the series, *What Your First Grader Needs to Know*, was published in 1991. In 1997, *What Your Kindergartner Needs to Know* was published for the benefit of the preceding year group. The present volume, *What Your Year 1 Child Needs to Know*, represents, with small alterations, the text of *What Your Kindergartner Needs to Know*. In the USA children start full-time education in most states at Kindergarten when they are five rising six, whereas in the UK children of that age would be starting in Year 1. After consulting widely with teachers and educationists, we took the view that the material was largely appropriate for Year 1 students, although they will have already been in school for a year, given that UK schools now start their intake with Reception when children are four rising five.

To quote Professor Hirsch: share the knowledge!

Robert Whelan
General Editor, Civitas Core Knowledge Project

General Introduction to the Core Knowledge Series

I. WHAT IS YOUR CHILD LEARNING IN SCHOOL?

A parent of identical twins sent me a letter in which she expressed concern that her children, who are in the same grade in the same school, are being taught completely different things. How can this be? Because they are in different classrooms; because the teachers in these classrooms have only the vaguest guidelines to follow; in short, because the school, like many in the United States, lacks a definite, specific curriculum.

Many parents would be surprised if they were to examine the curriculum of their child's elementary school. Ask to see your school's curriculum. Does it spell out, in clear and concrete terms, a core of specific content and skills all children at a particular grade level are expected to learn by the end of the school year?

Many curricula speak in general terms of vaguely defined skills, processes and attitudes, often in an abstract, pseudo-technical language that calls, for example, for children to 'analyze patterns and data', or 'investigate the structure and dynamics of living systems', or 'work cooperatively in a group'. Such vagueness evades the central question: what is your child learning in school? It places unreasonable demands upon teachers, and often results in years of schooling marred by repetitions and gaps. Yet another unit on dinosaurs or 'pioneer days.' *Charlotte's Web* for the third time. 'You've never heard of the Bill of Rights?' 'You've never been taught how to add two fractions with unlike denominators?'

When identical twins in two classrooms of the same school have few academic experiences in common, that is cause for concern. When teachers in that school do not know what children in other classrooms are learning on the same grade level, much less in earlier and later grades, they cannot reliably predict that children will come prepared with a shared core of knowledge and skills. For an elementary school to be successful, teachers need a common vision of what they want their students to know and be able to do. They need to have *clear, specific learning goals*, as well as the sense of mutual accountability that comes from shared commitment to helping all children achieve those goals. Lacking both specific goals and mutual accountability, too many schools exist in a state of curricular incoherence, one result of which is that they fall far short of developing the full potential of our children. To address this problem, I started the non-profit Core Knowledge Foundation in 1986. This book and its companion volumes in the Core

Knowledge Series are designed to give parents, teachers – and through them, children – a guide to clearly defined learning goals in the form of a carefully sequenced body of knowledge, based upon the specific content guidelines developed by the Core Knowledge Foundation (see below, 'The Consensus Behind the Core Knowledge Sequence').

Core Knowledge is an attempt to define, in a coherent and sequential way, a body of widely used knowledge taken for granted by competent writers and speakers in the United States. Because this knowledge is taken for granted rather than being explained when it is used, it forms a necessary foundation for the higher-order reading, writing and thinking skills that children need for academic and vocational success. The universal attainment of such knowledge should be a central aim of curricula in our elementary schools, just as it is currently the aim in all world-class educational systems.

For reasons explained in the next section, making sure that all young children in the United States possess a core of shared knowledge is a necessary step in developing a first-rate educational system.

II. WHY CORE KNOWLEDGE IS NEEDED

Learning builds on learning: children (and adults) gain new knowledge only by building on what they already know. It is essential to begin building solid foundations of knowledge in the early grades when children are most receptive because, for the vast majority of children, academic deficiencies from the first six grades can *permanently* impair the success of later learning. Poor performance of American students in middle and high school can be traced to shortcomings inherited from elementary schools that have not imparted to children the knowledge and skills they need for further learning.

All of the highest-achieving and most egalitarian elementary school systems in the world (such as those in Sweden, France and Japan) teach their children a specific core of knowledge in each of the first six grades, thus enabling all children to enter each new grade with a secure foundation for further learning. It is time American schools did so as well, for the following reasons:

(1) Commonly shared knowledge makes schooling more effective.

We know that the one-on-one tutorial is the most effective form of schooling, in part because a parent or teacher can provide tailor-made instruction for the individual child. But in a non-tutorial situation – in, for example, a typical classroom with twenty-five or more students – the instructor cannot effectively impart new knowledge to all the students unless each one shares the background knowledge that the lesson is being built upon.

Consider this scenario: in third grade, Ms. Franklin is about to begin a unit on early explorers – Columbus, Magellan and others. In her class she has some students who were in Mr. Washington's second-grade class last year and some students who were in Ms. Johnson's second-grade class. She also has a few students who have moved in from other towns. As Ms. Franklin begins the unit on explorers, she asks the children to look at a globe and use their fingers to trace a route across the Atlantic Ocean from Europe to North America. The students who had Mr. Washington look blankly at her: they didn't learn that last year. The students who had Ms. Johnson, however, eagerly point to the proper places on the globe, while two of the students who came from other towns pipe up and say, 'Columbus and Magellan again? We did that last year.'

When all the students in a class *do* share the relevant background knowledge, a classroom can begin to approach the effectiveness of a tutorial. Even when some children in a class do not have elements of the knowledge they were supposed to acquire in previous grades, the existence of a specifically defined core makes it possible for the teacher or parent to identify and fill the gaps, thus giving all students a chance to fulfill their potential in later grades.

(2) Commonly shared knowledge makes schooling more fair and democratic.

When all the children who enter a grade can be assumed to share some of the same building blocks of knowledge, and when the teacher knows exactly what those building blocks are, then all the students are empowered to learn. In our current system, children from disadvantaged backgrounds too often suffer from unmerited low expectations that translate into watered-down curricula. But if we specify the core of knowledge that all children should share, then we can guarantee equal access to that knowledge and compensate for the academic advantages some students are offered at home. In a Core Knowledge school, *all* children enjoy the benefits of important, challenging knowledge that will provide the foundation for successful later learning.

(3) Commonly shared knowledge helps create cooperation and solidarity in our schools and nation.

Diversity is a hallmark and strength of our nation. American classrooms are usually made up of students from a variety of cultural backgrounds, and those different cultures should be honoured by all students. At the same time, education should create a school-based culture that is common and welcoming to all because it includes knowledge of many cultures and gives all students, no matter what their background, a common foundation for understanding our cultural diversity.

In the next section, I will describe the steps taken by the Core Knowledge Foundation to develop a model of the commonly shared knowledge our children need (which forms the basis for this series of books).

III. THE CONSENSUS BEHIND THE CORE KNOWLEDGE SEQUENCE

The content in this and other volumes in the Core Knowledge Series is based on a document called the *Core Knowledge Sequence*, a grade-by-grade sequence of specific content guidelines in history, geography, mathematics, science, language arts and fine arts. The *Sequence* is not meant to outline the whole of the school curriculum; rather, it offers specific guidelines to knowledge that can reasonably be expected to make up about *half* of any school's curriculum, thus leaving ample room for local requirements and emphases. Teaching a common core of knowledge, such as that articulated in the Core Knowledge Sequence, is compatible with a variety of instructional methods and additional subject matters.

The *Core Knowledge Sequence* is the result of a long process of research and consensus building undertaken by the Core Knowledge Foundation. Here is how we achieved the consensus behind the *Core Knowledge Sequence*.

First we analysed the many reports issued by state departments of education and by professional organisations – such as the National Council of Teachers of Mathematics and the American Association for the Advancement of Science – that recommend general outcomes for elementary and secondary education. We also tabulated the knowledge and skills through grade six specified in the successful educational systems of several other countries, including France, Japan, Sweden and West Germany.

In addition, we formed an advisory board on multiculturalism that proposed a specific knowledge of diverse cultural traditions that American children should all share as part of their school-based common culture. We sent the resulting materials to three independent groups of teachers, scholars and scientists around the country, asking them to create a master list of the knowledge children should have by the end of grade six. About 150 teachers (including college professors, scientists, and administrators) were involved in this initial step.

These items were amalgamated into a master plan, and further groups of teachers and specialists were asked to agree on a grade-by-grade sequence of the items. That sequence was then sent to some one hundred educators and specialists who participated in a national conference that was called to hammer out a working agreement on an appropriate core of knowledge for the first six grades.

This important meeting took place in March 1990. The conferees were elementary school teachers, curriculum specialists, scientists, science writers, officers of national organisations, representatives of ethnic groups, district superintendents and school principals from across the country. A total of twenty-four working groups decided on revisions in the *Core Knowledge Sequence*. The resulting provisional *Sequence* was further fine-tuned during a year of implementation at a pioneering school, Three Oaks Elementary in Lee County, Florida.

In only a few years, many more schools – urban and rural, rich and poor, public and private – joined in the effort to teach Core Knowledge. Based largely on suggestions from these schools, the *Core Knowledge Sequence* was revised in 1995: separate guidelines were added for kindergarten, and a few topics in other grades were added, omitted, or moved from one grade to another, in order to create an even more coherent sequence for learning. Revised editions of the books in the Core Knowledge Series reflect the revisions in the *Sequence*. Based on the principle of learning from experience, the Core Knowledge Foundation continues to work with schools and advisors to 'fine-tune' the Sequence, and is also conducting research that will lead to the publication of guidelines for grades seven and eight, as well as for preschool. (*The UK Core Knowledge Sequence* can be downloaded from the Civitas Core Knowledge website www.coreknowldge.org.uk.)

IV. THE NATURE OF THIS SERIES

The books in this series are designed to give a convenient and engaging introduction to the knowledge specified in the *Core Knowledge Sequence*. These are resource books, addressed primarily to parents, but which we hope will be useful tools for both parents and teachers. These books are not intended to replace the local curriculum or school textbooks, but rather to serve as aids to help children gain some of the important knowledge they will need to make progress in school and be effective in society.

Although we have made these books as accessible and useful as we can, parents and teachers should understand that they are not the only means by which the *Core Knowledge Sequence* can be imparted. The books represent a single version of the possibilities inherent in the *Sequence*, and a first step in the Core Knowledge reform effort. We hope that publishers will be stimulated to offer educational videos, computer software, games, alternative books and other imaginative vehicles based on the *Core Knowledge Sequence*.

These books are not textbooks or workbooks, though when appropriate they do suggest a variety of activities you can do with your child. In these books, we address your child directly, and occasionally ask questions for him or her to think about. The earliest books in the series are intended to be read aloud to children. Even as children become able to read the books on their own, we encourage parents to help their children read more actively by reading along with them and talking about what they are reading. You and your child can read the sections of this book in any order, depending on your child's interests or depending on the topics your child is studying in school, which this book may sometimes complement or reinforce. You can skip from section to section and re-read as much as your child likes.

We encourage you to think of this book as a guidebook that opens the way to many paths you and your child can explore. These paths may lead to the library, to many other good books, and, if possible, to plays, museums, concerts and other opportunities for knowledge and enrichment. In short, this guidebook recommends places to visit and describes what is important in those places, but only you and your child can make the actual visit, travel the streets and climb the steps.

V. WHAT YOU CAN DO TO HELP IMPROVE EDUCATION

The first step for parents and teachers who are committed to reform is to be sceptical about oversimplified slogans like 'critical thinking' and 'learning to learn'. Such slogans are everywhere and, unfortunately for our schools, their partial insights have been elevated to the level of universal truths. For example: 'What students learn is not important; rather, we must teach students to learn *how* to learn.' 'The child, not the academic subject, is the true focus of education.' 'Do not impose knowledge on children before they are developmentally ready to receive it.' 'Do not bog children down in mere facts, but rather, teach critical-thinking skills.' Who has not heard these sentiments, so admirable and humane, and – up to a point – so true? But these positive sentiments in favor of 'thinking skills' and 'higher understanding' have been turned into negative sentiments against the teaching of important knowledge. Those who have entered the teaching profession over the past forty years have been taught to scorn important knowledge as 'mere facts', and to see the imparting of this knowledge as somehow injurious to children. Thus it has come about that many educators, armed with partially true slogans, have seemingly taken leave of common sense.

Many parents and teachers have come to the conclusion that elementary education must strike a better balance between the development of the 'whole child' and the more limited but fundamental duty of the school to ensure that all children master a core of knowledge and skills essential to their competence as learners in later grades. But these parents and teachers cannot act on their convictions without access to an agreed upon, concrete sequence of knowledge. Our main motivation in developing the *Core Knowledge Sequence* and this book series has been to give parents and teachers something concrete to work with.

It has been encouraging to see how many teachers, since the first volume in this series was published, have responded to the Core Knowledge reform effort.

Parents and teachers are urged to join in a grassroots effort to strengthen our elementary schools. The place to start is in your own school and district. Insist that your school clearly state the core of *specific* knowledge and skills that each child in a grade must learn. Whether your school's core corresponds exactly to the Core Knowledge model is less important than the existence of some core – which, we hope, will be as solid, coherent, and challenging as the *Core Knowledge Sequence* has proven to be. Inform members of your community about the need for such a specific curriculum, and help make sure that the people who are elected or appointed to your local school board are independent minded people who will insist that our children have the benefit of a solid, specific, world class curriculum in each grade.

Share the knowledge!

E. D. Hirsch, Jr.
Charlottesville, Virginia

Language
and Literature

Reading, Writing and Your Year 1 Child

PARENTS: Before we present a selection of poems and stories for your child, we want to address you directly. This section, Reading, Writing and Your Year 1 Child, is intended to help you understand how children are – or should be – taught to read and write in a good Year 1 classroom, and to suggest a few ways that you can help at home.

Teaching Children to Read: The Need for a Balanced Approach

In Key Stage 1, schools must attend, first and foremost, to the crucial mission of early education: teaching children to read. To emphasise reading is not to suggest that the other two R's – 'riting and 'rithmetic – are any less important, only to distinguish reading as, in many ways, the skill of skills, the critical ability required for most other learning.

Everyone agrees that children should learn to read. But, as suggested by the subtitle of a classic study of the teaching of reading – Jeanne Chall's *Learning to Read: The Great Debate* – not everyone agrees about how to achieve that goal. Many studies have demonstrated, however, that while fashions come and go in education, pulling schools toward one extreme or another, there is a reasonable middle ground that is best for children.[1]

This middle ground balances two approaches that some educators, who advocate the use of either one approach or the other, mistakenly see as mutually exclusive. The first approach emphasises the systematic teaching of the 'nuts and bolts' of written language: phonics and decoding skills (turning written letters into spoken sounds), spelling, handwriting, punctuation, grammar, vocabulary, sentence structure, paragraph form, and other rules and conventions. The second approach emphasises the need for children to be nourished on a rich diet of poetry, fiction, and non-fiction. It focuses attention on the meanings and messages conveyed by written words, and insists that children be given frequent opportunities to use language in creative and expressive ways.

Schools need to embrace *both* of these approaches. It is important to pay attention to the 'nuts and bolts': educators need to take steps to balance a worthwhile emphasis on literature and creative expression with an equally necessary emphasis on the basic how-to skills of reading and writing.

---

[1] See, for example, Marilyn Jager Adams, *Beginning to Read: Thinking and Learning About Print* (Cambridge: MIT Press, 1990). For a discussion of the debate in the UK see Melanie Phillips, *All Must Have Prizes* (Little, Brown and Company, 1996).

While parents can support a child's growth as a reader and a writer, especially by reading aloud regularly at home, schools, not parents, are responsible for teaching children to read and write. We will now discuss what it means to learn to read and write, as well as appropriate goals for reading and writing in Year 1.

Learning to Read and Write

To learn to read is to learn to understand and use our language, specifically our written language. Learning to read is not like learning to speak. When children learn to talk, it all seems to happen so *naturally*. With apparently little explicit instruction, children learn – just by hearing others talk – to understand the meaning of the sounds communicated to them: 'Time to brush your teeth.' 'Look at the butterfly!' 'I love you.' They learn to make specific sounds that convey certain meanings: 'Pretty!' 'I'm thirsty.' 'Can we go to the park today?'

While speech seems to come naturally, reading is a very different story. It is not enough just to see or hear others reading. Learning to read takes effort and instruction, because reading is not a natural process. While children do have a natural hunger to understand the meanings and messages conveyed by written words, our written language is not a natural thing – it is an artificial code. There is no natural reason why when you see this mark – A – you should hear in your mind a sound that rhymes with 'day'. But you do, because you have learned the code. A few children seem to figure out this code for themselves, but most children need organised, systematic, direct instruction in how to decode the words on the page, that is, to turn the written symbols, the letters, into the speech sounds they represent.

All codes follow certain rules or conventions. In the code of written English, individual letters represent certain sounds. The letter 't' makes the sound heard at the beginning of 'turtle', the letter 'm' makes the sound heard at the beginning of 'mitten'. Groups of letters can be combined in particular ways to make other sounds. The letters 'ea' can make the sound heard in 'team' and 'each'. Letter-sound patterns written in a precise left-to-right order make words: 'team' means something different from 'meat'.

The key to helping children unlock the code of our written language is to help them understand the relationships between individual letters, and combinations of letters, and the sounds they make. It is true that sometimes these relationships seem odd: consider, for example, the different sounds of the letters 'ough' in 'though' and 'enough'. Despite these occasional oddities, there is a logic to the written English alphabet: its basic symbols, the letters, represent the basic speech sounds, or 'phonemes', of our spoken language.

The relationships between letters and sounds exhibit many regular patterns, as in, for example, 'cat', 'hat', 'sat', 'mat', 'fat', 'rat'.

So, part of learning to read means learning the predictable letter-sound patterns in written words. Learning these letter-sound patterns enables a child who confronts a page of print to decode the written words into the sounds of the spoken language that they represent. The other side of the coin is learning the basic skills of writing, which enable a child who faces a blank page to encode the sounds of spoken language by putting on paper the corresponding written letters to form words, and by following other conventions of writing (such as capitalisation and punctuation) that allow us to get across our meanings, even when the person to whom we are communicating is not present before us.

All of this talk about decoding and encoding may sound very mechanical and a little intimidating. It should be kept in mind that instruction in decoding and encoding is all in the service of meaning and understanding. If children are to communicate their ideas, thoughts, and desires in writing, as well as to understand what others are saying in print – whether it's a traffic sign, a film poster, a letter from a relative, or a story by A.A. Milne, Roald Dahl or Dr. Seuss – then they need to have the tools to encode and decode written English.

A Goal for Year 1

Children will have begun the process of learning to read in, or even before, their Reception year. Some children learn to read and write more readily than others. This is to be expected, since prior to Year 1, children have had different degrees of exposure to language and literature. Some have rarely seen a book. Others know the alphabet, have been read to nightly, and play language games on home computers. Yet, even given the best opportunities, some children will not learn to read and write as easily as others. Parents should not get anxious about who reads 'first'. Learning to read is not a race: no medals are given to the earliest reader.

Regardless of precisely when a child starts to read and write, all children need early instruction, and some may need extra guidance. Part of what a good Year 1 programme does is to provide challenging tasks for advanced students as well as extra practice and assistance for the children who need it. If a child is having difficulty, a school should not rationalise his difficulty by saying that the child is 'not developmentally ready'. You do not wait for readiness to happen. Rather, the child who is less ready should be given appropriate preliminary experiences to help him benefit from formal reading instruction, followed up by even more support, encouragement, and practice in the areas posing difficulty.

In reading and writing, a reasonable goal for Year 1 is to have *all children beginning to read and write on their own by the end of Year 1*. To achieve that goal, schools need to take a balanced approach that emphasises both meaning and decoding. A good Year 1 programme motivates children by offering them many occasions to communicate in speech and writing, and by giving them many opportunities to hear meaningful and well-told literature, including poetry, fiction, and non-fiction. Such literature gives children insight into a world of meaning expressed in words which they may not be able to read on their own but which they understand when the words are read aloud and discussed by an adult.

But for children to learn to read, it's not enough just to have good books read aloud to them. Listening to books does help children acquire a sense of what makes up a story, and it motivates them to want to read. But it will not teach them how to read the words on the page.

If children are to gain access on their own to the world of meaning, they must first be given the keys. Schools can give them these keys by providing explicit and systematic instruction in decoding written language. Children need repeated practice in working with letters and sounds in order to develop a good initial understanding of how language works. This does not mean mindless drill; rather, it means providing repeated and varied opportunities for children to work and play with letters and sounds.

What Does a Good Year 1 Programme Do?

Here are some things a good Year 1 programme does to help children meet the goal of beginning to read and write on their own.

- A good programme helps children develop their oral language, including speaking and listening. Children are asked to talk about books that have been read to them, to ask and answer questions, and sometimes to retell or summarise the story.

- A good programme provides a classroom environment in which children are surrounded by written language that is meaningful to them, such as posters with the children's names and birthdays, name labels on desks or cupboards, and word labels on objects in the classroom ('door', 'blackboard', 'map', etc.). Children also have their attention drawn to familiar uses of written language in everyday life, such as signs, recipes, invitations and announcements of upcoming events.

- A good programme builds on children's knowledge of the alphabet that has begun in Reception. Most children should already recognise and name the lower-case letters of the alphabet. In Year 1 they need to become equally familiar with all uppercase letters. A good Year 1 programme provides regular handwriting practice. Through this, children refine letter size and legibility and learn to make appropriate use of the space on a page to present written information. (See the handwriting charts on pages 7–8.)

● A good programme explicitly and systematically develops children's phonemic awareness, that is, the understanding that the sound of a word can be thought of as a string of smaller, individual sounds. In its simplest form this means saying and hearing the word 'mat' as a single sound; but when saying it slowly, you can recognise three separate sounds: mmm-aaa-ttt. Most children will have learnt this skill in Reception. In Year 1, a good programme teaches more complex phonics, including sounds made by two or more letters together, such as 'ay' in 'play'.

Here are accepted models for writing the small (lowercase) letters and the capital (uppercase) letters. Your child's school may offer models that differ in minor details from these; if so, follow the school's models. The directional arrows indicate a sequence of pencil strokes to follow. Have your child begin at the dot and form small letters in one continuous stroke, without lifting the pencil from the paper (except to cross the 'f', 't' and 'x' and to dot the 'i' and 'j').

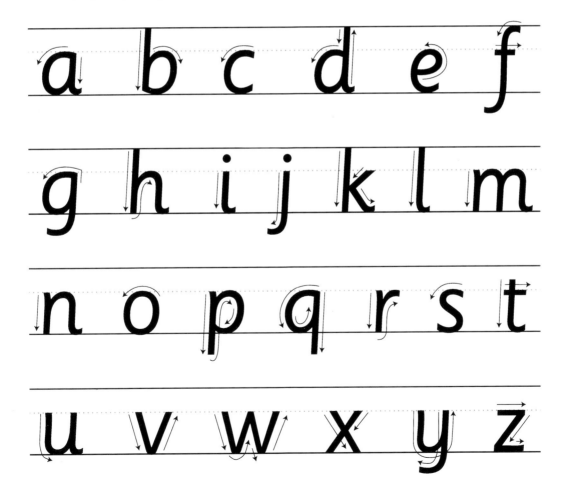

A B C D E F

G H I J K L

M N O P Q R

S T U V W X

Y Z

Here is how a left-handed child should hold a pencil.

Here is how a right-handed child should hold a pencil.

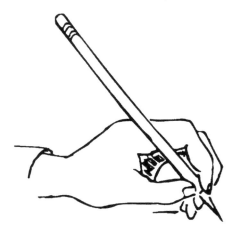

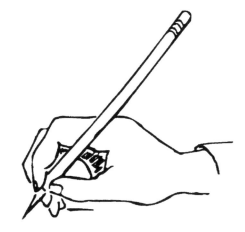

- Through a variety of listening activities, a good programme regularly asks children to pay attention to the sounds in words so that they begin to distinguish the smaller units of sound that make up a single word. For example, they may be asked to clap along with the separate syllables as they say a word: 'happy – hap[clap] – py[clap]; yesterday yes[clap] - ter[clap]-day[clap].' They may be asked to listen to the syllables of a word, then blend them together and say the whole word aloud; for example, they hear 'pic-nic', and say 'picnic'. They are asked to listen to and compare words, and recognise similarities and differences in their sounds. For example, does 'mat' rhyme with 'mate'? Does 'mat' rhyme with 'bat'? Does 'moon' start with the same sound as 'soon'? Does 'moon' start with the same sound as 'mop'?

    (*Parents take note:* some schools discourage children from sounding out words and urge them instead to 'guess' the words based on 'clues' from pictures or what's going on in the story. This is a serious mistake. Children need to learn a systematic, reliable way to figure out words that they don't know, and this can come only from giving them explicit instruction in the code of our written language.)

- A good programme provides a solid understanding of the basic principle underlying our written language - the *alphabetic principle*: that the sounds we hear in words are represented by letters written from left to right. Individual letters represent specific sounds, and groups of letters may also be combined to form specific letter-sound patterns (such as the letters 'ch' in 'check', 'chick' and 'chimp'). While there is no single universally accepted sequence for teaching the letter-sound patterns of the English language, a good Year 1 programme gives children regular practice with the initial consonant letter-sound patterns (for example, the *mmm* sound made by the letter 'm' in 'mitten', or the *sss* sound made by the letter 's' in 'sun'), and at least some of the short vowel letter-sounds (for example, the sound made by the letter 'a' in 'apple' and the letter 'o' in 'olive'). For more examples, see the typical 'Letter-Keyword Chart' pictured on page 11.

- Whatever sequence a school follows, it is important that the instruction be systematically organised to make *explicit* the letter-sound patterns and present them in a way that builds logically and sequentially, *not* in a haphazard or occasional fashion. Phonics instruction is most effective when it is regular, if not daily, with one skill building on another and with plenty of practice and review.

● As children master individual letter-sound patterns and become able to sound out words like 'bat', 'cat', 'ham' and 'Sam', a good programme provides phonetically controlled reading materials. These are simple stories written in a controlled vocabulary that corresponds to the letter-sound patterns a child has been taught in preparation for reading the story. For example, after being taught some consonants and the short 'a' sound (as in 'apple'), a child might read a simple story about 'Mat and Sam' or 'Mac, Tab and the Hat'. While such stories are of course not literature, they are very helpful in teaching children to read, especially in providing the early and tremendously satisfying experience of being able 'to read it all by myself'. In preparation for reading these stories, children also need to be taught to recognise some 'sight words', words that occur frequently in books but do not conform to the usual letter-sound patterns, such as 'of', 'was', 'do', 'the'.

Letter-Keyword Chart

Keywords are often used to introduce children to some basic letter sounds. If your child can recognise and name the letters of the alphabet, then you can use this chart by following this pattern: letter-name/keyword/ sound. For example, point to the ball and say the letter name, 'b', then the word, 'ball', then the sound, *buh*. Have your child repeat after you: 'm' – 'mitten' – mmm; 's' – 'sun' – sss; and so on. Note that for the vowels – 'a', 'e', 'i', 'o', 'u', – this chart presents keywords with short vowel sounds, as in 'igloo' and 'olive'. You can tell your child that the vowels are special letters that can make different sounds. In some words the vowels have long sounds and 'say their own names', for example 'a' as in 'hay', 'e' as in 'see', 'i' as in 'pie', 'o' as in 'no' and 'u' as in 'unicorn'.

A good programme recognises that reading and writing reinforce each other, and it provides children with many opportunities to communicate in writing. This means not only having the children copy letters and words in a workbook, or writing down words the teacher dictates – all of which are valuable practice that should take place regularly – but also occasionally having the children write letters, short stories, captions to pictures, and the like. Of course, Year 1 children will often want to say more than they can write correctly, so in these cases the children should be encouraged to use phonetic spelling, that is, 'to spell it the way they think it sounds' (so that a child may write, for example, 'bot' for 'boat'). This occasional practice of phonetic spelling is beneficial for Year 1 children because it engages them in actively thinking about the sounds of words and how they are represented, and can make them more interested in writing and more willing to put their thoughts on paper. Of course, children need regular practice with conventional, correct spellings as well.

That, in brief, describes some of what a good Year 1 programme will do to help all children achieve the goal of beginning to read and write on their own by the end of Year 1. Some children will surpass this goal; others may come close but not quite achieve it. But every child should receive appropriate instruction, materials, and support, and should be guided and encouraged to do his or her best to meet the goal.

What Parents Can Do to Help

As parents, you can help your Year 1 child take the first steps in learning to read and write. Here are a few suggestions:

Without question, the single most important and helpful thing you can do is to set aside fifteen or twenty minutes regularly, daily if possible, to *read aloud to your child*. See pages 17–18 in this book for suggested activities to accompany reading aloud. Engage your child in 'playing' with language. Such play can be spontaneous. Tell 'knock-knock' jokes. Ask riddles. Try tongue twisters. While driving in the car, you can play rhyming games and memory games, recite (or sing) favourite nursery rhymes, and point to different signs and talk about what they mean. While shopping for groceries, you can help your child cross items off a list, point to labels and talk about what they mean, and engage in impromptu word games: 'Here's a tin of beans. Let's think of words that rhyme with 'tin'. Help your child make the connection between oral and written language by encouraging her to dictate words for you to write: 'You say it and I'll write it'. You can start by asking her to dictate something short, such as a title for a drawing she has done. Encourage her to watch as you repeat aloud, word for word, what she has said while you simultaneously print the words. Once you've printed the whole title, reread what you've written while pointing to each word. Later, you can encourage your child to dictate something longer, like a story. You can ask him to tell the story of something he has experienced (a birthday party, going to the park or zoo, visiting a relative, baking biscuits) or a 'made-up' adventure (such as 'My Day with a Dragon'). Or you can ask him to retell a favourite story that you have read to him. He may want to look at the book's illustrations to help guide his retelling.

You can send an important message about the value you place on reading and writing by talking with your child about the schoolwork she brings home. Set aside time to look at her papers with her. Be supportive; praise the effort and don't worry about the errors, such as the inevitable misspelled words. (In school, the teacher should be observing your child's progress and working to correct any consistent pattern of errors.)

Suggested Resources

The resources recommended here are meant to complement, not substitute for, the reading books and associated materials that schools use to teach reading and writing. Our suggestions are directed to parents, though some teachers may find these additional resources helpful as well, especially if their school has adopted a philosophy or set of materials that neglects the systematic early teaching of decoding skills and the conventions of written language.

The following list is intended to help you get started in locating a few of the many good resources available. There are *many* phonics materials available from many sources; in recommending a few here, we do not mean to exclude others. The recommendations here are for materials that are time-tested and/or readily available, generally at a reasonable cost, and usable by those without special training in the teaching of reading and writing.

Besides the books suggested below, other useful supplies are generally available from online teacher resource sites and some toy shops:

● magnetic letters and letter flash cards
● letter-picture cards (cards with simple pictures and a corresponding letter, for example, the letter 'a' with a picture of an apple) and word-picture cards
● simple bingo or lotto games to practise recognising letters and words
● workbooks to practise handwriting
● alphabet activity books

Alphabet books

Alphabet books are appropriate for preschool age children. We list them here because Year 1 children still enjoy them and benefit from them. There are dozens of good alphabet books; here are just a few favourites.

- *ABC* by Quentin Blake (Red Fox 2002). Quentin Blake's quirky illustrations coupled with a simple text make learning fun.

- *The Most Amazing Hide-and-Seek Alphabet Book* by Robert Crowther (Walker 2005) is an interactive and delightful ABC to which children will often return.

- *Astonishing Animal ABC* by Charles Fuge (Gullane 2011) offers hilarious pictures and a rollicking text.

- *ABC Animal Rhymes for You and Me* by Giles Andreae (Orchard 2010) is a rhyming romp through the alphabet, guaranteed to make learning enjoyable.

Beginner Readers

- *The Blue Banana Series* (Egmont). Authors include Bel Mooney and Michael Morpurgo. Bananas are a reading series which provide quality stories for a range of readers. These books are designed for independent reading but many of the titles are also suitable for use in school for guided reading. Although designed to look like a series, they provide a great deal of variety in terms of genres, authors and illustrations. They are attractively produced with colour illustrations and are written in natural language without the controlled vocabulary of some reading schemes. Because of the variation in demand and the difference in expectation between each of the colour strands, the series is not intended to be used as a scheme. However, the books provide valuable and enjoyable reading practice for children at the appropriate level and usefully support children's growing independence as readers.

- *Leap Frog Series* (Franklin Watts). Authors include Penny Dolan and Anne Cassidy. Brightly illustrated early reading books by excellent authors and illustrators, perfect for newly independent readers. These books have been compiled in consultation with literacy experts and are suitable for new readers.

- *Fast Fox Slow Dog Series* by Allan Ahlberg (Puffin).

Other Resources

- Be sure to check what reading course your child is following at school to ensure the supplementary work you do at home complements their learning in class. *The Butterfly Book* by Irina Tyk (Civitas, 2007) is an easily accessible, structured, phonics-based reading course with simple instructions for parents, teachers and children to follow. Similarly, *Jolly Phonics* provides a thorough foundation in reading and writing, teaching the letter-sounds in an enjoyable, multisensory way.

- *The Cat in the Hat; Green Eggs and Ham; One Fish Two Fish Red Fish Blue Fish* by Dr. Seuss (Collins). These are just a few of many beginner books with lots of rhyming words and repetition. Read them aloud over and over. As children grow familiar with them, they are likely to chime in on such lines as 'I do not like them, Sam-I-Am!' If they are ready to read these on their own, that's great - but do not expect it of a Year 1 child!

- Picture books with predictive text encourage children to learn a rhyming story by heart, which is useful for revisiting later and for practising skills. Introduce children to such titles as *Little Rabbit Foo Foo* by Michael Rosen (Walker); *Hairy Maclary from Donaldson's Dairy* by Lynley Dodd (Puffin); *Room on the Broom* by Julia Donaldson (Macmillan) and *Each Peach Pear Plum* by Allan Ahlberg (Puffin).

- Children need a variety of stories to widen their vocabulary and introduce them to new concepts. Take them to the library to enable them to choose a range of books, and always allow them to revisit favourites. Look out for books by exciting new authors such as Polly Dunbar, Emily Gravett, Mini Grey and Oliver Jeffers.

- Reading aloud to children is an essential activity right through the primary school. While your child is learning the nuts and bolts of reading you can introduce some exciting longer stories alongside the picture books you will be sharing with them. Humphrey Carpenter's *Mr Majeika Series* (Puffin) and Jenny Valentine's *Iggy and Me* (Collins) series are lovely, as well as Jill Tomlinson's *The Owl who was Afraid of the Dark* (Egmont) and Dick King-Smith's *Sophie Stories* (Walker). Read aloud for as long as your children will allow you to. It's very important for them to hear how words come off the page, and to use their imagination to put the words into pictures.

- *The Ultimate First Book Guide*, published by A & C Black and edited by Leonie Flynn, Daniel Hahn and Susan Reuben covers all aspects of the reading process. It enables parents to understand how reading develops as well as suggesting over 500 excellent books to look out for.

More

- For further information about children's books parents might consider joining the Federation of Children's Book Groups. Annual membership entitles families to a copy of Carousel magazine three times a year, which provides excellent reviews of current children's literature, as well as revisiting old favourites. See **fcbg.org.uk** for details.

- As well as public libraries, many independent children's bookshops can offer expert advice about children's reading and suggest excellent titles to suit each child's individual needs. See **www.ncbc.co.uk** for example.

Literature

Introduction: Worlds of Meaning

There is one simple practice that can make a world of difference for your Year 1 child: read aloud to your child often, daily if possible. Reading aloud opens the doors to a world of meaning that most children are curious to explore but cannot enter on their own.

In reading aloud, you can offer your child a rich and varied selection of literature, including poetry, fiction, and non-fiction. Good literature brings language to life and offers children new worlds of adventure, knowledge, and humour.

Year 1 children enjoy traditional rhymes and fairy tales, like those found in the following pages. Even as adults, we find bits and pieces of fairy-tale lore entering our language, as when a sports commentator refers to the triumph of an underdog team as 'a Cinderella story', or when a successful businessman is described as having 'a Midas touch'.

For children, fairy tales can delight and instruct, and provide ways of dealing with the darker human emotions, like jealousy, greed and fear. As G. K. Chesterton observed, fairy tales 'are not responsible for producing in children fear, or any of the shapes of fear... The baby has known the dragon intimately ever since he had an imagination. What the fairy tale provides for him is a St. George to kill the dragon.' And, as the celebrated writer of children's tales, Wanda Gág, wrote in 1937: 'a fairy story is not just a fluffy puff of nothing... nor is it merely a tenuous bit of make believe... Its roots are real and solid, reaching far back into man's past... and into the lives and customs of many people and countries.' Whatever the geographical origin of the traditional tales we tell here – Europe, Africa, Asia, etc. – the stories have universal messages and lasting appeal across cultures and generations.

There are also, of course, many good books for young children by modern and contemporary writers, such as Michael Morpurgo, Joan Aiken, Dr. Seuss, Maurice Sendak, Michael Rosen, Jack Prelutsky, Laurent de Brunhoff, Jill Tomlinson, Allan Ahlberg and many others. Your local library has a treasury of good books, and you might want to consult the lists of recommended works in such guides as:

● *The Rough Guide to Children's Books for 5-11 Year Olds* by Nicholas Tucker (Rough Guides Ltd). These guides examine the best children's books available for 5-11 year olds. They include reviews of recommended titles, ranging from picture books through classic tales and poetry to stories dealing with contemporary issues, with a brief synopsis of each and an evaluation of its special qualities and educational advantages. The guides are subdivided by age and subject matter.

- *Great Books to Read Aloud* by Jacqueline Wilson (Corgi Childrens). This is a guide for books for parents to read aloud to their children. The book features reading tips from experts and sample extracts from brilliantly entertaining stories for all age groups. With an introduction by Children's Laureate Jacqueline Wilson, it also features tips on reading aloud from children's reading experts.

Beyond stories and poems, you can share appropriate works of non-fiction with your child. Year 1 children are fascinated by illustrated books that explain what things are and how they work, by biographies of famous people when they were children, by books about animals and how they live.

Read-Aloud Activities

Try to set aside a regular time for reading aloud, a time free from other obligations or distractions (including the television, which must be off). When you read aloud, don't feel embarrassed about hamming it up a bit. Be expressive; try giving different characters different voices.

If your child is not used to hearing stories read aloud, you may want to begin by reading some poems or some of the shorter selections in this book. If your child starts to squirm as you read longer stories, take a break from reading and get your child involved: have him look at a picture, or ask him some questions, or ask him to tell you what he thinks about what has happened so far, or have him draw a picture to go with the part of the story you've read.

When you read aloud, most of the time your child will be involved in the simple pleasure of listening. At other times you can involve your child in some additional activities to encourage comprehension and interest. Remember, these activities are not tests. Use them with a gentle touch; relax, have fun together.

- Let your child look through the book before you read it. Let him skim the pages and look at pictures.

- Direct your child's attention to the book's title page. Point to the author's name and read it as written, for example, 'Written by Emily Gravett'. If the book is illustrated, also read the illustrator's name, for example, 'Illustrated by Kate Greenaway'. Discuss what the words 'author' and 'illustrator' mean, and what authors and illustrators do (see also pages 52 and 91 of this book). As you read more and more books, talk with your child about her favourite authors or illustrators. Look in the library for more works by your child's favourite authors and illustrators.

- Sometimes let your child pick the books for reading aloud. If your child has picked a book or books from the library, she may soon learn the lesson that 'you can't tell a book by its cover'. If you begin a book that she has chosen and she expresses dislike or lack of interest, don't force her to finish hearing it. Just put the book aside with the understanding that 'maybe we'll like this better later'.

- As you read, run your finger below the words as you say them. This will help your child to associate spoken words with written words, and also expose him to the left-to-right direction of print. In rereading a selection, you can direct your child's attention to individual words as you say them aloud. This helps give your child a sense of words as individual units of speech and thought. Occasionally you can try reading a short sentence aloud, pronouncing each word very distinctly, and then asking your child how many words are in the sentence.

- After reading a story, discuss the sequence of events. 'Can you tell me what happened first? What did he do next?' You can draw three or four simple pictures representing scenes in the story, then ask your child to arrange the pictures in the proper sequence as she retells the story.

- After reading a poem or a story or a segment of a longer book, help your child recall details by asking questions. Keep in mind the five Ws: Who? What? When? Where? Why? For example, after reading 'Jack and Jill': Who went up the hill? Why? What happened to Jack? To Jill? (Maintain a playful, conversational tone; this is not a test!)

- Engage your child in a discussion of the story by asking questions that go beyond recall of details and take her into interpretation. For example: 'Why did all the other ducks make fun of the ugly duckling? How do you think he felt when they made fun of him?'

- Children often have favourite books that they want to hear again and again. Occasionally, when you reread a beloved and familiar story, pause and let your child supply the next word or words from memory. For example, when you say the words of the Big Bad Wolf – 'Little pig, little pig, let me come in!' – let him continue: 'Not by the hair of my chinny chin chin.'

- Help your child memorise a favourite nursery rhyme.

- Act out a story or scenes from a story. Your child doesn't need to memorise a set script; she can use her own language to express a character's thoughts. A few simple props can help: paper bags for masks, old shirts for costumes, a broomstick for a horse – all can be transformed by your child's active imagination.

Familiar and Favourite Poems

PARENTS: Here you will find a selection of traditional Mother Goose rhymes and other favourite poems. Children delight in hearing them read aloud, and they will enjoy and take pride in learning a few of their favourite rhymes by heart.

We also suggest some activities to go along with the poems. By playing with rhyming words, your child can sharpen her awareness of the sounds of spoken words. The activities are for speaking aloud; your child is not expected to read any words.

Activities for Poetry

● Read a rhyming poem aloud to your child. Then reread it and emphasise the rhyming words. Read the poem again and ask your child to 'fill in the blank' with the rhyming word. For example:

'Jack be nimble, Jack be quick. Jack jump over the candle _____.' ('stick')

● Read a rhyming poem to your child several times. As you talk about the poem, give your child one member of a pair of rhyming words from the poem, then ask what rhymes with it. For example, after many readings of 'Twinkle, Twinkle, Little Star', you might ask, 'What rhymes with star?' ('are') and, 'What rhymes with high?' ('sky'). Later you can extend this activity by asking, for example, 'Can you think of any other words that rhyme with star?' ('far', 'bar', 'car', etc.)

● Ask your child to be the 'mistake finder'. Say a poem that has grown familiar through repetition, but replace a rhyming word with a 'wrong' word that doesn't rhyme. Tell your child to clap when she hears a mistake. (Be sure to use a familiar poem so your child can do this activity successfully.) For example:

'One, two,
 Buckle my shoe;
 Three, four,
 Shut the gate.'

At times you can also ask her to correct your 'mistake' by supplying the right rhyming word. Ask your child to repeat a word you say and then say a rhyming word. For example:

You say: cat
Child says: cat, bat

Here are some words to start with:

cat	bed	map	pig	fan
game	toe	pin	fun	bug
cake	bump	boat	light	ball

You can extend this activity by asking your child to say as many words as he can think of that rhyme with the word you say.

SOME POETRY COLLECTIONS FOR CHILDREN

- *The Puffin Book Of Fantastic First Poems* selected by June Crebbin (Puffin) is a highly accessible collection, divided into seven sections in which children can read about animals, playtime, families, mealtimes, outings, curling up for bed or just plain nonsense. It features some of the best work from over 60 favourite poets and is packed tight with bright illustrations which perfectly capture the essence of the words. From Robert Louis Stevenson and Walter de la Mare right up to date with Roger McGough and Michael Rosen.

- *Please Mrs Butler* by Allan Ahlberg (Puffin) is a collection of funny poems about the experience of being in the classroom.

- *Twinkle Twinkle Chocolate Bar* compiled by John Foster (Oxford University Press) is a beautifully illustrated must-have collection of poems for the young.

- *Rumble Roar Dinosaur* by Tony Mitton (Macmillan). Children will love discovering a whole host of dinosaurs in this fun-filled picture book. Each spread features a short rhyming poem by Tony Mitton, in which a different dinosaur introduces itself. Mixing humour with information, the poems include details about where each dinosaur lived, what it ate and how it got around.

Time to Rise

by Robert Louis Stevenson

A birdie with a yellow bill

Hopped upon the window-sill.

Cocked his shining eye and said:

'Ain't you 'shamed, you sleepy-head?'

Happy Thought

by Robert Louis Stevenson

The world is so full

of a number of things,

I'm sure we should all

be as happy as kings.

Hickory, Dickory, Dock

Hickory, dickory, dock,

The mouse ran up the clock.

The clock struck one,

The mouse ran down,

Hickory, dickory, dock.

Early to Bed

**by Benjamin Franklin,
from *Poor Richard's Almanack***

Early to bed and early to rise,

Makes a man healthy, wealthy,

and wise.

Diddle, Diddle, Dumpling

Diddle, diddle, dumpling, my son John,
Went to bed with his trousers on;
One shoe off, and one shoe on,
Diddle, diddle, dumpling, my son John.

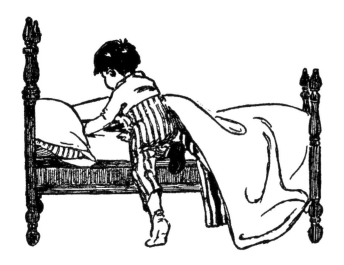

A Diller, a Dollar

A diller, a dollar,
A ten o' clock scholar
What makes you come so soon?
You used to come at ten o' clock
But now you come at noon!

Hey Diddle, Diddle

Hey, diddle, diddle,
The cat and the fiddle,
The cow jumped over the moon;
The little dog laughed
To see such fun,
And the dish ran away with the spoon.

Little Bo Peep

Little Bo Peep has lost her sheep,
And can't tell where to find them;
Leave them alone, and they'll come home,
Wagging their tails behind them.

Little Boy Blue

Little Boy Blue,
Come blow your horn,
The sheep's in the meadow,
The cow's in the corn;
But where is the boy
Who looks after the sheep?
He's under a haystack,
Fast asleep.

Baa, Baa, Black Sheep

Baa, baa, black sheep,
Have you any wool?
Yes, sir, yes, sir,
Three bags full.
One for the master,
And one for the dame,
And one for the little boy
Who lives down the lane.

One, Two, Buckle My Shoe

One, two,

Buckle my shoe;

Three, four,

Shut the door;

Five, six,

Pick up sticks;

Seven, eight,

Lay them straight;

Nine, ten,

A big fat hen;

Eleven, twelve,

Dig and delve;

Thirteen, fourteen,

Maids a-courting;

Fifteen, sixteen,

Maids in the kitchen;

Seventeen, eighteen,

Maids in waiting;

Nineteen, twenty,

My plate's empty.

Rain, Rain, Go Away

Rain, rain, go away,

Come again another day.

It's Raining, It's Pouring

It's raining, it's pouring,

The old man is snoring.

He bumped his head

And went to bed,

And couldn't get up in the morning.

The Wind

by Christina Rossetti

Who has seen the wind?

Neither I nor you;

But when the leaves hang trembling

The wind is passing through.

Who has seen the wind?

Neither you nor I;

But when the trees bow down their heads

The wind is passing by.

The More It Snows

by A. A. Milne

The more it

SNOWS-tiddely-pom,

The more it

GOES-tiddely-pom

The more it

GOES-tiddely-pom

On

Snowing.

And nobody

KNOWS-tiddely-pom,

How cold my

TOES-tiddely-pom

How cold my

TOES-tiddely-pom

Are

Growing.

Monday's Child

Monday's child is fair of face,

Tuesday's child is full of grace,

Wednesday's child is full of woe,

Thursday's child has far to go,

Friday's child is loving and giving,

Saturday's child works hard for a living,

But the child who is born on the Sabbath day

Is bonny and blithe and good and gay.

Roses Are Red

Roses are red,

Violets are blue,

Sugar is sweet,

And so are you.

Mary, Mary, Quite Contrary

Mary, Mary, quite contrary

How does your garden grow?

With silver bells, and cockle shells,

And pretty maids all in a row.

Boat

by Michael Rosen
illustrated by Quentin Blake

Made a boat
from sticks and cloth –
put it on the water
to see it float.

Go boat, go boat
sail across that sea.
Go boat
and sail on back to me.

It's sea and sky all the way over
my boat flies out across the water
but always comes on back to me.

It's a good boat
go boat.
She's a sail boat
my boat.

Go boat, go boat
sail across that sea.
Go boat
and sail on back to me.

Jack and Jill

Jack and Jill went up the hill
To fetch a pail of water;
Jack fell down and broke his crown,
And Jill came tumbling after.

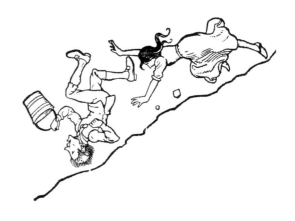

Jack Be Nimble

Jack be nimble,
Jack be quick,
Jack jump over
The candlestick.

There Was a Little Girl

There was a little girl
Who had a little curl
Right in the middle of her forehead;
When she was good, she was very, very good,
And when she was bad, she was horrid.

Little Miss Muffet

Little Miss Muffet
Sat on a tuffet,
Eating her curds and whey;
Along came a spider,
Who sat down beside her
And frightened Miss Muffet away.

Georgie Porgie

Georgie Porgie, pudding and pie,
Kissed the girls and made them cry;
When the boys came out to play,
Georgie Porgie ran away.

Humpty Dumpty

Humpty Dumpty sat
on a wall,
Humpty Dumpty had
a great fall.
All the king's horses,
And all the king's men,
Couldn't put Humpty together again.

Little Jack Horner

Little Jack Horner
Sat in a corner,
Eating his Christmas pie;
He put in his thumb,
And pulled out a plum,
And said, 'What a good boy am I!'

Mary Had a Little Lamb
from the poem by Sarah Josepha Hale

Mary had a little lamb,
Its fleece was white as snow;
And everywhere that Mary went,
The lamb was sure to go.

It followed her to school one day,
That was against the rule;
It made the children laugh and play
To see a lamb at school.

And so the teacher turned it out,
But still it lingered near,
And waited patiently about
Till Mary did appear.

'Why does the lamb love Mary so?'
The eager children cry.
'Why, Mary loves the lamb, you know',
The teacher did reply.

Hot Cross Buns!

Hot cross buns!
Hot cross buns!
One a penny, two a penny,
Hot cross buns!

If you have no daughters,
Give them to your sons;
One a penny, two a penny,
Hot cross buns!

Simple Simon

Simple Simon met a pieman
Going to the fair;
Said Simple Simon to the pieman,
'Let me taste your ware.'

Says the pieman to Simple Simon,
'Show me first your penny';
Says Simple Simon to the pieman,
'Indeed, I have not any.'

Old Mother Hubbard

Old Mother Hubbard
Went to the cupboard
To get her poor dog a bone,
But when she got there,
The cupboard was bare,
And so her poor dog had none.

Old King Cole

Old King Cole

Was a merry old soul,

And a merry old soul was he;

He called for his pipe,

And he called for his bowl,

And he called for his fiddlers three.

Sing a Song of Sixpence

Sing a song of sixpence,

A pocket full of rye;

Four and twenty blackbirds

Baked in a pie.

When the pie was opened,

The birds began to sing;

Wasn't that a dainty dish

To set before the king?

The king was in his counting-house

Counting out his money;

The queen was in the parlour

Eating bread and honey.

Ladybird, Ladybird

Ladybird, ladybird,

Fly away home,

Your house is on fire,

And your children are gone.

The maid was in the garden

Hanging out the clothes,

Along came a blackbird

And pecked off her nose.

Three Blind Mice

Three blind mice,

Three blind mice,

See how they run!

See how they run!

They all ran after the farmer's wife,

Who cut off their tails with a
carving knife,

Did you ever see such a sight in your life,

As three blind mice?

Jack Sprat

Jack Sprat could eat no fat,

His wife could eat no lean,

And so between the two of them

They licked the platter clean.

See-saw, Margery Daw

See-Saw, Margery Daw

Jenny shall have a new master;

She shall have but a penny a day,

Because she can't work any faster.

A. RACKHAM

The Three Little Kittens

by Eliza Lee Follen

Three little kittens lost their mittens

And they began to cry,

'Oh, mother dear,

We very much fear

That we have lost our mittens'.

'Lost your mittens!

You naughty kittens!

Then you shall have no pie!'

'Mee-ow, mee-ow, mee-ow.'

'No, you shall have no pie!'

'Mee-ow, mee-ow, mee-ow.'

The three little kittens found their mittens

And they began to cry,

'Oh, mother dear,

See here, see here!

See, we have found our mittens!'

'Put on your mittens,

You silly kittens,

And you may have some pie.'
'Purr-r, purr-r, purr-r,
Oh, let us have the pie!
Purr-r, purr-r, purr-r.'

The three little kittens put on their mittens,
And soon ate up the pie;
'Oh, mother dear, We greatly fear
That we have soiled our mittens!'
'Soiled your mittens!
You naughty kittens!'
Then they began to sigh,
'Mee-ow, mee-ow, mee-ow.'
Then they began to sigh,
'Mee-ow, mee-ow, mee-ow.'

The three little kittens washed their mittens,
And hung them out to dry;
'Oh, mother dear,
Do not you hear
That we have washed our mittens?'
'Washed your mittens!
Oh, you're good kittens!
But I smell a rat close by,
Hush, hush! Mee-ow, mee-ow, mee-ow.'
'We smell a rat close by,
Mee-ow, mee-ow, mee-ow.'

There Was an Old Woman Who Lived in a Shoe

There was an old woman who lived in a shoe.

She had so many children she didn't know what to do;

She gave them some broth without any bread;

And spanked them all soundly and put them to bed.

Star Light, Star Bright

Star light, star bright,

First star I see tonight,

I wish I may, I wish I might,

Have the wish I wish tonight.

Aesop's Fables

A fable is a special kind of story that teaches a lesson. People have been telling some fables over and over again for hundreds of years. It is said that many of these fables were told by a man named Aesop [EE-sop], who lived in Greece a very, very long time ago.

Aesop knew bad behaviour when he saw it, and he wanted people to be better. But he knew that we don't like to be told when we're bad. That is why many of his fables have animals in them. The animals sometimes talk and act like people. In fact, the animals behave just as well and just as badly as people do. That's because, even when a fable is about animals, it is really about people. Through these stories about animals, Aesop teaches us about how we should act as people.

At the end of the fable, Aesop often tells us a lesson we should learn. The lesson is called the *moral* of the story.

Here are four of Aesop's fables. The first three end by telling you the moral of the story. But the last one does not tell you the moral. When you read the last fable (about 'The Grasshopper and the Ant'), talk about what you think the moral of that story is.

The Dog and His Reflection

A hungry dog stole a juicy piece of meat from a butcher's shop and ran away as fast as his legs would carry him. As he was crossing a bridge he looked down and saw his own reflection in the clear water of the stream. The foolish dog thought that he was looking at another dog, holding another piece of meat. Not content with what he had, he lunged forward to grab the other dog's piece of meat – only to drop his own! It sank to the bottom of the river, and he was left with no dinner.

MORAL: If you are greedy, you may lose everything.

The Lion and the Mouse

A mighty lion was sleeping under the shade of a spreading tree when a little mouse accidentally ran across him. The lion awoke and, quick as a flash, brought down his great paw upon the tiny little mouse. The mouse was terrified, thinking that the lion was about to kill him.

'Please spare me,' he pleaded with the lion. 'I didn't mean to wake you, and I am such a weak little creature compared with you, who are called the King of Beasts, that it would do you no credit to kill me. If you let me go, one day I might be able to help you.'

The lion took pity on the mouse and released him, although he thought to himself that it was unlikely that such a tiny mouse would ever be able to help such a great beast as himself.

Shortly afterwards, the lion was hunting in the forest when he walked into a trap. The nets of hunters closed around him, and he found that the more he struggled, the tighter the ropes bit into his great and powerful limbs. The lion's terrible roars could be heard through all the forest, and the mouse pricked up his tiny little ears. He recognised the voice of his friend, who had spared his life, and he hurried to find out what was wrong.

'Don't worry, my friend,' said the mouse to the lion, 'I will soon have you free of these ropes.'

He set to work with his sharp little teeth until the ropes fell away from the lion. The noble beast was free, and learned that kindness can always be repaid, even by very little friends!

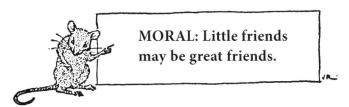

MORAL: Little friends may be great friends.

The Hare and the Tortoise

Once there was a hare who was so proud of how fast she could run that she pitied the animals who were slower than herself. 'What a poor creature you are,' she said to the tortoise. 'You move so slowly you look as if you are standing still. I can run over hills and valleys while you are struggling to cross the path. If we were to have a race, I would run so far ahead of you, you could never catch up.' 'Don't be too sure of that,' said the tortoise. 'Let's try it and see who wins.' 'Agreed!' said the hare, and they decided on the course of the race. Off went the hare, who was soon out of sight of the tortoise. 'Well, well,' she thought, 'I knew it would be so. I am so far ahead, I can afford to have a little rest.' Seeing some inviting ferns, she curled herself up in the middle of them and fell sound asleep. But while she slept, the steady tortoise came along behind her, saw her sleeping, and overtook her! By the time the hare woke up, the tortoise had won the race. How cross she was!

MORAL: Slow and steady wins the race. (Being the most talented doesn't always mean you'll come out on top. Hard, steady work is very important, too.)

The Grasshopper and the Ant

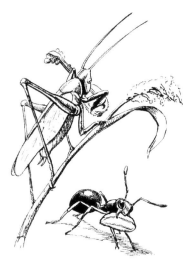

It was a glorious summer's day and the sun was high in the sky. A grasshopper was relaxing in a field of corn when he saw a tiny ant scurrying past him carrying a grain of corn.

'My dear little friend,' said the grasshopper, 'why are you struggling with that grain of corn, which is larger than you are, on such a beautiful day? You should be relaxing in the sun like me. Such days are too beautiful for work.'

'I work every day to store up food for the winter,' said the ant, 'for the sun will not always be shining, and we need to look to the future.'

The next day was another hot one, but once again the hard-working little ant spent it carrying grains of corn back to his underground home. The grasshopper was so happy to be warm and free that he sang his grasshopper song all day long, rubbing his long legs together.

'Chirrup, chirrup,' he sang, as the ant struggled to and fro. 'Will you not rest, little friend, and sing some happy summer songs on this lovely day?'

'Indeed no,' said the ant, 'I must add to my store of food for the winter, for the sun will not always be shining, and we need to look to the future.'

The next day was even hotter than the one before, with not a cloud in the sky, and the grasshopper was so happy he did a little grasshopper dance, springing from leaf to leaf and from one blade of grass to another.

'Chirrup, chirrup,' he sang, 'do you not feel like dancing, little ant, for very joy of being alive on such a glorious day?'

'Indeed it would be fine to dance,' said the ant, 'but the winter is coming and I must be wise. The sun will not always be shining, and we need to look to the future.'

The days went by, and summer turned to autumn, and then to winter. Soon the ground was hard and bare, and snow fell thickly all around. The grasshopper was hungry. There were no leaves for him to chew, no grass to nibble, and no corn to swallow. He went to the door that led to the ant's little house underground and knocked.

'May I have some of your corn?' he asked. 'I am so hungry I cannot long survive in this cold weather.'

'But how did you spend the summer?' asked the ant.

'Why, I spent it relaxing, singing and dancing,' said the hungry grasshopper.

'In that case,' said the ant, 'I find that he who spends the summer relaxing and singing and dancing, must spend the winter feeling hungry.'

What do you think the moral of this story is?

Stories

The Three Little Pigs

There was an old sow with three little pigs, and as she had not enough to keep them, she sent them out to seek their fortune. The first that went off met a man with a bundle of straw, and said to him:

'Please, sir, give me that straw to build a house.'

Which the man did, and the little pig built a house with it. Presently along came a Big Bad Wolf and knocked at the door, saying: 'Little pig, little pig, let me come in.'

To which the pig answered: 'Not by the hair of my chinny chin chin!'

The Big Bad Wolf answered: 'Then I'll huff, and I'll puff, and I'll blow your house down!'

So he huffed, and he puffed, and he blew his house down, and ate up the little pig.

The second little pig met a man with a bundle of sticks, and said to him: 'Please sir, give me some sticks to build a house.'

Which the man did, and the pig built his house. Then along came the Big Bad Wolf and said: 'Little pig, little pig, let me come in.'

'Not by the hair of my chinny chin chin!'

'Then I'll puff, and I'll huff, and I'll blow your house down!'

So he huffed, and he puffed, and he puffed, and he huffed, and at last he blew the house down, and he ate up the little pig.

The third little pig met a man with a load of bricks, and said: 'Please sir, give me those bricks to build a house with.'

So the man gave him the bricks, and he built his house with them. Then the Big Bad Wolf came along, as he had to the other little pigs, and said: 'Little pig, little pig, let me come in.'

'Not by the hair of my chinny chin chin!'

'Then I'll huff, and I'll puff, and I'll blow your house down.'

Well, he huffed and he puffed, and he huffed and he puffed, and he puffed and he huffed; but he could not blow the house down.

Then the wolf was very angry indeed, and declared he would eat up the little pig, and that he would come down the chimney after him. When the little pig saw what the wolf was about to do, he hung up a pot full of water in his fireplace and made up a blazing fire under it. Soon the water was bubbling and boiling merrily in the pot and, just as the wolf was coming

down the chimney, the little pig took off the cover, and in fell the Big Bad Wolf. The little pig put on the cover again and boiled him up until he made a tasty stew. Then he lived happily ever afterwards.

Goldilocks and the Three Bears

Once upon a time, there was a little girl who lived with her grandmother in a cottage near the woods. She had a head of beautiful golden curls and so she was often known as Goldilocks.

Grandmother was going to market one Saturday morning and as she left the cottage she said: 'Now, Goldilocks, you must not leave the house, some say there are great bears in the forest that like to eat little girls for lunch!'

Goldilocks was usually a good little girl, who did what her grandmother told her, but it was such a beautiful day that she soon forgot her grandmother's warning and ran outside to explore.

She wandered about the woods chasing butterflies until she was tired and hungry, at which point she realised she was quite lost. So, deciding that there was nothing else for it, she wandered even deeper into the forest until she came upon a little cabin.

With great relief, she knocked on the door, but there was no answer. Timidly she opened the door. It seemed that nobody was at home. Now, you might think that she should turn right around and go home, but Goldilocks was so tired and hungry that she completely forgot her manners and walked right on into the house!

She went in and saw the table which had been set for three, for there were three bowls of different sizes, filled to the brim with lovely, steaming porridge. Goldilocks, being very hungry lifted a big spoonful of the porridge from the biggest bowl, but it was too salty. Then she tasted the porridge in the middle-sized bowl, but it was too sweet. Then she tasted the porridge in the little bowl and that tasted just right, so she licked the bowl clean!

Now she was feeling even more tired, so she went up the stairs. This led to a large room in which there were three beds in a row. The first was a very big bed and Goldilocks hopped in. But it was too hard and bumpy so she did not like it. She tried the next bed but it was so deep that she sank right down into it and had to clamber back up. So over she went to the smallest bed. It was just right! It was so comfortable that she dropped off into a sound sleep at once.

Now it so happened that the owners of this little cabin were a family of three bears, who had been out for a walk in the woods to build up an appetite for dinner. The big Daddy Bear marched hungrily to his place at the table and said: 'SOMEONE HAS BEEN EATING MY PORRIDGE!' Then the middle-sized Mummy Bear got to her bowl and said: 'SOMEONE HAS BEEN EATING MY PORRIDGE TOO!' Then the little Baby Bear said: '*Someone has been eating my porridge and has finished it all off!*'

Not having anything else to eat in the house, the bears ended up being so grumpy that they decided the best thing would be to go to bed early. When they went upstairs Daddy Bear stopped in his tracks and said: 'SOMEONE HAS BEEN LYING IN MY BED!' Then Mummy Bear noticed that her bed had also been disturbed and said: 'SOMEONE HAS BEEN LYING IN MY BED TOO!' And then Baby Bear cried out in alarm: '*Someone has been lying in my bed – and SHE'S STILL IN IT!*' He said this so loudly that Goldilocks woke up. When she saw that she was surrounded by bears she was so frightened that she jumped through the open window, climbed down the drainpipe and went running and screaming through the woods all the way home. The bears hurried downstairs, not knowing what to make of it, and watched as her golden head went bobbing away through the woods and they haven't seen her since.

The Three Billy-Goats Gruff

Once upon a time there were three Billy-Goats all named 'Gruff'. They longed more than anything to go up a particular hillside that was covered with thick green grass. To get to the hillside they had to cross a bridge over a little brook. And under this bridge lived a great ugly Troll, with eyes as big as saucers, and a nose as long as a poker.

So first of all, up came the smallest Billy-Goat Gruff to cross the bridge.

'*Trip, trap! Trip, trap!*' went the bridge.

'WHO'S THAT TRIP-TRAPPING OVER MY BRIDGE?' roared the Troll.

'Oh, it is only I, the tiniest Billy-Goat Gruff. I'm going up to the hill-side to make myself fat,' said the Billy-Goat, with such a small voice.

'Oh ho! I'm coming to gobble you up', said the Troll.

'Oh, no! Please don't eat me. I'm too little,' said the Billy-Goat, 'Wait a bit until my brother Billy-Goat Gruff comes, he's much bigger.'

'Well, be off with you', said the Troll.

A little while after came the second Billy-Goat Gruff to cross the bridge.

'*Trip, trap! Trip, trap! Trip, trap!*' went the bridge.

'WHO'S THAT TRIP-TRAPPING OVER MY BRIDGE?' roared the Troll.

'Oh, it's only me, the second Billy-Goat Gruff. I'm going up to the hillside to make myself fat', said the Billy-Goat, who hadn't such a small voice.

'Oh ho! I'm coming to gobble you up', said the Troll.

'Oh, no! Don't eat me, wait a little until my brother, the Big Billy-Goat Gruff comes, he's much bigger.'

'Very well! Be off with you', said the Troll.

But just then up came the Big Billy-Goat Gruff.

'*TRIP, TRAP! TRIP, TRAP! TRIP, TRAP!*' went the bridge, for the Billy-Goat was so heavy that the bridge creaked and groaned under him.

'WHO'S THAT TRAMPING OVER MY BRIDGE?' roared the Troll.

'IT IS I! THE BIG BILLY-GOAT GRUFF', said the Billy-Goat, who had an ugly hoarse voice.

'Now I'm coming to gobble you up', roared the Troll.

And the Big Billy-Goat Gruff said:

'Well, come along! I've got two spears,
 And I'll poke your eyeballs out of your ears;
 I've got besides two monstrous stones,
 And I'll crush you to bits, body and bones.'

And so he flew at the Troll, and poked his eyes out with his horns, and crushed him to bits, body and bones. He tossed him out into the brook, and after that he went up to the hillside. There the Billy-Goats got so fat they could hardly walk home again.

'Snip, snap, snout

This tale's told out.'

The King with Horse's Ears
An Irish Folktale

The story I'm going to tell you is not one you hear every day. It's a story about a king who allowed his hair to be cut and his beard to be trimmed only once a year. He lived on the western borders of Old Ireland, and his name was a queer one – Labhras.

Mysteriously, the unfortunate barbers who were granted the task of taming the wild mass of flowing hair were never heard from again when the task was finished. About seven unlucky fellows disappeared, and after that not a barber in the land would come within the castle gates. So the king made a law, that all the barbers throughout the country were to draw straws, and he who pulled the short straw was ordered to come to the castle to carry out the task.

One year the short straw was drawn by the unlucky son of a poor widow woman, and it was announced throughout the town. When the poor mother heard the news she nearly fainted with worry, but as she knew that wouldn't save the poor fellow's life, she thought better of it and ran up the road as fast as she could until she came to the castle gates.

She broke through the guards and came into the big stone hall, where the king was to be found dealing with kingly matters.

'What brings this mad woman here?' he said flying into a rage. 'Go,' said he to the butler, 'and put the guards into the dungeon, for letting me be disturbed at my royal court!' and turning to the old woman he said: 'What do you want, you unfortunate old woman?'

'Oh, please your noble majesty,' she said, 'don't take my son away from me. If you do, who will I have to take care of me?'

'Who is your son?' he said; 'and what has he got to do with me?'

'Oh, he is the unfortunate one who is to cut your majesty's hair tomorrow! And I am sure after that I'll never see him again!'

And the woman was so pathetic in her distress and her sobs that the old king took pity on her and agreed to let her have her son back safe and sound.

The following day the poor barber came in, like a dog with its tail between his legs. He stood, bowing and bowing and thanking the King for his mercy.

The King looked at him straight in the eye and said: 'My good fellow, you'll be free to go where you please after cutting my hair, but you must first take an oath and swear to me, by the king's hand, that you will never tell any creature who has ears and a tongue what you'll see this day!'

So he sat down on his throne, took off his golden crown, with his eyes fixed on the barber; and when the crown was off, up flew two long brown horse's ears (but they were as long as if they belonged to a donkey!).

The poor lad never quite knew how he managed the job without bursting into a fit of laughter. At one point he almost clipped the edge of one ear, but the King let out such a roar that it almost terrified him to death.

When he had finished the job, the servant handed him five gold coins and the King said, 'Now, my lad, if I ever hear a word of this, I will surely hunt you down and hang you!'

When the boy returned home, the poor mother was there, looking out the door, to see if her son would ever come back to her; and at last, there he was coming down the street, pulling one leg after the other. And when he came in, he tumbled head over heels into his bed. The poor mother begged him to tell her what was the matter, but he could not say a word about what he had seen, for fear the King would find out and hang him.

At last, after two days and nights, the doctor came; and as sure as he did, he told the boy to put out his tongue, and let him feel his pulse.

'Doctor,' says the poor fellow, 'there's no use in trying to blindfold the devil in the dark: I have a secret. If I can't tell it, I'll die; and if I do tell it, I'll not be allowed to live.'

When he heard the precise instructions given to the boy, that the secret was not to be told to any creatures with tongues and ears on them, he said to the poor barber boy: 'Go into the wood and make a split in the bark of one of the trees, tell your secret into the cut, and see how you'll feel after that.'

The doctor was hardly out of the house when the boy was up, and creeping off to the wood. He was afraid to stop, for fear he'd be seen, until he was deep in the forest, where two paths crossed one another. There was a nice big oak tree at the spot, and so he went no farther; but cut the bark in a downward gash, stooped down, and whispered into it: 'Labharas the King has horse's ears.'

Well, the poor fellow was hardly done whispering, when he felt as if a mountain was lifted off his back. With the five gold coins he and his mother lived like royalty for a long time; but the end of the year was drawing near, and it was coming to the time when he'd have to cut the King's long hair again, and he began to grow very distressed.

Before the day came, however, there was great coming and going; for the other three kings of Ireland were invited, along with all the lords and ladies that chose to travel so far, to listen to a great match of harp-playing between the King's famous harpist and anyone who was brave enough to play against him.

Now, a week before the match, the harpist found some cracks in his instrument and so he went into the wood to look for a nice tree to cut down, so that he could make himself a new one.

Where should he end up but at that very oak tree the barber had told his secret to! He cut it down, and carved it into the finest harp that you ever did see, and when he tried it he was enchanted by the beautiful music it played!

So at last the great day came, and the streets were filled with coaches and horses, and the big stone hall in the castle was crammed. The King was on his high throne, and the three other kings were before him, and behind him, and at one side of him; and in the centre all the harpists were sitting surrounded by the gentlemen and ladies of the court; and the ordinary people, like you and I, were to be found at the back, so that the hall was packed so full of people that you could hardly move.

So the King gave the word of command, and up got his famous harpist. The music he made was so mournful that those who couldn't cover their faces put a cross look on themselves to hide their grief.

This didn't please the King; so he waved his hand, and the harpist struck up a jig, but there was no room for dancing. So instead everyone that had a cap flung it in the air and stamped their feet. But being afraid that the crowd would trample on each other and on the other harpists for dancing room, he changed his tune and made music so sweet that everyone shut their eyes and leaned back and hoped that it would never end.

But all good things must come to an end, and the harpist let his arms fall on his knees, and every one sighed and groaned for being brought back to the world again.

Then the other four harpists each took their turn, and, sure enough, fine music flew out from under these hands; but none was as good as that of King Labhras's harpist. So when they stopped, the king said to his harpist: 'Give us one more tune to finish.'

'My King,' said the harpist, 'I'm afraid that it wasn't my fingers that struck out that music; it was the music that stirred my fingers. There's some magic in the instrument, and I fear it will play a trick on us.'

'Nonsense!' said the King, 'play away!'

Well, his fingers hardly touched the strings, when they felt like sandpaper and the harp let out a huge roar, as if thunder were breaking over the roof, and a thousand men were smashing stones. A loud voice began to shout out from the strings that were keeping hold of the harpist fingers: 'Labhras the King has horse's ears!'

Well, to be sure! How the people were frightened, and how they looked at the unfortunate King, who didn't know whether he was standing on his feet or his head, and would have given half of Ireland to be ten miles underground at that moment.

He put up his poor hands to his head, not knowing what he was doing, and pulled off the golden crown. Up flew the two long hairy ears! At first there was a gentle tittering, and then someone laughed and shortly the whole crowd was roaring with laughter, the tears running down their cheeks! King Labhras was hardly able to stand it and soon had to be carried off to bed!

So Labhras gave up his kingship, for a person having such a blemish in those days could not be a king. The clan elected the young man to be their next king. He was a good king who reigned long and well, and he had no secrets from his people. He also took the name of Labhras, which in Gaelic is also the name for the bay tree.

WHAT IS AN ILLUSTRATOR?

 Do you like to draw? This is Quentin Blake: he loves to draw. In fact, drawing is his job. He's an artist – a special kind of artist called an illustrator.

An illustrator makes the pictures – the illustrations – that go in a book. Illustrations can be drawings, paintings, even paper cut-outs.

Quentin drew the pictures for the poem 'Boat' by Michael Rosen on pages 28–29. Before an illustrator draws a picture, they begin by imagining, by making pictures in their mind. When someone reads you a story, do you sometimes see pictures of what's happening in your mind? That's what an illustrator does: they see pictures in their mind – and then they draw them.

'What you really do when you start to draw,' says Quentin, 'is you imagine that you are that person and you go into the reactions you think you would be having. I find myself doing the faces as I'm drawing them. I like drawing anything that is doing something. I like activity. Dragons are good because you can arrange them in interesting ways across the page, get people to ride on them, that sort of thing.'

When you sit down with a book that has pictures, find out who the illustrator is. And the next time you draw or paint, think about those 'pictures in your mind' from some of your favourite stories.

The Little Red Hen

Once a hard-working little red hen lived on a farm with a dog, a cat, and a pig. One day she decided to make bread.

'Who will help me cut the wheat to make my bread?' she asked.

'Not I', said the dog.

'Not I', yawned the cat.

'Not I', grunted the pig.

'Then I will do it myself', said the little red hen.

When she had cut the wheat, the little red hen asked, 'Who will help me take the wheat to the miller for grinding?'

'Not I', growled the dog.

'Not I', hissed the cat.

'Not I', snorted the pig.

'Then I will do it myself', said the little red hen.

When the wheat had been ground into flour, the little red hen asked, 'Who will help me make the flour into bread dough?'

'Not I', sighed the dog.

'Not I', whined the cat.

'Not I', sniffed the pig.

'Then I will do it myself', said the little red hen.

When she had mixed the dough, the little red hen asked, 'Who will help me bake the bread?'

'Not I', muttered the dog.

'Not I', murmured the cat.

'Not I', grumbled the pig.

'Then I will do it myself', said the little red hen.

And so, all by herself, she baked a fine loaf of bread.

'Now,' said the little red hen, 'who will help me eat the bread?'

'I will!' barked the dog.

'I will!' purred the cat.

'I will!' grunted the pig.

But the little red hen said, 'No you won't. I cut the wheat all by myself. I took it to the miller all by myself. I mixed the dough and baked it all by myself. And now I shall eat the bread – all by myself!'

Chicken Little

Once upon a time there was a dear little chicken named Chicken Little. One morning as she was scratching in her garden, an acorn fell off a tree and hit her on the head.

'Oh, dear me!' she cried, 'the sky is falling. I must go and tell the King.' And away she ran down the road.

By and by she met Henny Penny going to the shops. 'Where are you going in such a hurry?' asked Henny Penny.

'I'm going to tell the King the sky is falling', answered Chicken Little.

'How do you know the sky is falling?' asked Henny Penny.

'Because a piece of it fell on my head', she replied.

'Then we must go and tell the King at once!' said Henny Penny. So on Chicken Little went, followed by Henny Penny. Turning up a shady lane they met Goosey Loosey.

'Where are you two going in such a hurry?' asked Goosey Loosey.

'Oh, we are going to tell the King the sky is falling', answered Henny Penny.

'How do you know?'

'Chicken Little told me', said Henny Penny.

'A piece of it fell on my head', cried Chicken Little.

'May I go with you?' asked Goosey Loosey.

'Certainly', answered Chicken Little.

Then away went the three, Chicken Little, Henny Penny and Goosey Loosey.

After a while, they came to a pond where they met Ducky Lucky.

'Where are you three going?' he asked.

'The sky is falling and we are going to tell the King', answered Goosey Loosey.

'How do you know?' asked Ducky Lucky.

'Henny Penny told me', said Goosey Loosey.

'Chicken Little told me', said Henny Penny.

'A piece of it fell on my head', cried Chicken Little.

'May I go with you?' asked Ducky Lucky.

'Certainly', they answered.

By and by whom should they meet but Turkey Lurkey, carrying a basket of gooseberries to market.

'Where are you four going?' she asked.

'The sky is falling and we are going to tell the King', answered Ducky Lucky.

'How do you know it is falling?' asked Turkey Lurkey.

'Goosey Loosey told me', answered Ducky Lucky.

'Henny Penny told me', said Goosey Loosey.

'Chicken Little told me', said Henny Penny.

'A piece of it fell on my head', cried Chicken Little.

'May I go with you?' asked Turkey Lurkey.

'Certainly', said Chicken Little.

Then Turkey Lurkey followed Chicken Little, Henny Penny, Goosey Loosey and Ducky Lucky until they met Foxy Loxy.

'Where are you five going?' asked Foxy Loxy with a sly grin.

'The sky is falling and we're going to tell the king', answered Turkey Lurkey.

'How do you know?' asked Foxy Loxy.

'Ducky Lucky told me so', answered Turkey Lurkey.

'Goosey Loosey told me', answered Ducky Lucky.

'Henny Penny told me', said Goosey Loosey.

'Chicken Little told me', said Henny Penny.

'A piece of it fell on my head', cried Chicken Little.

'If the sky is falling, surely it would be better to get to safety? Come into my den where you can shelter', said Foxy Loxy.

So Chicken Little, Henny Penny, Goosey Loosey, Ducky Lucky and Turkey Lurkey followed Foxy Loxy into his den and they were never heard from again!

Little Red Riding Hood
(A tale from the Brothers Grimm)

Once upon a time there was a dear little girl who was loved by all, but by no one more than her grandmother, who would have done anything for the child. Once she sent her a red velvet cloak, with a hood lined with red silk, that suited her so well that she refused to wear anything else and so she became known as 'Little Red Riding Hood'.

One day her mother gave her a freshly baked cake and told her to take it to her grandmother, who was feeling poorly. Her mother warned her: 'Go quickly and take care not to run off the path. Do not stop until you get there.'

'I will do just as you say, Mother', said Little Red Riding Hood and started on her way.

The grandmother lived out in the woods, not far from the village. Little Red Riding Hood had just entered the woods when she came across a huge wolf. Little Red Riding Hood was not at all afraid because she did not know what a wicked creature this wolf was.

'Good morning, Little Red Riding Hood', he said.

'Good morning to you too, Mr. Wolf', she answered kindly.

'Where might you be heading so early this morning?' he asked.

'To visit my grandmother, Mr. Wolf.'

'And what's that you've got in your basket?'

'A freshly baked cake, for you see, Grandmother is feeling unwell and this will help to make her feel better.'

'And where does your poor grandmother live, Little Red Riding Hood?'

'Her house can be found a little deeper in the woods, not too far from here, standing under the three large oak trees – surely you must know it?' replied Little Red Riding Hood.

The wolf thought to himself: 'What a tender young girl this is! What a nice juicy mouthful she will be – much tastier than the old grandmother I'm sure, but not enough for a meal. I must be crafty so as to catch them both!'

They began to walk deeper into the woods together. After a while the wolf said: 'Look at all those pretty flowers growing. Why don't you stop and pick some for your grandmother – they are sure to cheer her up! How sweetly the little birds are singing, how pleasant it is here; and yet you are walking so quickly it is as if you were late for school!'

Little Red Riding Hood looked up and saw the beautiful flowers swaying gently in the breeze and listened to the birds sweetly chirping, and she thought to herself: 'I am sure Grandmother would love some wild flowers for her bedside– they are sure to cheer her up.' So she ran from the path into the wood and when she had picked one, she saw an even prettier one further on and ran after it and so she wandered deeper and deeper into the wood.

The wolf meanwhile ran straight to the grandmother's house and knocked on the door.

'Who is it?' called the grandmother.

'It is I, Little Red Riding Hood, I have brought you some cake', replied the wolf in a high voice.

'Lift the latch, dear, I am too weak to get up.'

The wolf lifted the latch, flung the door open and, without saying a word, pounced upon the grandmother and gobbled her up!

Then the crafty wolf dressed in the grandmother's nightclothes and put on her glasses and hopped into the grandmother's bed.

Little Red Riding Hood, after picking all the flowers she could carry, suddenly remembered her grandmother and set out on the path again.

When she arrived at her grandmother's house she was surprised to find the door open and, as she went inside, she suddenly got a very strange feeling.

She called out: 'Hello... Grandmother?' but received no answer, so she went into the bedroom and there lay her grandmother with her night cap pulled far down over her face and the covers right up to her chin, looking very strange indeed.

'Oh! Grandmother,' she gasped, 'what big ears you have!'

'All the better to hear you with, my dear', was the reply.

'But Grandmother, what big eyes you have!' she said.

'All the better to see you with, my dear.'

'But, Grandmother, what large hands you have!'

'All the better to hug you with, my dear,' said the wolf.

'Oh! But Grandmother, what terribly big teeth you have!'

'All the better to EAT you with!' cried the wolf.

And scarcely had the wolf said this, when he leapt from the bed and swallowed up poor Little Red Riding Hood whole!

The wolf was now feeling very full and so he decided to lie back down on the bed, where he promptly fell asleep, snoring very loudly. A hunter who was passing the house heard the snores and thought to himself: 'My, the old woman sounds terrible! I'd better go and check if she needs anything.'

So the hunter went into the room and when he saw the wolf lying on the bed he cried: 'Ah! At last I've found you, you wicked beast.' He was just about to shoot the wolf when it occurred to him that the wolf had probably eaten the grandmother and that she might still be saved. So instead he took a pair of scissors and cut open the stomach of the sleeping wolf.

Out popped Little Red Riding Hood! 'Oh thank you Mr. Hunter, how frightened I have been, it was so dark inside the wolf – I thought I might never get out!' she cried. The hunter was so surprised – but he was even more surprised when the old grandmother came out from the wolf's stomach as well!

Little Red Riding Hood fetched some great stones which they put into the wolf's belly and sewed him up again. When the wolf awoke, he tried to run away, but the stones were so heavy that he fell down dead at once!

And Little Red Riding Hood thought to herself: 'As long as I live, I will never leave the path when my mother has told me not to.'

The Tiger, the Brahmin and the Jackal

This story is a folktale from India where many people follow the Hindu religion. A Brahmin is a holy man and a teacher.

 nce upon a time, a tiger was caught in a trap. He tried in vain to get out through the bars, and rolled and bit with rage and grief when he failed.

By chance, a poor Brahmin came by.

'Let me out of this cage, oh pious one!' cried the tiger.

'No way!' replied the Brahmin mildly, 'You would probably eat me if I did.'

'Not at all!' swore the tiger with many oaths; 'On the contrary, I should be forever grateful, and serve you as a slave!'

Now when the tiger sobbed and sighed and wept and swore, the pious Brahmin's heart softened, and at last he decided to open the door of the cage. Out popped the tiger, and, seizing the poor man, cried: 'What a fool you are! What is to prevent me from eating you now, since after being cooped up for so long I am terribly hungry!'

The Brahmin pleaded and begged for his life, so the tiger eventually said: 'We shall ask three things for their opinion as to whether it is right that I should eat you or not.'

So the Brahmin first asked a fig tree what it thought of the matter, but the fig tree replied coldly: 'What have you to complain about? Don't I give shade and shelter to everyone who passes by, and don't they in return tear down my branches to feed their cattle? Don't whimper – be a man!'

Then the Brahmin, sad at heart, went farther afield till he saw a buffalo turning a well-wheel; but it answered: 'You are a fool to expect gratitude! Look at me! Whilst I gave milk they fed me on delicious cotton-seed and oil-cake, but now that I can give milk no longer, they tie me up here and give me horrible food!'

The Brahmin, even sadder, asked the road to give him its opinion.

'My dear sir,' said the road, 'how foolish you are to expect anything else! Here am I, useful to everybody, yet all, rich and poor, great and small, trample on me as they go past, giving me nothing but the ashes of their pipes and the husks of their grain!'

On this the Brahmin turned back sorrowfully, and on the way he met a jackal, who called out, 'Why, what's the matter, Mr. Brahmin? You look as miserable as a fish out of water!'

The Brahmin told him all that had occurred. 'How very confusing!' said the jackal, when the recital was ended; 'Would you mind telling me over again, for everything has got so mixed up?'

The Brahmin told it all over again, but the jackal shook his head in a distracted sort of way, and still could not understand.

'It's very odd,' said he, sadly, 'but it all seems to go in at one ear and out at the other! I will go to the place where it all happened, and then perhaps I shall be able to give a judgment.'

So they returned to the cage, by which the tiger was waiting for the Brahmin, and sharpening his teeth and claws.

'You've been away a long time!' growled the savage beast, 'but now let us begin our dinner.'

'Our dinner!' thought the wretched Brahmin, as his knees knocked together with fright; 'what a remarkably delicate way of putting it!'

'Give me five minutes, my lord!' he pleaded, 'in order that I may explain matters to the jackal here, who is somewhat slow in his wits.'

The tiger consented, and the Brahmin began the whole story over again, not missing a single detail, and spinning as long a yarn as possible.

'Oh, my poor brain! Oh, my poor brain!' cried the jackal, wringing its paws. 'Let me see!

How did it all begin? You were in the cage, and the tiger came walking by—'

'Pooh!' interrupted the tiger, 'what a fool you are! I was in the cage.'

'Of course!' cried the jackal, pretending to tremble with fright; 'Yes! I was in the cage – no I wasn't – dear, dear, where are my wits? Let me see – the tiger was in the Brahmin, and the cage came walking by – no, that's not it, either! Well, don't mind me, but begin your dinner, for I shall never understand!'

'Yes, you shall!' returned the tiger, in a rage at the jackal's stupidity; 'I'll make you understand! Look here – I am the tiger-'

'Yes, my lord!'

'And that is the Brahmin-'

'Yes, my lord!'

'And that is the cage –'

'Yes, my lord!'

'And I was in the cage – do you understand?'

'Yes-no – Please, my lord—'

'Well?' cried the tiger impatiently.

'Please, my lord! How did you get in?'

'How! Why in the usual way, of course!'

'Oh, dear me! My head is beginning to whirl again! Please don't be angry, my lord, but what is the usual way?'

At this the tiger lost patience, and, jumping into the cage, cried: 'This way! Now do you understand how it was?'

'Perfectly!' grinned the jackal, as he dexterously shut the door, 'And if you will permit me to say so, I think matters will remain as they were!'

The Bremen Town Musicians
(A tale from the Brothers Grimm)

Once upon a time there was an old donkey, who for many years had carried heavy sacks of corn to and from the mill. But now his strength was leaving him and he was getting too old to carry the heavy bags. His master tried to think how he could get rid of his donkey so that he would no longer have to feed him; but the donkey, fearing what his master might do, ran away and took the road to Bremen.

On the way he heard a man playing music in the street and he thought to himself: 'I can surely be as good a musician as that.'

After he had been walking for some time he came upon an old hound dog gasping for breath as if he had been running for a week.

'What are you gasping for, old boy?' asked the donkey.

'As I am old and can no longer go on the hunt, my master wants to kill me because I am no longer of use to him, so I have run away.'

'Why don't you join me?' suggested the donkey. 'I am going to be a street musician in Bremen. I can play the flute, you can play the drum.'

The hound agreed and on they went.

Before long, they came to a cat, sitting on the path with a face as long as three rainy days!

'Now then, Mr. Tom, what can be the matter?' asked the donkey.

'Who can be happy when their life is in danger?' answered the cat. 'Because I am now getting old, and my teeth are worn, I can no longer hunt for mice. My mistress has thrown me out because all I can do is sit by the fire and purr. What am I to do?'

'Come with us to Bremen!' said the donkey at once. 'You know a lot about music of the night, you can be a town musician with us.'

And so the cat went with them on the road to Bremen. A while later the three musicians came upon a cockerel, perched on a farmyard gate, crowing with all his might.

'What on earth is the matter? Why are you making so much noise?' asked the donkey.

'I have overheard the cook saying she intends to roast me for Sunday dinner. This evening I am to have my head cut off! So I am crowing while I still can,' said the cockerel.

'You must come with us! We are going to Bremen, you have a good voice and will make a great singer for our band!'

The cockerel agreed and all four went on together. They could not reach the city of Bremen in one day and in the evening they were travelling through a forest, where they decided they must pass the night. The donkey and the hound laid themselves down under a large tree, the cat settled himself on a large branch and the cockerel flew right to the top branches, where he would be safest.

From the top of the tree the cockerel could see a little spark of light in the distance, so he called to his companions that there must be a house not far off. The donkey said: 'If so, we should get up and go there, for we would surely be more comfortable there.'

The hound thought that a few bones with some meat on them would do him good too!

So they made their way to the place where the light shone and soon arrived at a well-lit house. The donkey, who was the tallest, went to the window and looked in.

'What do you see?' asked the cockerel.

'A table covered with good things to eat and drink! But there are some robbers sitting at the table enjoying themselves.'

The animals tried to think of a way to drive away the robbers and at last they thought of a plan. The donkey stood on his hind legs, the hound jumped on the donkey's back, the cat climbed upon the dog and the cockerel flew up and perched upon the head of the cat.

When this was done they began to perform their music together: the donkey brayed, the hound barked, the cat mewed and the cockerel crowed; then they burst through the window of the room so that the glass shattered loudly. The robbers had never heard such a horrible din and, thinking that a ghost had come in to haunt them, fled in great fear out into the forest. The four companions sat down at the table and ate as if they had been starved for a month!

As soon as the four musicians were finished, they put out the light and found themselves a place to sleep. The donkey laid himself down upon some straw in the yard, the hound on the mat behind the door, the cat upon the hearth near the warm fire and the cockerel perched himself upon a beam of the roof. They were so tired from the night's adventure that they went straight to sleep.

Later that night, when the robbers saw from their hideaway that the light was no longer burning in their house and all appeared quiet, their captain ordered one of them to go and examine the house.

The man, finding all still, went into the kitchen to light a candle, and not seeing the cat lying by the dying fire, stepped on his tail. The angry cat flew in his face, spitting and scratching. The messenger was dreadfully frightened and ran to the back door, but the dog, who lay there, sprang up and bit his leg; and as he ran across the yard by the straw-heap, the donkey gave him a great kick with his hind foot. All of this woke the cockerel, who cried down from the beam 'Cock-a-doodle-doo!'

The robber ran back as fast as he could to his captain and said, 'Ah, there is a horrible witch sitting in the house, who spat on me and scratched my face with her long claws; and by the door stands a man with a knife who stabbed me in the leg; and in the yard there lies a black monster, who beat me with a wooden club; and above on the roof sits a ghost calling out "Catch a crook or two!"'

The robbers did not trust themselves in the house again; but it suited the four musicians of Bremen so well that they did not care to leave it any more and, as far as I know, they are living there to this day.

The Ugly Duckling

A tale from the original by Hans Christian Andersen

It was lovely summer weather in the country and the golden corn, the green oats and the haystacks piled up in the meadows looked beautiful. The cornfields and meadows were surrounded by large forests, in the midst of which were deep lakes.

In a sunny spot by a pleasant old farmhouse, close by a deep river, grew great burdock leaves, so high that under the tallest of them a little child could stand upright. The spot was as wild as the centre of a thick wood. In this snug hiding place sat a duck on her nest, watching for her young ducklings to hatch. She was beginning to get tired of her task, for she had been sitting for a long time, and she did not have visitors very often because the other ducks preferred to swim about in the river rather than to climb the slippery banks and sit under a big leaf to talk with her.

At length one shell cracked, and then another, and from each egg came a living creature that lifted its head and cried, 'peep, peep'. 'Quack, quack', said the mother, and then they all quacked as well as they could, and looked about them on every side at the large green leaves.

'How large the world is', said the young ducks, when they found how much more room they now had than while they were inside the eggshell. 'Do you imagine this is the whole world?' asked the mother; 'It stretches far beyond the garden to the field, but I have never been any further. Well then, are you all out? No, I declare, the largest egg still lies there. I wonder how long this is to last, I am quite tired of it,' and she seated herself again on the nest.

'Well, how are you getting on?' asked an old duck, who paid her a visit.

'One egg is not hatched yet,' said the duck, 'it will not break. But just look at all the others, are they not the prettiest little ducklings you have ever seen?'

'Let me see the egg that will not break,' said the duck; 'Ah yes! I have no doubt it is a turkey's egg. I was tricked by such an egg once myself and I had such trouble with the little one. I quacked and clucked, but I just could not get it to swim. Take my advice, leave it where it is and teach the other children to swim.'

'I think I will sit on it a little while longer,' said the duck; 'as I have sat so long already, a few more days will be nothing.'

'Please yourself', said the old duck, and she went away.

At last the large egg broke, and a young one crept forth crying, 'peep, peep.' It was very large and very ugly. The duck stared at it and exclaimed: 'It is very large and not at all like the others. I wonder if it really is a turkey. We shall soon find out, however, when we go to the water. It must go in, if I have to push it myself.'

On the next day the weather was delightful, and the sun shone brightly on the green burdock leaves, so the mother duck took her young brood down to the water, and jumped in with a splash. 'Quack, quack', cried she, and one after another the little ducklings jumped in. The water closed over their heads, but they came up again in an instant, and swam about quite prettily with their legs paddling under them as easily as possible, and the ugly duckling was also in the water swimming with them.

'Oh,' said the mother, 'that is not a turkey; how well he uses his legs, and how upright he holds himself! He is my own child, and he is not so very ugly after all if you look at him properly. Quack, quack! Come with me now, I will introduce you to the farmyard, but you must keep close to me or you may be trodden upon; and, above all, beware of the cat!'

When they reached the farmyard, they could hear a horrible noise, a commotion of quacks, honks, hisses, clucks and gobbles. 'Now keep together,' said the mother, 'and bow to the old duck yonder. She is a great lady. Now, bow your necks children and say "Quack!"'

The ducklings did as they were told, but the other ducks stared, and said, 'Look, what a strange-looking fellow one of them is; we don't want him here', and then one flew out and bit him in the neck.

'Let him alone,' said the mother, 'he is not doing any harm.'

'Yes, but he is so big and ugly,' said the spiteful duck, 'and therefore he must be turned out.'

Then the great lady duck spoke up and said, 'All of your children are pretty except this one. He has not turned out well. It's a pity you can't hatch him over again.'

'Oh,' said the mother, 'that cannot be, Your Highness. And though he is not handsome, he is a good child and a fine swimmer and I think that, in time, he will grow to look more like the others.'

'Well, make yourselves at home dears,' said the old duck.

And so they made themselves comfortable; but the poor duckling, who had crept out of his shell last of all, and looked so ugly, was bitten and pushed and made fun of, not only by the ducks, but by all the farmyard animals. 'He is too big', they all said, and the turkey puffed himself out like a ship in full sail and flew at the duckling, until he was quite red in the face, so that the poor little thing did not know where to go, and was quite miserable because he was so ugly and laughed at by the whole farmyard.

So it went on from day to day and it became worse and worse. The poor duckling was set upon by everyone; even his brothers and sisters were unkind to him, and would say, 'Ah, you ugly creature, I wish the cat would get you', and his mother said she wished he had never been born. The ducks pecked him, the chickens beat him, and the girl who fed the hens kicked him with her feet. So at last he ran away.

He flew and flew, until he came out on a large moor, inhabited by wild ducks where he remained the whole night, feeling very tired and sorrowful.

In the morning, when the wild ducks rose in the air, they stared at their new comrade. 'What sort of a duck are you?' they all said, coming round him.

He bowed to them, and was as polite as he could be, but he did not reply to their question. 'You are exceedingly ugly', said the wild ducks.

Poor thing! All he wanted was permission to lie among the rushes, and drink some of the water on the moor and to be left alone. After he had been in the marsh for two days, there came two wild geese. 'Listen, friend,' said one of them to the duckling, 'you are so ugly that we like you! Why don't you join us? Not far from here is another marsh, in which there are some pretty geese, really lovely maidens. It is a chance for you to get a wife; you may be lucky, ugly as you are.'

Then suddenly – BANG!-BANG! – shots sounded in the air, and the two wild geese fell dead among the rushes, and the water was tinged with blood. The blue smoke from the guns rose like clouds over the dark trees, and as it floated away across the water, a number of dogs bounded in among the rushes, which bent beneath them wherever they went. How they terrified the poor duckling! He turned away his head to hide it under his wing, and at the same moment a large, terrible dog passed quite near him. His jaws were open, his tongue hung from his mouth, and his eyes glared.

He thrust his nose close to the duckling, showing his sharp teeth, and then, 'splash, splash', he went into the water without touching him, 'Oh,' sighed the duckling, 'how thankful I am for being so ugly; even a dog will not bite me.'

It was late in the day before all became quiet, but even then the poor young thing did not dare to move. He waited quietly for several hours, and then, after looking carefully around him, hastened away from the marsh as fast as he could. He ran over field and meadow till a storm rose, so strong that he had to fight just to move ahead.

Towards evening, he reached a poor little cottage that seemed ready to fall down. The storm was so violent that the duckling could go no farther; he sat down by the front doorstep, and then he noticed that there was a narrow opening near the bottom of the door large enough for him to slip through, which he did very quietly, and sheltered for the night.

A woman, a tom cat and a hen lived in this cottage. The tom cat, whom the mistress called 'My little son', was a great favourite; he could raise his back, and purr. The hen had very short legs, so she was called 'Chickie short legs'. She laid good eggs and her mistress loved her as if she had been her own child. In the morning, the strange visitor was discovered, and the tom cat began to purr, and the hen to cluck.

Now the cat and the hen thought they were the cleverest creatures in the whole world. The duckling certainly did not agree, but he was too afraid to question them.

'Can you lay eggs?' the hen asked.

'No', said the ugly duckling.

'Can you raise your back, or purr?' said the tom cat.

'No.'

'Then you should just keep quiet and listen when sensible people are speaking.'

So the duckling sat in a corner, feeling very low-spirited, until the sunshine and the fresh air came into the room through the open door, and then he began to feel such a great longing for a swim on the water that he could not help telling the hen.

'What an absurd idea,' said the hen. 'If you could purr or lay eggs, you wouldn't have such strange ideas.'

'But it is so delightful to swim about on the water,' said the duckling, 'and so refreshing to feel it close over your head when you dive down to the bottom.'

'Delightful, indeed!' said the hen, 'why you must be crazy! Ask the cat, he is the cleverest animal I know; ask him how he would like to swim about on the water, or to dive under it? Humph!'

'You don't understand me', said the duckling.

'We don't understand you? Who can understand you, I wonder? Do you consider yourself more clever than the cat, or me? I advise you, therefore, to lay eggs, and learn to purr as quickly as possible.'

'I believe I must go out into the world again', said the duckling.

'Well then, go!' said the hen.

So the duckling left the cottage, and soon found water on which it could swim and dive, but was avoided by all other animals, because of its ugly appearance. Autumn came, and the leaves in the forest turned to orange and gold. Then, as winter approached, the wind caught them as they fell and whirled them in the cold air. The clouds, heavy with hail and snow-flakes, hung low in the sky, and the raven stood on the ferns crying, 'croak, croak'.

All this was very sad for the poor little duckling. One evening, just as the sun set amid radiant clouds, there came a large flock of beautiful birds out of the bushes. The duckling had never seen any like them before. They were swans, and they curved their graceful necks, while their soft plumage shone with dazzling whiteness.

They uttered a singular cry, as they spread their glorious wings and flew away from those cold regions to warmer countries across the sea. As they mounted higher and higher in the air, the ugly little duckling felt quite a strange sensation as he watched them.

He whirled himself in the water like a wheel, stretched out his neck towards them, and uttered a cry so strange that he frightened himself. He could not stop thinking about those noble and beautiful birds.

As the winter grew colder and colder, the duckling was obliged to swim about on the water to keep it from freezing, but every night the space on which he swam became smaller and smaller. At length it froze so hard that the ice in the water crackled as he moved, and the duckling had to paddle with his legs as well as he could, to keep the space from closing up. He became exhausted at last, and lay still and helpless, frozen fast in the ice.

Early in the morning, a farmer, who was passing by, saw what had happened. He broke the ice in pieces with his wooden shoe, and carried the duckling home to his wife. The warmth revived the poor little creature; but when the children wanted to play with him, the duckling thought they would do him some harm; so he started up in terror, fluttered into the milk-pan, and splashed the milk about the room. Then the woman clapped her hands, which frightened him still more. He flew first into the butter-cask, then into the flour-tin, and out again. What a condition he was in! The children laughed and shrieked, and tumbled over each other, in their efforts to catch him; but luckily he escaped. The door stood open; the poor creature could just manage to slip out among the bushes, and lie down quite exhausted in the newly fallen snow.

It would be very sad if I were to tell you all the hard times the poor little duckling had during the hard winter; but when it had passed, he found himself lying one morning on a moor, amongst the rushes. He felt the warm sun shining, and heard the lark singing, and saw that all around was beautiful spring.

Then the young bird felt that his wings were strong, as he flapped them against his sides, and rose high into the air. They took him onwards, until he found himself in a large garden, before he well knew how it had happened. The apple trees were in full blossom, and everything looked beautiful in the freshness of early spring. From a thicket close by came three beautiful white swans, rustling their feathers, and swimming lightly over the smooth water. The duckling remembered the lovely birds, and felt a strange sadness.

'I will fly to those royal birds,' he exclaimed, 'and they will kill me, because I am so ugly, and dare to approach them; but it does not matter: it is better to be killed by them than pecked by the ducks, beaten by the hens, pushed about by the maiden who feeds the poultry, or starved with hunger in the winter.'

Then he flew to the water, and swam towards the beautiful swans. The moment they espied the stranger, they rushed to meet him with outstretched wings.

'Kill me', said the poor bird; and he bent his head down to the surface of the water, and awaited death.

But what did he see in the clear stream below? His own image – no longer a dark, grey bird, ugly to look at, but a graceful and beautiful swan. To be born in a duck's nest, in a farmyard, is of no consequence to a bird, if it is hatched from a swan's egg. He now felt glad at having suffered sorrow and trouble, because he was now able to enjoy so much more all the pleasure and happiness around him; for the great swans swam round the newcomer, and stroked his neck with their beaks, as a welcome.

Into the garden presently came some little children, who threw bread and cake into the water.

'See,' cried the youngest, 'there is a new one!' The rest were delighted, and ran to their father and mother, dancing and clapping their hands, and shouting joyously, 'There is another swan come; a new one has arrived.'

Then they threw more bread and cake into the water, and said: 'The new one is the most beautiful of all; he is so young and pretty.' And the old swans bowed their heads before him.

Then he felt quite embarrassed, and hid his head under his wing; for he did not know what to do, he was so happy, and yet not at all proud. Then he rustled his feathers, curved his slender neck, and cried joyfully, from the depths of his heart: 'I never dreamed of such happiness as this, while I was an ugly duckling.'

Tug-of-War

PARENTS: This is a folk tale from Africa. People in different parts of Africa tell it with different small animals – a tortoise, a porcupine, a rabbit – as the central character. All versions share a theme (found also in the American Brer Rabbit Tales, which have their roots in Africa) of the large, strong characters outwitted by the small, clever ones.

If your child is not familiar with the game of tug-of-war, you may want to describe it before you read this story aloud.

A long time ago, Turtle was walking through the jungle. As he slowly crossed the river, he was chased out by Hippopotamus, who was trying to take a nap. 'Get out of here quickly, Turtle! Move, move!' he snapped grumpily.

Once Turtle got out of Hippo's way as quickly as he could, he crossed Elephant's path. 'Look out Turtle! You are moving so slowly that I almost stepped on you!' said Elephant.

This made Turtle very grumpy. He was always being mistreated by all the other jungle animals.

'Well, you need to watch where you are going!' yelled Turtle. 'I may be slow but I am strong and mighty too!'

Elephant laughed. 'Oh Turtle, I could have easily stepped right on you and crushed you flat. You had better watch that sharp tongue of yours.'

'In that case,' said Turtle 'I challenge you to see who is the strongest. I challenge you to a tug-of-war!'

'A tug-of-war?' chuckled Elephant. He laughed so hard the earth shook for miles around. 'Why – you haven't got a chance!'

'Maybe I do and maybe I don't,' said Turtle, 'but if you're so sure, what have you got to lose? We will each take a hold of this vine here. You take one end and I'll go down to the river with the other. When I say, "Pull oh mighty beast, pull", we will both pull. You try to drag me into the jungle and I will try to drag you into the river. If the vine breaks then we are equals and will call each other "friend".'

'Fine by me,' said Elephant, 'I'll show you who's mighty.'

Turtle hurried all the way down to the river where Hippo was attempting to continue his afternoon nap.

'Hippo, you chased me out of the river earlier and now I am here to show you that I am mighty too', yelled Turtle.

Hippo emerged from the water. 'Oh yeah?' he said with a laugh.

'Yeah. You think that because you're so much bigger than me, that makes you better. Well let's have a tug-of-war to find out! You hold one end of this vine here and I'll hold the other. When I say, "Pull oh mighty beast, pull", you try to pull me into the water. And I will try to pull you into the jungle. We will keep pulling until one of us wins. If the vine breaks we will call each other "friend".'

Hippo laughed and said, 'You must have no brains at all! All right then, but I'll pull you down before you have time to think! It's about time I taught you some manners.'

Turtle walked halfway back into the jungle and yelled at the top of his lungs, 'PULL OH MIGHTY BEAST, PULL!' and he gave the vine a mighty shake.

When Elephant and Hippo felt this they began to pull and where quite surprised when they felt the strong tug at the other end. So they began to pull and pull with all their might. Neither of them would budge.

'Turtle is quite strong', thought Elephant.

'Turtle can pull much harder than I imagined', thought Hippo.

But they both kept pulling.

Turtle sat himself down in the shade of a big tree and munched on some grass, chuckling to himself as he watched the rope move ever so slightly one way and then ever so slightly the other way. Then he yawned and had a little nap.

He woke up a few hours later feeling refreshed and looked up to see the rope just as before, moving ever so slightly one way and then ever so slightly the other way.

Feeling that each beast had had enough, Turtle cut the vine. Both Hippo and Elephant tumbled apart. BUMP-BUMP-BUMP-BOOM!

Turtle ran over to Elephant and found him sprawled on the ground, rubbing his head with his trunk. 'You are strong, Turtle. I will allow you to roam the jungle with me from now on', said a tired Elephant.

Then Turtle ran down to Hippo who said grumpily: 'I won't chase you out of the water anymore. I will share my river with you, and call you my, uh, my – friend,' said an exhausted Hippo.

And from that day forward, Turtle was free to roam about the jungle, as fast or as slow as he pleased. And he also became one of the most respected animals in the jungle.

Cinderella

Once upon a time, there was a rich man whose wife fell ill. As she felt the end of her life drawing near, she called her only daughter to her bedside and said: 'Dear child, I will always look down on you from heaven and protect you. You must remember to always be good and kind.' Then she sank back, closed her eyes and with a sigh departed this life.

Every day the little girl went to her mother's grave and wept and always remembered to be good and kind. When winter came the snow spread a white sheet over the ground like a blanket; and when the sun came in the spring and melted it away, the little girl's father married a new wife. And so the little girl had a step-mother. Now was the beginning of a bad time for the little girl.

The new wife brought two of her own daughters by her previous husband into the house with her. They were both very beautiful, but proud and hateful at heart. 'Is the stupid goose to sit here with us?' they would say. They took her pretty clothes away from her and made her wear an old grey dress and wooden shoes.

The step-mother was just as hateful as her daughters and could not stand the good, kind girl. She forced her to do hard work from morning until night, carry the water, cook the dinner and light all the fires. In the evening she had no bed to go to, but had to sleep by the fireside among the ashes and cinders, so she always looked dusty and dirty and came to be called 'Cinderella'.

It happened that the King announced that he was going to hold a ball, to which all the beautiful young girls in the country were invited, in order that his son might choose himself a bride. When the step-sisters heard the announcement, they shrieked in excitement!

'For my part,' said the eldest, 'I will wear my red velvet suit with French trimming.'

'And I,' said the youngest, 'shall have my gold-flowered gown, and my diamond belt, which is quite out of the ordinary.'

They called Cinderella and said: 'Comb our hair for us, brush our shoes and fasten our buckles, for we are going to the ball at the palace.' Anyone but Cinderella would have tied their hair in knots, but she was very good and kind as always, and dressed them beautifully. Cinderella obeyed, but silently wept, because she too would have liked to go with them to the ball.

At last the happy day came for them to go to the palace. Cinderella followed them with her eyes as long as she could, and when she had lost sight of them, she began to weep. But it seemed she was not alone. A gentle voice asked her: 'What may be the matter dear?'

She looked up and saw her godmother peering down at her with a kind face. 'I wish I could–I wish I could–'; but she was not able to speak the rest, being interrupted by her tears and sobbing.

This godmother of hers, who happened to be a fairy, said to her: 'You wish to go to the ball– is that it?'

'Y–es', cried Cinderella, with a great sigh.

'Well then,' said her fairy godmother, 'because you are so good and kind, off to the ball you shall go! Run into the garden, and bring me in a big, orange pumpkin.'

Cinderella went immediately to gather the finest pumpkin she could find, and brought it to her fairy godmother, not being able to imagine how this pumpkin could make her go to the ball. Her fairy godmother scooped out all the inside of it, having left nothing but the rind; which she then struck with her wand, and instantly the pumpkin was turned into a fine coach, gleaming with gold.

'Now dear,' said the fairy godmother, 'bring me the mousetrap from the house.' Cinderella went to fetch the mousetrap, where she found six live mice. Ordering Cinderella to lift the trapdoor up a little, she gave each mouse, as it scurried out, a little tap with her wand. Each mouse was, at that moment, turned into a fine horse, which altogether made a very fine set of six horses of a beautiful mouse-coloured dapple-grey.

Next, with a tap of her wand, she turned a big rat into a fat, jolly coachman who had the smartest whiskers you ever did see.

'Well, are you not pleased?' said the fairy godmother.

'Oh yes!' cried Cinderella, 'but... must I go in these nasty rags?'

Her godmother only just touched her with her wand, and, at the same instant, her clothes were turned into cloth of gold and silver, all set with jewels. This done, she gave her a pair of glass slippers, the prettiest in the whole world. Cinderella got up into her coach, but her godmother warned her not to stay past midnight. 'When the clock strikes twelve, the coach will once again be a pumpkin, the horses mice and your clothes will once again become rags.'

She promised her fairy godmother she would not forget to leave before midnight; and then away she went, scarcely able to contain herself for joy.

At the palace, the King's son was told that a beautiful princess, whom nobody knew, had arrived. So he went to meet her. As he led her into the room, there was a great hush as everyone turned to look upon the unknown beauty. The prince asked Cinderella to dance with him and everyone looked on in admiration – everyone, that is, except the two jealous step-sisters who glared enviously at Cinderella, though they had no idea who she was.

For Cinderella, the music, the dancing, the warm gaze of the prince – it all seemed like a wonderful dream. While Cinderella was having such a wonderful time, she completely forgot about her promise to her fairy godmother. Suddenly she heard the clock strike twelve and the great bell of the palace began to toll...one...two...three...

'Oh no!' Cinderella gasped. 'What time is it?'

'Why, it's midnight', replied the prince.

Cinderella grew pale and she turned and ran from the ballroom, down a long hallway and down a long staircase to where her carriage awaited her. At the foot of the staircase she stumbled and one of her delicate glass slippers came off. But Cinderella could not stop. Already the clock had sounded the eleventh stroke of midnight – and she felt her silk gown turning back into the rough cloth. Her golden coach had turned back into a pumpkin, and the horses became little mice once again, so she ran all the way home as fast as she could. When she got there she realised she was still wearing one glass slipper!

The following morning Cinderella asked the two sisters if they had a nice time at the ball and if they had had the chance to dance with the Prince.

They told her that they had a perfectly horrid time because the prince had done nothing but look at the mysterious unknown princess all evening and not given either of them a second glance. Strangely, though, the beautiful princess had hurried away immediately when it struck twelve, and so quickly that she dropped one of her little glass slippers, the prettiest in the world, which the Prince had found after chasing after his beauty.

Later that day the Prince announced to the sound of trumpets that he would marry the girl whose foot would fit the slipper. He sent his men to try the slipper upon foot after foot.

At last they came to the house of Cinderella and her step-sisters. Each sister by turn tried to cram her foot into the delicate glass slipper, but it would not fit. Cinderella, who saw all this, stepped forward and said: 'Let me see if it will not fit me.'

Her sisters burst out laughing: 'You! Go back to the cinders where you belong!'

But the gentleman who was sent to try the slipper said that he had orders to try the slipper on every maiden in the kingdom. He placed the slipper on Cinderella's foot – and it was a perfect fit! The step-sisters could hardly believe it! And they were even more shocked when, from her pocket, Cinderella drew the other glass slipper.

And now her two sisters recognised Cinderella as the beautiful lady whom they had seen at the ball. They threw themselves at her feet and begged her to forgive them for treating her so badly. Cinderella being so kind-hearted forgave them at once and pulled them into a warm embrace.

Cinderella married the Prince and even invited her step-mother and step-sisters to live at the palace. And there, Cinderella and the Prince lived happily ever after.

The Wolf and the Seven Little Kids
A tale from the Brothers Grimm

There was once upon a time an old mother goat who had seven little kids, which she loved as much as any mother ever loved her children. One day she needed to go into the forest to fetch some food. So she called all seven to her and said: 'Dear children, I have to go into the forest. While I am away you must be on your guard against the wolf; if he gets in, he will gobble you up – skin and all! The beast often disguises himself, but you will know him at once by his rough voice and his black feet.'

The kids said: 'Don't worry, Mother, we will take good care of ourselves.' So the mother goat bleated goodbye and went off to find some food.

It was not long before there was a knock at the door. Someone called: 'Open the door, dear children; your mother is here, and has brought something back with her for each of you.' But the little kids knew at once that it was the wolf by his rough voice. 'We will not open the door,' they cried. 'You are not our mother. She has a soft, pleasant voice, unlike yours which is rough and horrible. You must be the wolf!'

Then the wolf went away to a shopkeeper and bought himself a great lump of chalk, which he ate to make his voice soft. Then he went back to the little house, knocked at the door and said softly: 'Open up, dear children, your mother is here and has brought something back with her for each of you.' But the wolf had laid his black paws against the window, and the children saw them and cried: 'We will not open the door, our mother has not got big, black, hairy feet like you. You must be the wolf!'

Then the wolf ran to a baker and said: 'I have hurt my feet, rub some dough over them for me.' And when the baker had rubbed his feet over, he ran to the miller and said: 'Sprinkle some white flour over my feet for me.'

Now the miller thought to himself: 'The wolf is up to no good. He wants to deceive someone,' and refused; but the wolf said: 'If you won't do it, I will eat you up in one bite!'

The miller was afraid, and so he made the wolf's paws white with flour for him. So the wicked wolf went for the third time to the door, knocked at it and said, 'Open the door for me children, your dear mother has come home and brought every one of you something back from the forest.'

The little kids cried: 'First you must show us your paws so we can see if you are our mother.' So the wolf put his paws in through the window and when the kids saw that they were white, they believed it was their mother and opened the door. But who should come in but the wolf!

The kids were terrified and wanted to hide themselves. One sprang under the table, the second into the bed, the third into the stove, the fourth into the kitchen, the fifth into the cupboard, the sixth under the washing-bowl and the seventh climbed into a big grandfather clock.

But the wolf found them all, and one after the other swallowed them whole. The youngest, who was hiding in the grandfather clock, was the only one he did not manage to find.

The wolf, feeling satisfied, strolled into the forest and laid himself down under a tree and fell asleep.

Soon afterwards the mother goat came home with some food for her kids, and what a sight she saw there! The house door stood wide open. The table, chairs and benches were thrown down, the washing bowl lay broken to pieces and the quilts and pillows were pulled off the bed. She called out for her children, but they were nowhere to be found. She called each one by name, but they did not answer. At last, when she called the name of the youngest, a tiny voice squeaked: 'Dear mother, I am in the big clock.' She took the kid out and it told her that the wolf had tricked them and eaten all his brothers and sisters. How she cried and cried for her poor children!

Still crying, she wandered outside with the youngest kid and when they came to the meadow they saw the wolf lying under the tree, snoring so loudly that the branches were shaking. The mother looked at the wolf in anger and suddenly she saw that something was moving and struggling in his huge belly. 'Heavens!' she said, 'is it possible that my poor children, whom this beast has swallowed whole, may still be alive?'

The youngest kid ran home as fast as he could to fetch the scissors as well as a needle and thread. The mother goat quickly snipped open the monster's stomach and hardly had she made one cut, than one little kid thrust its head out; and when she cut further still, all six sprang out, one after another, all still alive and kicking!

'Now,' said the mother to her kids, 'go and look for some big stones, and we will fill the wicked beast's stomach with them while he is still asleep.' The seven kids dragged the stones to her and she packed them into his stomach and sewed him up again as quickly as she could.

At last, when the wolf awoke, he stood up, and feeling very thirsty went to the well to get a drink. But when he began to walk and move about, the stones in his stomach knocked against each other and rattled. Then he cried:

'What rumbles and tumbles
 Against my poor bones?
 I thought it was six kids,
 It feels more like six stones!'

And when he got to the well and bent over to take a drink, the heavy stones made him fall in. He sank to the bottom and was never seen again.

King Midas and the Golden Touch

A myth from ancient Greece, adapted from
Nathaniel Hawthorne's *Wonder Book*

Once upon a time, there lived a very rich King whose name was Midas. King Midas was fonder of gold than of anything else in the world. One of the main reasons he loved being King so much was so that he could wear a golden crown. If he loved anything as much, or half as much as gold, it was his little daughter Marygold. When little Marygold ran to meet him, with a bunch of buttercups and dandelions, he used to say: 'Oh child! If these flowers were as golden as they look, they would be worth picking!'

King Midas had once loved flowers himself. He had planted a garden, in which grew the biggest and most beautiful roses that anyone had ever seen or smelt. These roses were still growing in the garden, but now, if he looked at them at all, it was only to calculate how much the garden would be worth if each of the rose-petals were a thin plate of gold.

At length, Midas came to love gold so much that he could scarcely bear to see or touch any object that was not gold. He passed a large portion of every day in a dark and dreary underground room where he kept his wealth and it was here that he was most happy.

Midas was enjoying himself in his treasure-room one day when a shadow fell over the heaps of gold; and, looking up suddenly, what should he behold but the figure of a stranger who seemed to shine with a golden glow.

As Midas knew that he had carefully turned the key in the lock, and that no human strength could possibly break into his treasure-room, he knew that his visitor must have magic power. But Midas felt no fear because the stranger had a kind smile.

'You are a wealthy man, my friend Midas!' he observed. 'I doubt whether any other four walls on earth contain so much gold as you have in this room.'

'Yes I have a lot of gold,' answered Midas, 'but it is not enough!'

'What?' exclaimed the stranger, 'then you are not satisfied?'

Midas shook his head.

'And pray what would satisfy you?' asked the stranger.

'Only this,' replied Midas, 'I want everything that I touch to be changed into gold!'

'The Golden Touch!' he exclaimed. 'Are you quite sure that this will satisfy you?'

'How could it not?' said Midas.

'Be it as you wish, then,' replied the stranger, waving his hand. 'Tomorrow, at sunrise, you will find yourself gifted with the Golden Touch.'

The figure of the stranger then became very bright, and Midas closed his eyes. On opening them again, he found that the figure had gone.

The next morning when the sun had hardly peeped over the hills, King Midas was wide awake, and, stretching his arms out of bed, began to touch the objects that were within reach.

He touched a chair and it turned to gold!

Midas ran about the room, touching everything that happened to be in his way. He touched one of the blankets, and it immediately turned to gold. He took up a book from the table. At his first touch, it turned to gold in his hands. He hurriedly put on his clothes, and was amazed to see himself in a magnificent suit of gold cloth, which retained its flexibility and softness, although it was very heavy. He drew out his handkerchief, on which little Marygold had stitched a design. That was also turned to gold, with the dear child's neat and pretty stitches running all along the border, in gold thread!

Somehow or other, this did not quite please King Midas. He would rather that his little daughter's work should have remained just the same as when she climbed onto his knee and put it into his hand. But he did not let this trouble him.

King Midas was so pleased by his good fortune and ran outside to the garden. Here he found a great number of beautiful roses in full bloom. He went from bush to bush, and touched each, until every individual flower and bud was changed to gold. By the time this work was completed, King Midas was feeling hungry, so he went to breakfast.

He tried to take a drink, but as soon as the liquid touched his lips it turned to gold. In despair, he helped himself to a boiled egg, which also turned instantly to gold. 'How am I to get any breakfast?' he cried.

King Midas next snatched a hot potato, and attempted to cram it into his mouth and swallow it in a hurry. But the Golden Touch was too quick for him. He found his mouth full, not of potato, but of red-hot metal, which so burnt his tongue that he roared aloud, both with pain and anger.

Just then he heard someone crying. It was Marygold.

'How now, my little lady!' cried Midas. 'What is the matter with you, this bright morning?'

Marygold held out her hand, in which was one of the roses which Midas had so recently turned into gold.

'And what is there in this beautiful golden rose to make you cry?' asked her father.

'Ah, dear father!' answered the child, as well as her sobs would let her; 'it is not beautiful, but the ugliest flower that ever grew! As soon as I was dressed I ran into the garden to gather some roses for you; because I know you like them, but all the beautiful roses have been ruined!'

'Oh, my dear little girl, don't cry!' said Midas and threw his arms affectionately about her. He bent down and kissed her. 'My precious, precious Marygold!' he cried.

But Marygold made no answer.

Alas, what had he done? The moment the lips of Midas touched Marygold's forehead, her sweet, rosy face had turned to yellow gold. Her beautiful brown ringlets the same. Little Marygold was a human child no longer, but a golden statue!

Midas cried out, wishing that he were the poorest man in the wide world, if the loss of all his wealth might bring back the faintest rose-colour to his dear child's face.

While he was despairing, he suddenly noticed a stranger standing near the door. Midas bent down his head, without speaking; for he recognised the same figure who had appeared to him the day before.

'Well, friend Midas,' said the stranger, 'pray how do you like the Golden Touch?'

Midas shook his head. 'I am very miserable', he said.

'And why might that be?' asked the stranger. 'Have you not everything that your heart desired?'

'Gold is not everything,' answered Midas. 'And I have lost all that my heart really cared for.'

'Then which of these two things do you think is really worth the most, the gift of the Golden Touch, or one cup of clear cold water?'

'O blessed water!' exclaimed Midas. 'It will never moisten my parched throat again!'

'The Golden Touch,' continued the stranger, 'or a crust of bread?'

'A piece of bread,' answered Midas, 'is worth all the gold on earth!'

'The Golden Touch,' asked the stranger, 'or your own little Marygold, warm, soft, and loving as she was an hour ago?'

'Oh my child, my dear child!' cried poor Midas wringing his hands. 'I would not have given that one small dimple in her chin for the power of changing this whole big earth into a solid lump of gold!'

'You are wiser than you were, King Midas!' said the stranger, 'Go then and plunge yourself into the river that glides past the bottom of your garden. Fill a vase with some of the water and sprinkle it over everything that you have touched. If you do this quickly and with a good heart, it may possibly repair your mischief.'

King Midas ran to the river bank and plunged headlong in, without waiting even to pull off his shoes.

King Midas filled a vase with water hastened back to the palace, where the first thing he did was to sprinkle the water by handfuls over the golden figure of little Marygold. No sooner did it fall on her than the rosy colour came back to the dear child's cheek and she began to sneeze and sputter. How astonished she was to find herself dripping wet, and her father still throwing more water over her!

'Father, stop!' she cried. 'See how you have wet my nice dress, which I put on only this morning!'

'Now I am truly happy!' said the King, much wiser than before. However, there were two things that reminded King Midas of the Golden Touch for the rest of his life. One was that the sands of the river sparkled like gold; the other was that little Marygold's hair had forever a golden sheen.

Snow White

(Adapted from the Brothers Grimm)

Once upon a time in the middle of winter, when the snowflakes were falling like feathers from heaven, a beautiful Queen sat sewing at her window, which had a frame of black ebony wood. As she sewed, she looked out at the snow and accidentally pricked her finger with the needle. Three drops of blood fell onto the snow that had gathered on the window ledge. The red on the white looked so beautiful, that she thought: 'If only I had a child as white as snow, as red as blood, and as black as this ebony frame.'

It was not long afterward that the Queen had a little daughter, with skin as white as snow, lips as red as blood and hair as black as ebony wood, and so they called her Snow White. But sadly, when the child was born the beautiful queen died.

After a few years had passed, the King married again. The new queen was very beautiful but she was terribly proud and could not bear to think that anyone might be more beautiful than she. She had a wonderful magic mirror, and when she stood in front of it and said:

'*Mirror mirror on the wall,*

Who is the fairest one of all?'

The mirror would answer her:

'*You, oh Queen, are the fairest one of all.*'

Then she would be satisfied, for she knew the mirror spoke only the truth.

Now, as Snow White grew up, she grew more and more beautiful, and when she was seven she was as beautiful as the day and more beautiful even than the proud queen herself. One day the queen went to the magic mirror and said:

'*Mirror, mirror on the wall,*

Who is the fairest of us all?'

And the mirror answered:

'*Though you are fair, oh Queen, it's true,*

Snow White is fairer still than you.'

When the queen heard this, she was shocked and turned green with envy, and from that moment she hated Snow White with a passion. Envy and pride grew in her heart like a weed and she could not rest day or night until one day she called a huntsman and said: 'Take the child away into the forest. Kill her and bring me back her heart as a token.'

The huntsman obeyed and took her away; but when he had drawn his knife, and was about to pierce Snow White's innocent heart, she began to weep and said: 'Dear huntsman, let me live! I will run away into the wild forest and never come back.'

And as she was so beautiful the huntsman had pity on her and said: 'Run then, poor child, run away and never come back.' And he thought to himself, it is likely that the wild beasts will eat her anyway. And just at that moment a young boar came running out of the woods and he stabbed it and cut out the heart and took it to the queen as proof that the child was dead.

Now Snow White was all alone in the great forest and so terrified that she looked at every leaf of every tree in terror. She began to run, over the sharp stones and through the thorn bushes. She ran for as long as her feet would carry her, until it was evening and she came across a little cottage in a clearing.

She went inside to rest herself. Everything in the cottage was very small; there was a table, on which were laid seven little plates; and on each plate a little spoon; moreover there were seven little knives and forks and seven little mugs. Against the wall stood seven little beds side by side, each covered with white sheets.

Little Snow White was so hungry and thirsty that she ate some vegetables and bread from each plate and drank a drop of wine out of each mug. Then she was so tired that she laid herself down on one of the little beds, but none of them suited her; one was too long, another too short, but at last she found that the seventh one was just right and so she went to sleep in it.

When it was quite dark, the owners of the cottage came back; they were seven dwarfs who worked every day digging in the mountains, with their shovels and their picks, for gold. They lit their seven little candles and saw that everything in their cottage had been disturbed.

The first dwarf said: 'Who has been sitting in my chair?'

The second said: 'Who has been eating off my plate?'

The third said: 'Who has been eating my vegetables?'

The fourth said: 'Who has been nibbling my bread?'

The fifth said: 'Who has been cutting with my knife?'

The sixth said: 'Who has been eating with my fork?'

The seventh said: 'Who has been drinking out of my mug?'

Then the first looked round and saw that there was a little dip in his bed and he said: 'Who has been getting into my bed?' The others came up and each called out, 'Somebody has been lying in my bed too!' When the seventh looked at his bed, he saw Snow White sleeping there. And he called to the others, who came running up to look. They held up their seven little candles and let the light fall on Snow White.

'Oh heavens!' they cried, 'what a lovely child!' and they were so in awe of her beauty that they did not wake her.

When morning came, Snow White awoke and was frightened when she saw the seven dwarfs. But they were ever so friendly and asked her what her name was.

'My name is Snow White', she answered.

'How have you come to be in our house?' asked the dwarfs. So Snow White told them that her step-mother had wished to have her killed but the huntsman had spared her life, and she described how she had run all day long until at last she had come upon the little cottage in the wood.

Then the dwarfs said: 'If you will take care of our little house, cook, clean and make the beds, you can stay here with us and we will take care of you and make sure you have everything you need.'

And Snow White agreed with all her heart. She kept the house in order for them. Every morning the dwarfs would go off and mine for gold while Snow White would be left alone to take care of the house. The dwarfs warned her: 'Beware of your step-mother, she will soon know that you are here, be sure not to open the door to anyone.'

Indeed, the queen, believing that she was again the first and most beautiful in the land, went to her magic mirror and said:

'*Mirror, mirror, on the wall,*

Who is the fairest one of all?'

And the mirror answered:

'*Oh Queen, you are of beauty rare,*

But over the hills where seven dwarfs dwell,

Snow White is still alive and well,

Incomparably fair.'

The queen was shocked, for she knew that the mirror only ever spoke the truth, which meant that Snow White must still be living! It filled her with rage to know that she was not the fairest in the land, so she thought again of a plan to kill Snow White. The queen dressed herself like an old woman so that no-one would recognise her. In this disguise she went over the seven mountains to the seven dwarfs and knocked at the door crying: 'Pretty things for sale, pretty things for sale!'

Snow White looked out of the window and called: 'Good morning, what have you to sell?'

'Good things, pretty things,' she answered, 'fine, brightly coloured, silk laces.'

'I may let the old woman in,' thought Snow White, 'what harm can she do me?' So she unbolted the door and bought the pretty laces.

'Child, let me lace you up properly' said the old woman. Snow White, seeing no reason to distrust the old woman, let herself be laced with the new laces. But the old woman laced her so tightly that Snow White could not breathe and fell down as though she were dead.

'Now,' said the evil queen, 'you are no longer the fairest in the land.' And she hurried off.

Soon the dwarfs came home and how shocked they were when they saw their dear little Snow White lying on the ground and thought she must be dead.

When they lifted her up they saw that she was laced much too tightly, so they cut the lace and she began to breathe again. When the dwarfs heard what had happened they said: 'The old woman was none other than the wicked queen! Take care and let no one come in when we are not with you.'

When the queen got home, she went straight to her magic mirror and said:

'Mirror, mirror on the wall,

Who is the fairest of us all?'

And the mirror answered:

'Oh Queen, you are the fairest of all I see,

But over the hills where seven dwarfs dwell,

Snow White is still alive and well,

And no one is so fair as she.'

The queen shook with anger. 'I will think of something that shall put an end to you', she said, and with the use of a witch's spell she made a poisonous comb. Then she disguised herself once again, this time as a different old woman. So she went over the seven mountains to the seven dwarfs' house and knocked on the door crying: 'Good things to sell, cheap, cheap, cheap!'

Little Snow White called out: 'Go away; I cannot let anyone in.'

'Surely you could look out of the window', replied the queen, and she held up the poisonous comb. Snow White liked it so much that, without thinking, she opened the door.

'Turn around and I shall comb your hair as it should be done', said the old woman. And as soon as she ran the comb through

Snow White's ebony hair, the poison began to work and the child fell down as if she were dead.

'Now my pretty, you are done for!' said the queen, and she went away.

Luckily the dwarfs came home early and saw the poisoned comb in Snow White's hair and pulled it out at once. As soon as they had removed it, Snow White woke up and told them what had happened. Then the dwarfs warned her again never to answer the door.

When the queen got home, she went straight to her mirror and said:

'Mirror, mirror on the wall,

Who is the fairest of us all?'

And the mirror answered:

'Oh Queen, you are the fairest of all I see,

But over the hills where seven dwarfs dwell,

Snow White is still alive and well,

And no one is so fair as she.'

When she heard the mirror say this she was overcome with rage. 'Snow White shall die,' she cried, 'even if it costs me my own life!'

She went into a quiet, secret room, where no one ever came, and made a poisonous apple. It was so big and red and shiny, that anyone who saw it would long to have a bite of it, but whoever ate a piece of it would surely die.

The queen made herself look like an old country woman and went over the seven mountains to the seven dwarfs' cottage. She knocked at the door. Snow White called out of the window: 'I cannot let anybody in. The seven dwarfs told me not to.'

'Alright, I'll go,' said the woman, 'but I shall leave you one of my apples.'

'No thank you,' said Snow White, 'I dare not take anything.'

'Child, you act as if my apples might be poisoned!' said the woman. 'Here, I'll take a bite of this apple myself, to show you it is safe!'

But the apple was so cleverly made that only one side was poisoned. Snow White longed for the fine apple, and when she saw that the woman had eaten part of it she could resist no longer, stretched out her hand and bit into the poisonous half. No sooner had she taken a bite of the apple than she fell down as if she were dead.

The queen cackled loudly and said: 'White as snow, red as blood, black as ebony you may be, but the dwarfs will not be able to save you this time!'

When she went home, she rushed to her mirror and asked:

'*Mirror, mirror on the wall,*

Who is the fairest one of all?'

And the mirror answered at last:

'*You are the now the fairest one of all.*'

The dwarfs came home that evening and found Snow White dead. They lifted her up and looked to see whether they could find anything poisonous, unlaced her, combed her hair, washed her with water but it was no use; the poor child was dead.

They sat around her, all seven of them, for three days. They would have buried her, but she looked so fresh and alive with her beautiful rosy cheeks that they said: 'We cannot bury her in the dark, cold ground.' So they made a coffin of clear glass, and laid her in it, writing her name on it in golden letters. Then they put the coffin upon the mountain and one of them always stayed by it to keep watch. Even the birds came and wept for Snow White.

Snow White lay for a long, long time in the coffin, and all the while she never changed but looked as if she were asleep, with skin as white as snow, lips as red as blood and hair as black as ebony.

Then one day a handsome Prince was riding through the woods. He stopped at the dwarfs' cottage to spend the night. From there he could see the coffin on the mountain and beautiful Snow White within it. He said to the dwarfs: 'Let me have the coffin, I will give you whatever you want for it.'

'We will not part with it for all the gold in the world', replied the dwarfs.

Then the Prince said: 'I beg you to give it to me, for I cannot live without looking upon the beautiful Snow White.' The dwarfs felt sorry for him and agreed to give him the coffin. The prince called his servants and told them to carry the coffin down from the mountain. As they were carrying it, they stumbled over a tree-stump, causing the poisonous piece of apple which had stuck in Snow White's throat to fall out of her mouth. And before long she opened her eyes and sat up exclaiming: 'Oh heavens! Where am I?'

The handsome Prince was so full of joy he said: 'You are with me,' and told her all that had happened. 'I love you more than anything else in the world; come with me to my father's palace and marry me.'

A splendid wedding was held for the Prince and Snow White. It so happened, however, that Snow White's wicked step-mother was also invited to the wedding feast. When she had dressed herself in her most beautiful clothes, she went to her mirror and asked:

'*Mirror, mirror on the wall,*

Who is the fairest of us all?'

And the mirror answered:

'*Though you are fair, oh Queen, it's true,*

The bride-to-be is fairer still than you.'

The wicked woman screamed with anger. At first she thought she would not go to the wedding, but she knew she would not be able to rest until she found out who the new bride was. When she saw that it was Snow White, she was filled with such a terrible rage that she swept from the palace in a great fury and was never heard from again. Snow White and the Prince lived happily ever after.

WHAT IS AN AUTHOR?

This is Michael Rosen. He's an author. An author writes books and poems. Many of these books tell stories. Michael loves to tell stories. He writes them down so he can share them with you.

Michael also loves to write poems – which makes him a special kind of author called a *poet*. You read one of Michael's poems on pages 28–29 of this book.

Michael has written many books and poems and has won awards for his writing. If you go to a library, you'll find lots of books that say, 'By Michael Rosen'.

How does Michael go about writing his poems? 'Well,' says Michael, 'sometimes I write on a piece of paper, sometimes on an old envelope, sometimes in a notebook, sometimes straight onto the computer. I think a bit. I write a bit. I think some more. I scribble out what I don't like. Scribble in some new bits. And then read it out to someone to see what they think.'

When you sit down with a book, find out who the author is. Do you have a favourite author? If you do, then the next time you're at the library, look for more books by that person.

Do you like to tell stories? Someday soon you'll learn to write them down, then you can be an author too!

In Which Pooh Goes Visiting and Gets into a Tight Place

A selection from *Winnie-the-Pooh* by A. A . Milne

Edward Bear, known to his friends as Winnie-the-Pooh, or Pooh for short, was walking through the forest one day, humming proudly to himself. He had made up a little hum that very morning, as he was doing his Stoutness Exercises in front of the glass: Tra-la-la, tra-la-la, as he stretched up as high as he could go, and then Tra-la-oh, help!-la, as he tried to reach his toes. After breakfast he had said it over and over to himself until he had learnt it off by heart, and now he was humming it right through, properly. It went like this:

Tra-la-la, tra-la-la,

Tra-la-la, tra-la-la,

Rum-tum-tiddle-um-tum.

Tiddle-iddle, tiddle-iddle,

Tiddle-iddle, tiddle-iddle,

Rum-tum-tum-tiddle-um.

Well, he was humming this hum to himself, and walking along gaily, wondering what everybody else was doing, and what it felt like, being somebody else, when suddenly he came to a sandy bank, and in the bank was a large hole.

'Aha!' said Pooh. (*Rum-tum-tiddle-um-tum.*) 'If I know anything about anything, that hole means Rabbit,' he said, 'and Rabbit means Company,' he said, 'and Company means Food and Listening-to Me-Humming and such like. *Rum-tum-tum-tiddle-um.*'

So he bent down, put his head into the hole, and called out:

'Is anybody at home?' There was a sudden scuffling noise from inside the hole, and then silence. 'What I said was, "Is anybody at home?"' called out Pooh very loudly.

'No!' said a voice; and then added, 'You needn't shout so loud. I heard you quite well the first time.'

'Bother!' said Pooh. 'Isn't there anybody here at all?'

'Nobody.'

Winnie-the-Pooh took his head out of the hole, and thought for a little, and he thought to himself: 'There must be somebody there, because somebody must have said "Nobody".'

So he put his head back in the hole, and said:

'Hallo, Rabbit, isn't that you?'

'No', said Rabbit, in a different sort of voice this time.

'But isn't that Rabbit's voice?'

'I don't think so,' said Rabbit. 'It isn't meant to be.'

'Oh!' said Pooh.

He took his head out of the hole, and had another think, and then he put it back, and said: 'Well, could you very kindly tell me where Rabbit is?'

'He has gone to see his friend Pooh Bear, who is a great friend of his.'

'But this is Me!' said Bear, very much surprised.

'What sort of Me?'

'Pooh Bear.'

'Are you sure?' said Rabbit, still more surprised.

'Quite, quite sure', said Pooh.

'Oh, well, then, come in.' So Pooh pushed and pushed and pushed his way through the hole, and at last he got in.

'You were quite right,' said Rabbit, looking at him all over. 'It is you. Glad to see you.'

'Who did you think it was?'

'Well, I wasn't sure. You know how it is in the Forest. One can't have anybody coming into one's house. One has to be careful. What about a mouthful of something?'

Pooh always liked a little something at eleven o'clock in the morning, and he was very glad to see Rabbit getting out the plates and mugs; and when Rabbit said, 'Honey or condensed milk with your bread?' he was so excited that he said, 'Both', and then, so as not to seem greedy, he added, 'But don't bother about the bread, please.'

And for a long time after that he said nothing… until at last, humming to himself in a rather sticky voice, he got up, shook Rabbit lovingly by the paw, and said that he must be going on.

'Must you?' said Rabbit politely. 'Well,' said Pooh, 'I could stay a little longer if it – if you –' and he tried very hard to look in the direction of the larder.

'As a matter of fact,' said Rabbit, 'I was going out myself directly.'

'Oh, well, then, I'll be going on. Goodbye.'

'Well, goodbye, if you're sure you won't have any more.'

'Is there any more?' asked Pooh quickly.

Rabbit took the covers off the dishes, and said no, there wasn't.

'I thought not', said Pooh, nodding to himself. 'Well, goodbye. I must be going on.' So he started to climb out of the hole. He pulled with his front paws, and pushed with his back paws, and in a little while his nose was out in the open again... and then his ears... and then his front paws... and then his shoulders... and then –

'Oh, help!' said Pooh. 'I'd better go back.'

'Oh, bother!' said Pooh. 'I shall have to go on.'

'I can't do either!' said Pooh. 'Oh, help and bother.'

Now by this time Rabbit wanted to go for a walk too, and finding the front door full, he went out by the back door, and came round to Pooh, and looked at him. 'Hallo, are you stuck?' he asked. 'N-no,' said Pooh carelessly. 'Just resting and thinking and humming to myself.'

'Here, give us a paw.' Pooh Bear stretched out a paw, and Rabbit pulled and pulled and pulled...

'Ow!' cried Pooh. 'You're hurting!'

'The fact is,' said Rabbit, 'you're stuck.'

'It all comes,' said Pooh crossly, 'of not having front doors big enough.'

'It all comes,' said Rabbit sternly, 'of eating too much. I thought at the time,' said Rabbit, 'only I didn't like to say anything,' said Rabbit, 'that one of us was eating too much,' said Rabbit, 'and I knew it wasn't me,' he said. 'Well, well, I shall go and fetch Christopher Robin.'

Christopher Robin lived at the other end of the Forest, and when he came back with Rabbit, and saw the front half of Pooh, he said, 'Silly old Bear', in such a loving voice that everybody felt quite hopeful again.

'I was just beginning to think,' said Bear, sniffing slightly, 'that Rabbit might never be able to use his front door again. And I should hate that', he said.

'So should I,' said Rabbit.

'Use his front door again?' said Christopher Robin. 'Of course he'll use his front door again.'

'Good,' said Rabbit.

'If we can't pull you out, Pooh, we might push you back.'

Rabbit scratched his whiskers thoughtfully, and pointed out that, when once Pooh was pushed back, he was back, and of course nobody was more glad to see Pooh than he was, still there it was, some lived in trees and some lived underground, and–

'You mean I'd never get out?' said Pooh.

'I mean,' said Rabbit, 'that having got so far, it seems a pity to waste it.'

Christopher Robin nodded.

'Then there's only one thing to be done,' he said. 'We shall have to wait for you to get thin again.'

'How long does getting thin take?' asked Pooh anxiously.

'About a week, I should think.'

'But I can't stay here for a week!'

'You can stay here all right, silly old Bear. It's getting you out which is so difficult.'

'We'll read to you,' said Rabbit cheerfully. 'And I hope it won't snow', he added.

'And I say, old fellow, you're taking up a good deal of room in my house – do you mind if I use your back legs as a towel-horse? Because, I mean, there they are – doing nothing – and it would be very convenient just to hang the towels on them.'

'A week!' said Pooh gloomily. 'What about meals?'

'I'm afraid no meals,' said Christopher Robin, 'because of getting thin quicker. But we will read to you.'

Bear began to sigh, and then found he couldn't because he was so tightly stuck; and a tear rolled down his eye, as he said: 'Then would you read a Sustaining Book, such as would help and comfort a Wedged Bear in Great Tightness?'

So for a week Christopher Robin read that sort of book at the North end of Pooh, and Rabbit hung his washing on the South end... and in between Bear felt himself getting slenderer and slenderer. And at the end of the week Christopher Robin said, 'Now!'

So he took hold of Pooh's front paws and Rabbit took hold of Christopher Robin, and all Rabbit's friends and relations took hold of Rabbit, and they pulled together...

And for a long time Pooh only said 'Ow!'...

And 'Oh!'…

And then, all of a sudden, he said 'Pop!' just as if a cork were coming out of a bottle. And Christopher Robin and Rabbit and all Rabbit's friends and relations went head-over-heels backwards… and on the top of them came Winnie-the-Pooh – free!

So, with a nod of thanks to his friends, he went on with his walk through the forest, humming proudly to himself. But Christopher Robin looked after him lovingly and said to himself, 'Silly old Bear!'

PARENTS: Find a copy of A.A. Milne's *Winnie-the-Pooh* for more stories about Pooh and his friends: Rabbit, Piglet, Eeyore, Kanga and Roo, and Christopher Robin—but not Tigger: that bouncy fellow is introduced in another book, *The House at Pooh Corner.*

The Velveteen Rabbit; or, How Toys Become Real

Adapted from the original by Margery Williams

There was once a velveteen rabbit, and in the beginning he was really splendid. He was fat and bunchy, as a rabbit should be; his coat was spotted brown and white, he had real thread whiskers, and his ears were lined with pink satin. On Christmas morning, when he sat wedged in the top of the Boy's stocking, with a sprig of holly between his paws, the effect was charming.

There were other things in the stocking, nuts and oranges and a toy engine, and chocolate almonds and a clockwork mouse, but the Rabbit was quite the best of all. For at least two hours the Boy loved him, and then there was a great rustling of tissue paper and unwrapping of parcels, and in the excitement of looking at all the new presents, the Velveteen Rabbit was forgotten.

For a long time he lived in the toy cupboard or on the nursery floor, and no one thought very much about him. He was naturally shy, and being only made of velveteen, some of the more expensive toys quite snubbed him. The mechanical toys were very superior and looked down upon everyone else; they were full of modern ideas and pretended they were real. But the Rabbit didn't even know that real rabbits existed; he thought they were all stuffed with sawdust like himself. So the poor little Rabbit was made to feel very insignificant and commonplace, and the only person who was kind to him at all was the Skin Horse.

The Skin Horse had lived longer in the nursery than any of the others. He was so old that his brown coat was bald in patches, and most of the hairs in his tail had been pulled out. He was wise, for he had seen many mechanical toys arrive to boast and swagger, and by and by break their mainsprings and pass away, and he knew that they were only toys and would never turn into anything else. For nursery magic is very strange and wonderful, and only those playthings that are old and wise and experienced like the Skin Horse understand all about it.

'What is REAL?' asked the Rabbit one day. 'Does it mean having things that buzz inside you and a stick-out handle?'

'Real isn't how you are made', said the Skin Horse. 'It's a thing that happens to you. When a child loves you for a long, long time, not just to play with, but REALLY loves you, then you become Real.'

'Does it hurt?' asked the Rabbit.

'Sometimes,' said the Skin Horse, for he was always truthful. 'When you are Real, you don't mind being hurt.'

'Does it happen all at once, like being wound up,' the Rabbit asked, 'or bit by bit?'

'It doesn't happen all at once,' said the Skin Horse. 'It takes a long time. Generally, by the time you are Real, most of your hair has been loved off, and your eyes drop out, and you get very shabby. But these things don't matter at all, because once you are Real, you can't be ugly.'

'I suppose you are Real!' said the Rabbit.

'The Boy's Uncle made me Real,' the Skin Horse said. 'That was a great many years ago; but once you are Real, you can't become unreal again. It lasts for always.'

The Rabbit sighed. He longed to become Real, to know what it felt like; and yet the idea of growing shabby and losing his eyes and whiskers was rather sad. He wished that he could become real without these uncomfortable things happening to him.

There was a person called Nana who ruled the nursery. Sometimes she took no notice of the playthings lying about, and sometimes she went swooping about like a great wind and hustled them away in cupboards. She called this 'tidying up', and the playthings all hated it. The Rabbit didn't mind it so much, for wherever he was thrown he came down soft.

One evening, when the Boy was going to bed, he couldn't find the china dog that always slept with him. Nana was in a hurry, so she simply looked about her, and seeing that the toy cupboard door stood open, she made a swoop.

'Here,' she said, 'take your old Bunny!' And she dragged the Rabbit out by one ear and put him into the Boy's arms.

That night, and for many nights after, the Velveteen Rabbit slept in the Boy's bed. At first he found it rather uncomfortable, for the Boy hugged him very tight, and sometimes he rolled over on him, and sometimes he pushed him so far under the pillow that the Rabbit could scarcely breathe. And he missed, too, those long moonlit hours in the nursery, when all the house was silent, and his talks with the Skin Horse. But very soon he grew to like it, for the Boy talked to him and made nice tunnels for him under the bed-clothes that he said were like the burrows the real rabbits lived in. And when the Boy dropped off to sleep, the Rabbit would snuggle down close under his little warm chin and dream, with the Boy's hands clasped close round him all night long.

And so time went on, and the little Rabbit was very happy – so happy that he never noticed how his beautiful velveteen fur was getting shabbier and shabbier, and his tail coming unsown, and all the pink rubbed off his nose where the Boy had kissed him.

Spring came, and they had long days in the garden, for wherever the Boy went, the Rabbit went too. He had rides in the wheelbarrow, and picnics on the grass, and lovely fairy huts built for him under the raspberry canes. And once, when the Boy was called away suddenly, the Rabbit was left out on the lawn until long after dusk, and Nana had to come and look for him with the candle because the Boy couldn't go to sleep unless he was there. He was wet through with the dew, and Nana grumbled as she rubbed him off with a corner of her apron.

'You must have your old Bunny!' she said. 'Fancy all that fuss for a toy!'

The Boy sat up in bed and stretched out his hands.

'Give me my Bunny!' he said. 'He isn't a toy. He's REAL!'

When the little Rabbit heard that, he was happy, for he knew that what the Skin Horse had said was true at last. The nursery magic had happened to him, and he was a toy no longer. He was Real. The Boy himself had said it.

That night he was almost too happy to sleep. And into his boot-button eyes, which had long ago lost their polish, there came a look of wisdom and beauty.

That was a wonderful summer!

Near the house where they lived there was a wood, and in the long June evenings the Boy liked to go there to play. He took the Velveteen Rabbit with him, and before he wandered off to play, he always made the Rabbit a little nest where he would be quite cosy. One evening, while the Rabbit was lying there alone, he saw two strange beings creep out of the tall grass near him.

They were rabbits like himself, but quite furry and brand-new. They must have been very well made, for their seams didn't show at all, and they changed shape in a queer way when they moved; one minute they were long and thin and the next minute fat and bunchy, instead of always staying the same as he did.

They stared at him, and the little Rabbit stared back. And all the time their noses twitched.

'Why don't you get up and play with us?' one of them asked.

'I don't feel like it,' said the Rabbit, for he didn't want to explain that he couldn't get up.

'Can you hop on your hind legs?' asked the furry rabbit.

That was a dreadful question, for the Velveteen Rabbit had no hind legs at all! The back of him was made all in one piece, like a pincushion. He sat still and hoped that the other rabbits wouldn't notice. But wild rabbits have very sharp eyes. And this one stretched out his neck and looked.

'He hasn't got any hind legs!' he called out. And he began to laugh.

'I have!' cried the little Rabbit. 'I have got hind legs! I am sitting on them!'

'Then stretch them out and show me, like this!' said the wild rabbit. And he began to whirl around and dance, till the little Rabbit got quite dizzy.

'I don't like dancing,' he said. 'I'd rather sit still.'

But all the while he was longing to dance, for a new tickly feeling ran through him, and he felt he would give anything to be able to jump about like these rabbits did.

The strange rabbit stopped dancing and came quite close.

'He doesn't smell right!' he exclaimed. 'He isn't a rabbit at all! He isn't real!'

'I am Real!' said the little Rabbit. 'I am Real! The Boy said so!' And he nearly began to cry.

Just then there was a sound of footsteps, and the Boy ran past near them, and with a flash of white tails the two strange rabbits disappeared. 'Come back and play with me!' called the little Rabbit. 'Oh, do come back! I know I am Real!'

But there was no answer. The Velveteen Rabbit was all alone. For a long time he lay very still, hoping that they would come back. But they never returned, and presently the sun sank lower and the little white moths fluttered out, and the Boy came and carried him home.

Weeks passed, and the little Rabbit grew very old and shabby, but the Boy loved him just as much. He loved him so hard that he loved all his whiskers off, and the pink lining to his ears turned grey, and his brown spots faded. He even began to lose his shape, and he scarcely looked like a rabbit anymore, except to the Boy. To him, he was always beautiful, and that was all that the little Rabbit cared about.

And then, one day, the Boy was ill.

His little body was so hot that it burned the Rabbit when he held him close. Strange people came and went in the nursery, and a light burned all night, and through it all the little Velveteen Rabbit lay there, hidden from sight under the bedclothes, and he never stirred, for he was afraid that if they found him, someone might take him away, and he knew that the Boy needed him.

It was a long, weary time, for the Boy was too ill to play. The little Rabbit snuggled down patiently, and looked forward to the time when the Boy would be well again and they would go out in the garden amongst the flowers and the butterflies and play splendid games in the raspberry thicket like they used to.

At last the Boy got better. He was able to sit up in bed and look at picture books while the little Rabbit cuddled close at his side. And one day they let him get up and dress.

It was a bright, sunny morning. They had carried the Boy outside, wrapped in a shawl, and the little Rabbit lay tangled up among the bedclothes, thinking.

The Boy was going to the seaside tomorrow. Now it only remained to carry out the doctor's orders. They talked about it all while the little Rabbit lay under the bedclothes and listened. The room was to be disinfected, and all the books and toys that the Boy had played with in bed must be burnt.

'Hurrah!' thought the little Rabbit. 'Tomorrow we shall go to the seaside!' For the Boy had often talked of the seaside, and he wanted very much to see the big waves coming in, and the tiny crabs, and the sand castles.

Just then Nana caught sight of him.

'How about his old Bunny?' she asked.

'That?' said the doctor. 'Why, it's a mass of scarlet fever germs! Burn it at once!'

And so the little Rabbit was put into a sack with the old picture books and a lot of rubbish, and carried out to the end of the garden. That was a fine place to make a bonfire, only the gardener was too busy just then to attend to it.

That night the Boy slept in a different bedroom, and he had a new bunny to sleep with him, but he was too excited to care very much about it. For tomorrow he was going to the seaside, and he could think of nothing else.

And while the Boy was asleep, dreaming of the seaside, the little Rabbit lay among the old picture books and rubbish, and he felt very lonely. The sack had been left untied, and so by wriggling a bit he was able to get his head through the opening and look out. Nearby he could see the thicket of raspberry canes in whose shadow he had played with the Boy on bygone mornings. He thought of those long sunlit hours in the garden – how happy they were – and a great sadness came over him. He thought of the Skin Horse, so wise and gentle, and all that he had told him. Of what use was it to be loved and lose one's beauty and become Real if it all ended like this? And a tear, a real tear, trickled down his shabby little velvet nose and fell to the ground.

And then a strange thing happened. For where the tear had fallen, a mysterious flower grew out of the ground. It had slender green leaves the colour of emeralds; and in the centre of the leaves, a blossom like a golden cup. It was so beautiful that the little Rabbit forgot to cry. And presently the blossom opened, and out of it there stepped the loveliest fairy in the whole world. Her dress was of pearl and dewdrops, and there were flowers round her neck and in her hair. And she came close to the little Rabbit and gathered him up in her arms and kissed him on his velveteen nose that was all damp from crying.

'Little Rabbit,' she said, 'I am the nursery magic Fairy. I take care of all the playthings that the children have loved. When they are old and worn out and the children don't need them any more, then I come and take them away with me and turn them into Real.'

'Wasn't I Real before?' asked the little Rabbit. 'You were Real to the Boy,' the Fairy said, 'because he loved you. Now you shall be Real to everyone.'

And she held the little Rabbit close in her arms and flew with him into the wood. It was light now, for the moon had risen. All the forest was beautiful. In the open glade between the tree trunks, the wild rabbits danced with their shadows on the velvet grass, but when they saw the Fairy, they all stopped dancing and stood round in a ring to stare at her.

'I've brought you a new playfellow,' the Fairy said. 'You must be very kind to him and teach him all he needs to know, for he is going to live with you for ever and ever!'

And she kissed the little Rabbit again and put him down on the grass.

'Run and play, little Rabbit!' she said.

But the little Rabbit sat quite still for a moment and never moved. For when he saw all the wild rabbits dancing around him, he suddenly remembered about his hind legs, and he didn't want them to see that he was made all in one piece. He did not know that when the Fairy kissed him that last time, she had changed him altogether. And he might have sat there a long time, too shy to move, if just then something hadn't tickled his nose, and before he thought what he was doing, he lifted his hind toe to scratch it.

And he found that he actually had hind legs! Instead of dingy velveteen, he had brown fur, soft and shiny, his ears twitched by themselves, and his whiskers were so long that they brushed the grass. He gave one leap, and the joy of using those hind legs was so great that he went springing about on them, jumping sideways and whirling round as the others did, and he grew so excited that when at last he did stop to look for the Fairy, she had gone.

He was a Real Rabbit at last, at home with the other rabbits.

Autumn passed and winter, and in the spring, when the days grew warm and sunny, the Boy went out to play in the wood behind the house. And while he was playing, two rabbits crept out and peeped at him. One of them was brown all over, but the other had strange markings under his fur, as though long ago he had been spotted, and the spots still showed through. And about his little soft nose and his round black eyes there was something familiar, so that the Boy thought to himself: 'Why, he looks just like my old Bunny that was lost when I had scarlet fever!'

But he never knew that it really was his own Bunny, come back to look at the child who had first helped him to be Real.

Two Tall Tales

PARENTS: There's a bit of truth in the two tall tales we tell here: both St. George and King Arthur were real people, or at least the stories told of them come from the deeds of real people. St. George was born in Turkey in about 280 AD and served in the Roman army. He was brave and strong, but also noble and honourable. Because he refused to give up his Christian faith he was put to death by the Roman emperor on 23 April. We still celebrate St. George's Day on 23 April. He was made patron saint of England by Henry V. In Shakespeare's play, Henry V leads his troops into battle with the famous line: 'Cry God for Harry, England and St. George!' His flag is a red cross on a white ground and forms the basis of the Union Jack (see page 136). King Arthur was a British leader who, in the sixth century, led the resistance to the invasion of the Saxons. However, whether King Arthur ever had a round table, or St. George ever fought a dragon, is another matter! Tall tales aren't known for being truthful: they present people and deeds bigger than life, but no bigger than the spirit of the people who love to tell tall tales.

St. George and the Dragon

St. George is the patron saint of England. That means that he is supposed to take care of England and its people when they are in trouble. Other countries have patron saints as well: Scotland has St. Andrew; Wales has St. David; and Ireland has St. Patrick. They all appear together with St. George in this story. It is a famous story about how he fought a dragon.

In the darkest depths of a thick forest lived Kalyb, an enchantress. Terrible were her deeds and few had the courage to challenge this evil witch. One day she used spells and charms to steal the son of the Lord High Steward of England away from his poor old nurse.

So upset was the Lord High Steward by the loss of his only son that he left England and in his grief and sorrow wandered from place to place until his hair was white as silver, until at last his life ended and he was finally able to rest.

Yet the child was marked from the beginning for great deeds; on his right hand was a blood-red cross and on his left leg a golden band. These signs so affected Kalyb, who knew that they meant that the child had a great destiny to fulfil, that she could not kill him as she had intended to do; and so he grew, each day becoming more handsome and strong until eventually he was the apple of her eye.

When he was fourteen he began to thirst for adventure, as all young boys do, but the wicked enchantress wanted to keep him in the forest with her forever. He wanted glory and could see the evil inside Kalyb, so she attempted to bribe him.

One day she led him to a castle and showed him six brave knights who were imprisoned in the tower. She said: 'Behold! These are the Six Champions and you shall be the seventh. Your name will be St. George of England. But only if you stay with me.'

But he would not. Then she led him to a magnificent stable where seven of the finest horses were kept. 'Six of these,' she said, 'belong to the Six Champions. The seventh and the best, the swiftest and most powerful in the world, whose name is Bayard, will be yours. But only if you stay with me.'

But he would not. Then she took him to an armoury, and strapped on his chest a breastplate of purest steel and placed on his head a helmet inlaid with gold. Then, taking a mighty sword, she placed it in his hand and said: 'This armour, which no weapon can pierce, and this sword called Ascalon, which will destroy all it touches, are yours. Surely now you will stay with me?'

But he would not. Finally, she tried to bribe him with her own magic wand, giving him power over all things in the enchanted forest. He threw it at a rock hoping it would break and end Kalyb's power.

To his surprise the rock opened, and in it was a view of a cave. He persuaded her to lead the way into this place of darkness and as she entered he waved the magic wand and closed the rock. The enchantress was sealed in her tomb and left to cry for all eternity.

And so St. George was freed from the enchanted forest, and rode to Coventry with the six other Champions: St. David of Wales, St. Andrew of Scotland, St. Patrick of Ireland, St. Denys of France, St. James of Spain and St. Anthony of Italy, all of whom he freed at once.

For nine months the Seven Champions exercised and trained in all the arts of war. So when spring returned, they were ready and set forth to seek foreign adventure. Thirty days and nights they rode until they came to a place with seven paths. The Seven Champions agreed to each take a separate path. They said farewell and with good spirit rode to their destiny.

St. George, on his charger Bayard, journeyed until he reached the sea where he boarded a ship bound for Egypt. He eventually arrived in a land that was deathly silent in the day and frighteningly dark at night. It was here that St. George met a poor hermit.

He asked the hermit for a bed so he could rest his tired limbs.

The hermit replied: 'You have come at a terrible time. Our land has been ravaged by a cruel dragon who demands the sacrifice of an innocent young girl every day. He has threatened to send a plague and scorch the earth so that no man or beast may live.

For four-and-twenty years he has terrified our land, and tomorrow it is the beautiful Sabia, daughter of the King, who must die.'

He explained that the King had promised to give his daughter in marriage, and the crown of Egypt, to any brave knight who would kill the dragon. 'For crowns I care not,' said St. George boldly, 'but the beautiful maiden will not die. I will slay the monster and save her from this cruel fate.'

The next day he rose at dawn and buckled his armour, laced his helmet and sharpened his sword. He mounted his trusted steed Bayard and had the old hermit guide him to the Valley of the Dragon.

On the way he met a procession of old women who were weeping and wailing. At the front was a beautiful damsel dressed in the finest Arabian silk; he knew it must be Sabia, the King's daughter.

He dismounted and bowed before the lady, asking her to return to her father's palace because he was going to kill the dreaded dragon. The beautiful Sabia, thanking him with tears and smiles, returned to the palace and St. George rode to meet the beast.

Soon the brave knight was at the dragon's lair and shouted for him to come out and fight. The dragon let out a mighty roar louder than thunder and spat venom from its mouth; its wings were burning flames and its eyes empty and cold.

From shoulder to tail it was forty feet long, its body covered in scales of glittering green, harder than brass with a great, golden belly. Its size and appearance would have made any other man tremble, but St. George steeled himself and prepared to fight. So fierce was the dragon's first charge that St. George nearly fell to the ground. He recovered himself and thrust his spear into the dragon's belly, but the spear shuddered and split into pieces. The monster roared and whipped both St. George and Bayard with its tail.

St. George was thrown from his horse, but by good fortune landed under a flowering orange tree. The fragrance from the tree had magical powers; no poisonous beast would dare come within seven feet of its branches. So the valiant knight lay there to recover his senses, until with eager courage he rushed back into combat.

Again he struck the dragon in the belly with his mighty sword, Ascalon; this time the dragon was wounded and purple poison spewed from its body and splattered St. George. The poison was so powerful that his breast plate and helmet burst into a thousand pieces.

St. George might have been killed, but again he sheltered under the branches of the orange tree. Here he prayed that God would help him in his fight against evil. Then with a bold and courageous heart he advanced and thrust his sword under the soft wing of the fiery dragon, where there were no scales. He pierced its heart and all the grass and flowers around him turned crimson with blood from the dying monster.

When the King heard what the knight had done, he offered him a large reward. But St. George was not interested in money and encouraged the King to give the money to the poor. Then he mounted his horse and rode off in search of further noble adventures.

You can see some more pictures of St. George and the Dragon in the Visual Arts chapter on pages 164 and 165.

King Arthur and the Knights of the Round Table
Adapted from *Our Island Story* by Henrietta Marshall (1905)

Many, many years ago England was ruled by a good and wise King called Uther Pendragon. He led the English people as they fought against the Saxon invaders. Even when he was so old and feeble that he could not stand, he was carried into battle on a sort of bed, and he still managed to frighten the Saxon enemy, so great was the power and fame of his courage. At last he died, and no one knew who was to be King after him.

And so the mighty nobles of Britain began to quarrel among themselves as to who should be king next. Each noble thought he had the best right, so the quarrelling was dreadful.

While they were all gathered together, fighting and shouting at each other, Merlin came among them, leading a tall, fair-haired boy by the hand. When the nobles saw Merlin, they stopped fighting and were silent. They knew how clever he was, and what incredible things he could do, and they were rather afraid of him.

Merlin stood quietly looking at them all from under his bushy eyebrows. He was a very old man. But he was tall and strong and splendid, with a long white beard and fierce, glittering eyes. It was no wonder that the Britons felt afraid of him.

'Lords of Britain,' said Merlin at last, 'why do you fight so? It would be better to prepare to do honour to your king. Uther Pendragon is indeed dead, but Arthur, his son, reigns in his stead.'

'Who is this Arthur? Where is he?' asked the nobles angrily. 'Uther Pendragon had no son.'

'Hear me,' said Merlin, 'Uther Pendragon had a son. It was told to me that he should be the greatest king who should ever reign in Britain. So when he was born, lest any harm should befall him, he was given into my care till the time should come for him to reign. He has dwelt in the land of Avilon, where the wise fairies have kept him from evil and whispered wisdom in his ear. Here is your king, honour him.'

Then Merlin lifted Arthur up and placed him upon his shoulders, so that all the people could see him. There was something so noble and splendid about Arthur, even though he was only a boy, that the great lords felt awed. Yet they would not believe that he was the son of Uther Pendragon. 'Who is this Arthur?' they said again. 'We do not believe what you say. Uther Pendragon had no son.'

Then Merlin's bright eyes seemed to flash fire. 'You dare to doubt the word of Merlin?' he shouted. 'Oh vain and foolish Britons, follow me.'

Taking Arthur with him, Merlin turned and strode out of the hall, and all the nobles followed him. As they passed through the streets, the people of the town followed too. On they went, the crowd growing bigger and bigger, till they reached the great door of the cathedral. There Merlin stopped, and the knights and nobles gathered around him; those behind pushing and pressing forward, eager to see what was happening.

There was indeed something amazing to be seen. In front of the doorway was a large stone which had not been there before. Standing upright in the stone was a sword, the hilt of which glittered with gems. Beneath it was written: 'Whoever can draw me from this stone is the rightful king of Britain.'

One after another the nobles tried to remove the sword. They pulled and tugged till their muscles cracked. They strained and struggled till they were hot and breathless, for each one was anxious to be king. But it was all in vain. The sword remained firm and fast in the rock.

Then last of all Arthur tried. He took the sword by the hilt and drew it from the stone quite easily.

A cry of wonder went through the crowd, and the nobles fell back in astonishment leaving a clear space round the king. Then as he stood there, holding the magic sword in his hand, the British nobles, one after another, knelt to Arthur, acknowledging him to be their lord.

Arthur was only fifteen when he was made king, but he was the bravest, wisest and best king that had ever ruled in Britain. As soon as he was crowned, he determined to free his kingdom from the Saxons. He swore a solemn oath that he would drive them out of the land. He made his knights swear the same solemn oath.

Then, taking the sword which he had won, and which was called Excalibur, and his mighty spear called Ron, he rode forth at the head of his army.

Twelve great battles did Arthur fight and win against the Saxons. He was always to be seen in the thick of the battle, in his armour of gold and blue, with a golden dragon and crown upon his helmet. He was so brave that no one could stand against him, yet so careless of danger that many times he would have been killed, had it not been for the magic might of his sword Excalibur, and of his spear Ron. And at last the Saxons were driven from the land and there was peace.

During these years, Arthur did much for his people. He taught them to love truth and goodness, and to be Christian and gentle. No king had ever been loved as Arthur was loved.

In those fierce and far-off days, when men spent most of their time fighting, it was very necessary for them to be brave and strong, in order to protect their dear ones, but they were very often cruel as well and nearly always fierce. Arthur taught people that it was possible to be brave yet kind, strong yet gentle. Afterwards people forgot this again, but in the days of Arthur the fame of his court and of his gentle knights spread far and wide.

Many stories are told of Arthur and his gentle, courteous knights, although they did not learn all their gentleness and their courtesy at once, as you shall hear.

Upon an Easter Day, Arthur called together all his knights and nobles, from his many kingdoms, to a great feast. They came from far and near, kings, earls, barons and knights, in splendid clothes, glittering with jewels and gold.

As they waited for the King they laughed and talked together. But secretly each heart was full of proud thoughts. Each man thought himself nobler and grander than any of the others.

The tables were spread for the feast. They were covered with white silk cloths. Silver baskets piled with loaves, golden bowls and cups full of wine stood ready, and, as the knights and nobles talked and waited, they began to choose where they would sit.

In those days, master and servants all sat together at the same table for meals. The master and his family sat at the top, and the servants and poor people at the bottom of the table. So it came to be considered that the seats near the top were the best. The further down the table any one sat, the less honour was paid him.

At this feast, no servants or poor people were going to sit at table, yet all the nobles wanted places at the top. 'We will not sit in the seats of beggars,' they said.

So they began to push each other aside, and to say: 'Make way, this is my seat.'

'No, I am more honourable than you. You must sit below me.'

'How dare you? My name is more noble than yours. That is my seat.'

'Give way, I say.'

At first it was only words. Soon it came to blows. They had come to the feast unarmed, so they had only their hands with which to fight, but as they grew angrier and angrier, they seized the bowls of wine and threw them at each other. Next the loaves of bread and the gold and silver cups were thrown about, the tables and benches were overturned, howls and yells filled the hall, and everything was in dreadful confusion.

When the noise was at its worst, the door opened and the King appeared. His face was stern and grand as he looked down on the struggling, yelling crowd.

'Sit ye, sit ye down quickly, every man in the place where he is,' he cried. 'Whoso will not, he shall be put to death.'

At the sound of their King's stern voice, the foolish nobles were filled with shame. Silently they sat down; the tables and benches were put back in their places and the feast began.

But Arthur was sad at heart. 'How can I teach my people to be gentle and kind, if my knights will not even sit in peace to eat?' he said to himself. Then as he sat sorrowfully wondering what he could do, Merlin came to him.

'Be not sad, oh King,' he said, 'but listen to my advice. Tell your carpenters to make a great round table at which there shall be a place for every knight. Then there can be no more quarrelling. For at a round table there is neither top nor bottom, so no knight can say that he sits above or below another. All shall be equal.'

Then Arthur was sad no longer. He did as Merlin advised, and had a great round table made, at which there was a seat for each one of his knights. After that there was no more quarrelling as to who should have the best place, for all were equal, and Arthur's knights became known as the Knights of the Round Table.

But, alas! the time of peace did not last. Again came days of war and strife. In a great and terrible battle, Arthur and nearly all his knights were killed. Once more the fierce Saxons swept over the land, filling it with sorrow and bloodshed, and the glory and beauty of knighthood were forgotten in Britain.

But some people think that Arthur did not die. They say that when he was wounded so that he could fight no more, the wise fairies came to take him back to fairyland. They say that he is still there, and that one day he will come again.

Other people say the stories about Arthur and his knights are not true, but at least we may believe that in those far-off, fierce, fighting days there was a king who taught his people that to be gentle was not cowardly and that to be cruel was not brave.

Sayings

PARENTS: Every culture has phrases and proverbs that make no sense when carried over literally into another culture. To say, for example, that someone has 'let the cat out of the bag' has nothing to do with setting free a trapped kitten. Nor – thank goodness – does it ever literally 'rain cats and dogs'!

The sayings and phrases in this section may be familiar to many children, who hear them at home. But the inclusion of these sayings and phrases may be helpful to parents and teachers who work with children from home cultures in which these are not familiar.

For Year 1 children, we have chosen to introduce a selection of very familiar sayings that are likely to have some connection to the child's world of experience.

April showers bring May flowers

People use this saying to mean that something unpleasant can cause something pleasant to happen, just as spring rains cause flowers to bloom.

Bob had caught chicken pox and he couldn't go to the fair. 'Cheer up, Bob,' said his mother. 'April showers bring May flowers: you have to stay home, but now we have time to work on that big new puzzle you've been wanting to put together.'

Better safe than sorry

People use this saying to mean it's better not to take a chance than to do something that might be very risky. They say this because you're less likely to be hurt or make a bad mistake when you're careful.

Alex dared Jimmy to walk on the railing of the old bridge. 'No way, Alex,' said Jimmy. 'It's a long fall into the river. Better safe than sorry.'

Do unto others as you would have them do unto you

This saying is called the Golden Rule. People use it to mean: treat people as you would like to be treated yourself. It comes from the Bible.

'Lilly, stop drawing on Priya's picture', said the babysitter. 'Would you like Priya to mess up your picture? Remember: do unto others as you would have them do unto you.'

A dog is man's best friend

Some people think that a dog is more than a pet. They think a dog can also be a really good friend. That's because dogs, like good friends, can be loyal and loving.

Peter had lost his lunch money and torn his favourite shirt. As he walked home, he was feeling sad, but then he heard his dog, Rusty, barking. Rusty jumped up and licked Peter with his big wet tongue. 'Rusty,' Peter laughed, 'it's true: a dog is man's best friend.'

The early bird gets the worm

This saying means that you can usually get ahead of others if you get going before they do. Sometimes people say it to someone who needs a little extra push to do what he is supposed to do.

'Hey, Raj,' said Peter, 'did you hear? Amy's Card Shop is opening early on Saturday, and the first fifty people in the shop get free football cards!'

'That's great!' answered Raj. 'Let's find out what time they open and be waiting at the door. The early bird gets the worm, you know.'

Great oaks from little acorns grow

This saying means that, just as a small acorn can grow into a towering oak tree, something that starts out small or not very important can turn out big or very important.

King John was a bad king who thought he could do just as he liked. The English barons were determined to make him admit that other people had rights, and he had to respect them. They made him sit down in a place called Runnymede and sign a piece of paper called Magna Carta, promising that he wouldn't do certain things. This made a lot of people start to think about how much power the king should have, and how much he should listen to the advice of other people. Over the centuries, many people have been inspired by Magna Carta to demand a say in how they are governed. Now our laws are made by parliament, which is made up of men and women we elect to act for us. Things have changed a lot – just as a great oak has changed a lot since it was an acorn!

Look before you leap

This saying means that you should be careful and think before you rush into doing something.

'Mum!' said Max with excitement. 'Ben says he'll swap me all his toy cars for my bike? Isn't that great?'

'I don't know, Max, is it?' asked his mother. 'You ride your bike every day, and a bike costs a lot more than toy cars. Do you really want to swap? You'd better look before you leap.'

A place for everything and everything in its place

This saying means you should put things where they belong. People use this saying when they want people to be neat.

When Yasmin came in from playing, she would always kick off her shoes in the hall. Her mother said, 'Yasmin, your shoes don't belong in the hall. Please put them in the cupboard. Remember: a place for everything and everything in its place!'

It's raining cats and dogs

People use this saying to mean that it is raining very, very hard.

'We'd better ride the bus home today. If we walk, we'll get soaked. It's raining cats and dogs!'

Practice makes perfect

People use this saying to mean that doing something over and over again makes you good at it.

Chloe liked taking piano lessons. She practised every day. Sometimes it was hard, but she felt proud when she learned to play her first song without making any mistakes. She understood now why her teacher always said, 'Practice makes perfect.'

Where there's a will, there's a way

This saying means if you want to do something badly enough, you'll find a way to do it.

Meg had tried and tried to jump the skipping rope fifty times in a row, but she always messed up after forty jumps. 'Agh!' she said to her friend Khadijah. 'I don't think I'll ever do fifty!'

'Oh yes you will', said Khadijah. 'Keep trying. Where there's a will, there's a way.'

History and Geography

Introduction

In Reception and Year 1, children often study aspects of their immediate world: the family, the school, the community, etc. While such local studies should be encouraged, we should also take advantage of children's natural curiosity and begin to broaden their horizons. By introducing Year 1 children to history and geography, we can foster their curiosity about the larger world and begin to develop their sense of the past and its significance. For young children, we need to emphasise the 'story' in history. By appealing to children's naturally active imaginations, we can ask them to 'visit' people and places in the past. We encourage you to go beyond these pages to help your child learn about history through art projects, drama, music, and discussions.

In the following pages, we introduce – let us emphasise, introduce – a variety of people and events. The children will encounter most of these people and events more fully in their later schooling. For example, we introduce the dates of the signing of Magna Carta in 1215 and the Declaration of Rights in 1689 as 'birthdays of our nation', on the premise that young children can understand the idea of a birthday. But we do not go into any detailed discussion of the ways in which power was transferred from the throne to the House of Commons, although we will be looking at these important events in more details in later volumes.

In beginning to tell children the story of the past, we have tried to be sensitive about the degree to which, and the manner in which, we expose children to the tragic aspects of history, such as Britain's involvement with the slave trade. In some cases, we have chosen to leave for later years some of the darker aspects of history. For example, we talk briefly about the English Civil War without going into any details about the terrible suffering on both sides. The goal in Year 1, then, is less to explore historical events or ideas in depth than to orient the child to the past and plant the seeds of knowledge that will grow in later years.

Suggested Resources

Our Island Story by Henrietta Marshall (Civitas/Galore Park Publishing 2005). The classic one-volume child's history of Britain from the Romans to Queen Victoria, first published in 1905.

Start-Up History Series (Evans). This series is an introduction to history for young children, who are encouraged to discover history on the page. Key information is presented through a combination of simple, clear text and strong visual images.

A visit to... by Rachael Bell (Heinemann Library). A visit to... helps primary learners understand what it's like to be a child in another land. Young readers will travel to famous sites, join in traditional celebrations and visit children's classrooms. Books feature: readable text including fact files, maps, photos and illustrations, as well as lists of some basic words in each language.

World Alphabet Series (Fran Lincoln Books). This photographic alphabet series of books introduces young readers to the culture of different countries. Ranging from food and drink to the lively celebrations, these books focus on both city and country life, and are the perfect way to introduce children to the world.

The Passport to the World Series (Albert Whitman & Company) is a collection of children's picture books, written by different authors and illustrated by different artists. Each book tells the story of a different child in a different country. Each is well written and beautifully illustrated and shows how a child might typically live, work, play, sleep, eat, dream and, if they are lucky enough, go to school.

World History and Geography

What a Ball! Our World

Step outside and what do you see? Look as far as you can. Do you see houses and gardens? Big blocks of flats? Green fields and hills? A river or the sea?

Whatever you see, it's all part of our world. The world stretches as far as you can see – in fact, a whole lot further!

Let's imagine that just outside there's a high tower. I mean really high. You can climb a ladder to the top, a ladder that's longer than the ladder of the highest slide you've ever climbed. Ready? Start climbing. Keep going – don't stop now. At last you've reached the top. Catch your breath!

Now you're way up high. You can see things you never saw from the ground. You can see how this big world of ours goes on and on and on. Maybe you can see your city or town stretching far, far away. Maybe you can see rows of houses (they look teeny from your perch on the top of the ladder), all lined up along streets that look like crisscrossed lines. Maybe you can see the tops of trees and a blue-green line that snakes along through them. What is that wavy line? A river!

Well, we can't stop here. I forgot to tell you: at the top of the ladder there's a rocket ship. Yes, it's waiting for you! Climb in! Put on your space suit and strap on the seat belts. Ready for countdown? Five, four, three, two, one – blast off!

You're off to the moon! Here you are, First Child on the Moon! Step outside your space ship (but keep your space suit on; there's no air to breathe on the moon). Now let's look back to where you came from – our world, the planet Earth. What do you see?

It's a ball! Seen from outer space, our world is a large bluish ball with patches of white swirling around it. What do you think those swirly white patches are? (They're clouds.) This is how our world, the planet Earth, looks from space.

This is how our world, the planet Earth, looks from space.

The planet Earth

Oceans and Continents

Now, imagine that you have on special space glasses that allow you to peek under all those clouds. If you could, then the Earth would look something like this.

Look at all that blue. It seems to be moving. What do you think it is? That's right – it's water. And what are those big green patches? Did you say, 'land'?

Right again.

Do you see that there's a lot more blue than green? Water, water, everywhere! Well, not quite everywhere, but our world is mostly under water. The biggest bodies of water are called oceans.

What about those big pieces of land poking through the oceans? They're called continents. There are seven of them. Each continent has its own name. The seven continents are:

Asia

Europe

Africa

North America

South America

Australia

Antarctica

As you can see from this map, each continent has a different shape. Run your finger slowly around the outline of each continent. Place a piece of white paper or tracing paper over the map, and with a pencil trace the outline of each continent. (But, since Antarctica is mostly hidden way down at the bottom of this map, you will want to trace it from the map on page 133.)

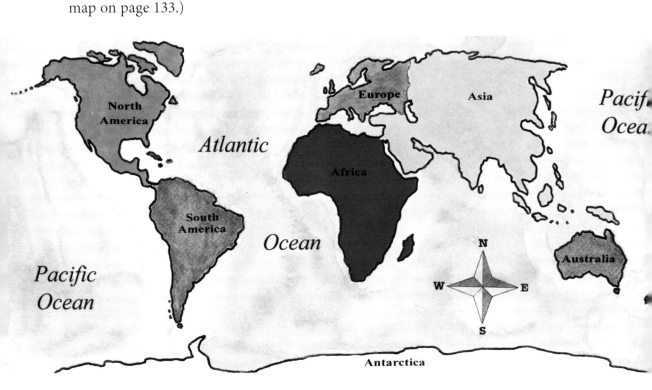

Maps and the Globe

Do you know what you're making when you draw the land shapes on a piece of paper? You're making a map. That's what maps are – drawings of the world. Maps give us pictures of the world to study. They help us see the shapes of land and water. Maps can also give us other information. Some maps show where mountains and rivers and lakes are, and give their names. Some show the names of highways and the locations of towns and cities.

This girl is using a globe

There's a special kind of map that isn't flat like paper. Instead, this map is round, like a big balloon. It's called a globe. A globe is a little model of our world. Of course, a globe is much, much smaller than our planet Earth, just as a Matchbox car is much smaller than a real car or a doll is much smaller than a real person.

At home, school or the library, look at a globe. Notice how much more water there is than land. Now find each of the seven continents. Use your finger to trace around the outline of each continent.

Which Way Are You Going?

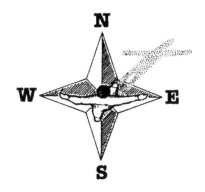

To help you find things on a map or globe, you need to know the four main directions that tell you where things are. Everything on earth is in a certain direction from where you are now. Let's learn the names of the four main directions. They are: **north**, **south**, **east** and **west**.

East is where the sun rises. If you don't know where that is, you can find out early tomorrow morning. West is where the sun sets. You can find out where that is late today or tomorrow.

North, South, East, West

Let's look at the directions on a map. In most maps, the top of a map is north. To go north, move your finger up on the map.

The bottom of a map is south. To go south, move your finger down.

The right of a map is east. To go east, move your finger to the right.

The left of a map is west. ('Left' and 'west' sound alike, which can help you remember.) To go west, move your finger to the left.

Have you heard of the North Pole and the South Pole? Those are the special names for the very top of our world, and for the very bottom. Which pole is at the top of our world? Can you find the North Pole on a globe? Can you find the South Pole on a globe?

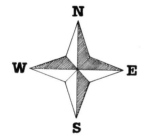 *Many maps use a picture like this to show the directions.*

Now try this. Here's a picture of a house. There is something near the house on each side. Which direction is each thing from the house?

● The dog is ___ of the house.

● The tree is ___ of the house.

● The cat is ___ of the house.

● The car is ___ of the house.

Around the World in Seven Ways

PARENTS: It is not important that Year 1 children be able to define or explain the difference between countries and continents. A complete understanding of the relevant geographical and political concepts requires a level of abstract reasoning that will develop in later years for most children. We provide the basic explanation below because children will hear about both countries and continents, and they can benefit from having at least a working response to their likely question, 'What's the difference?'

Let's learn about the seven continents. Do you remember their names? Let's say them aloud: Asia, Europe, Africa, North America, South America, Australia, Antarctica.

As you learn about the seven continents, you'll also hear about some different countries. Countries and continents – what's the difference? Well, countries are usually smaller than continents. For example, let's say you live in Britain (do you?). Then that's your country: Great Britain. But your country is only part of a bigger continent. Which continent? Europe.

Even though it is an island, Great Britain is a country on the continent of Europe. There are other countries on the continent of Europe. To the south of Britain, on the other side of the English Channel, is the country called France. To the west of Britain, on the other side of the Irish Sea, is the country called Ireland. Each one of these countries has different

Many countries use a flower to represent them. Can you see the rose (England); daffodil (Wales); thistle (Scotland); shamrock (Ireland); lily (France)?

leaders and different rules. Each country uses a different kind of money to Britain. Each country has a different flag. But all three countries are on the same continent: Europe.

Now let's learn about the seven continents and about some of the countries in each continent.

Asia

The largest continent in the world is Asia. Look at Asia on the map. Put your finger on Asia, but watch out! Asia is home to tigers, elephants and panda bears, and they might find your finger very interesting.

A wall runs for miles and miles across the country of China. This picture shows only a small part of the Great Wall of China. A powerful leader made his people build this wall a long time ago to defend their country from enemies. The wall has watchtowers and walkways. It's so wide that you can ride six horses side by side along its top.

Europe

Look at the map on page 120 and find Asia's neighbour, Europe. Asia and Europe touch each other. Compared to Asia, Europe is a small continent. Europe has beautiful buildings: wonderful palaces, churches, museums and more!

This is the Eiffel Tower, in the country called France. The Eiffel Tower is made of metal. You can ride to the top of the tower in a lift and look out over the great city of Paris.

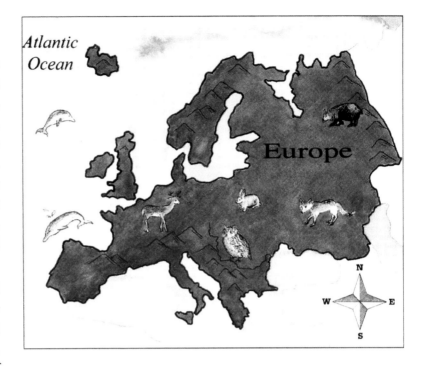

Here we are outside Buckingham Palace, which is in London. Who lives in a palace? Why, who else but a king, or a queen, or maybe both? For many, many years, the kings and queens of Britain have lived in Buckingham Palace. Nowadays, the king or queen doesn't rule Britain or make the laws but the British people still like to have a king or queen. Who are those red-coated fellows with fuzzy black hats standing outside the palace? They are the palace guards.

Look back to the map on page 120. Take your finger and move it down from Europe. You'll soon come to Africa. Use your fingers to measure Africa. See how much bigger Africa is than Europe? Africa is the world's second largest continent. (Do you remember the name of the largest continent?)

Africa spreads over much of the earth. It's a continent of amazing variety. 'Variety' means difference. Africa has lots of different kinds of weather and land.

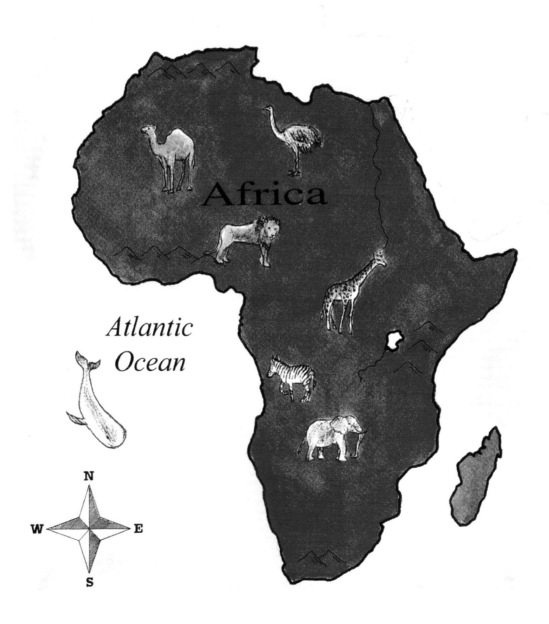

In one part of Africa, there are hot, dry deserts. In another part, there are big stretches of grassland. In another part, there are steamy jungles.

And if you think Africa has lots of different kinds of weather and land, wait till you see the animals. There are hippos and hyenas, leopards and lions, elephants and rhinos, crocodiles and ostriches – and that's just the beginning.

This picture shows a small part of a huge park in East Africa called the Serengeti (sair-in-GET-ee). Here you can find hungry giraffes munching on treetops, lions lounging on rocks and zebras, antelopes and cheetahs roaming across the grassland.

This is a picture of a market in Morocco, a country in North Africa. Do you see any fruits or vegetables you recognise?

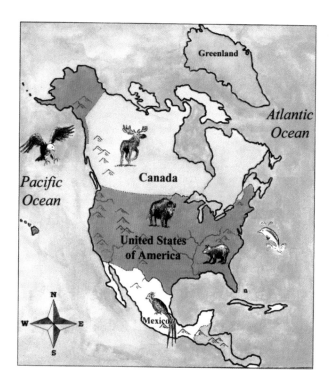

Look at the map on page 120. Put your finger on Africa. Pretend your finger is a ship. It's time to sail away from Africa. Go west, toward two big connected continents. To get there, you have to cross an ocean first. The name of this big ocean is the Atlantic Ocean.

Let your finger sail over the big waves of the Atlantic Ocean and take you to North America.

You've just crossed one big ocean, the Atlantic, to get to North America. Now, move your finger west across North America. Do you see another ocean on the western side of the continent? This is the Pacific Ocean.

A famous song says that the United States of America stretches 'from sea to shining sea' – and now you know the names of those two 'shining seas'!

Between the Atlantic and the Pacific oceans, on the continent of North America, you'll find deserts, prairies and forest. You'll find steamy swamps where alligators live and tall mountains where mountain lions roam. You'll find farms and cities, big and little.

One of the most beautiful places in the United States is the Grand Canyon. A long, long, long time ago – millions of years ago – a river ran through here and the water carved away the land. If you visit the Grand Canyon, there are places where you can go deep down into the canyon. Do you know how you get there? You ride on mules!

These women are doing a popular dance in Mexico. Look at how colourful their special dresses are. (Can you find Mexico on the map on page 128?)

These red-coated people from Canada are part of the Royal Canadian Mounted Police, who are known by the nickname 'Mounties'. The Mounties became famous for tracking down criminals and bad guys on horseback. People say that the Mounties 'always get their man', so watch out, bad guys! (Can you find Canada on the map on page 128?)

This big, brown bear, called a grizzly bear, is found in North America. Despite having very large, sharp teeth, grizzly bears like to eat fish like salmon.

South America

Look again at the map on page 120. Put your finger on the Pacific Ocean side of North America. Start near the top, then slide your finger down, down, down, following the outline of the land, until you reach another really big piece of land. Do you remember that on most maps north is up and south is down? So, as you slide your finger down, in what direction are you going? When you reach that other big piece of land, you're no longer in North America. You've reached the continent called South America.

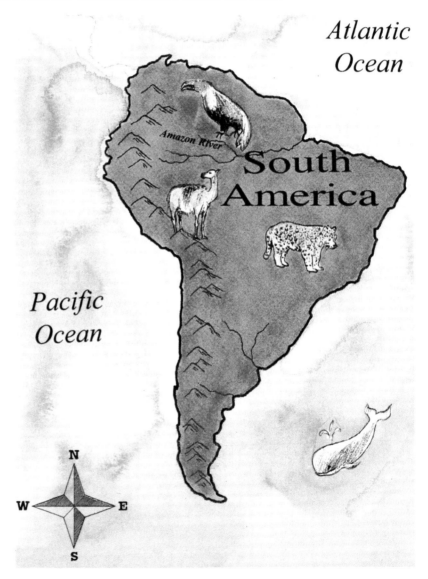

Keep sliding your finger down the Pacific Ocean side of South America. You're sliding over the Andes Mountains, the longest mountain range in the world. Do you see the special marks that the map here uses to show these mountains? The marks show you that the Andes Mountains run all the way down the Pacific side of South America. People live in these mountains and some of the people raise helpful furry animals called llamas. Llamas are patient and strong, but don't annoy them. If they get angry, they spit at you!

There's a lot more to South America than mountains. Look on the map on page 130 for a big river. The map uses a blue line to show this river. Of course, the line on the map is small, but this river is very, very big and very, very long. It's called the Amazon. The Amazon River begins high in the Andes Mountains, then goes on until it runs through a steamy jungle called a rainforest. The Amazon rainforest has anteaters and anacondas (huge snakes), jaguars and sloths, howler monkeys and vampire bats.

Here's a rainforest creature called a sloth. Hey, Mr. Sloth! Don't you have anything better to do than just hang around?

High in the Andes Mountains, there's a very old city called Machu Picchu. Long ago the people called Incas built this stone 'city in the clouds'.

Australia is the smallest continent. Australia is really a large island. (An island is a piece of land with water all around it.) People in Europe and North America sometimes call Australia the 'down under' continent because Australia is 'down under' Europe and North America. Australia is the home of some animals that you'll find on no other continent: kangaroos, koalas and wallabies. And there's one very unusual Australian animal that seems like a mixture of a bunch of animals: it's called a duckbill platypus. (The platypus is pictured on the map. Can you find it?)

Koalas remind some people of teddy bears, but they're not bears at all. They're actually the same kind of animal as the kangaroo. Both koalas and kangaroos are a kind of animal called marsupials – which means the mothers have their babies in pouches near their belly and can hop around with them everywhere.

At the very bottom of the world is the continent of Antarctica. Antarctica is the home of – well, almost nothing. It's blanketed by such thick snow and ice that almost no plants grow here and almost no animals can live here. Some animals who live between land and sea call Antarctica home – penguins, for example, and some seals and whales. But even these animals prefer to stay closer to the warmer islands that are around the continent of Antarctica.

So, if you're planning a holiday, Antarctica is not the place to go. These giant emperor penguins look like they're dressed for a fancy party!

Antarctica

Can you answer these questions about the continents?

1. Which is the biggest continent?

2. On which continent will you find the Andes, the longest mountain range in the world?

3. If you wanted to see a giraffe or zebra living in the wild (not in a zoo), which continent would you visit?

4. On which continent will you find these three countries: France, Great Britain and Ireland?

5. Koalas and kangaroos live on which continent?

After you've answered the questions, go to a globe or map. Point to and name each of the seven continents.

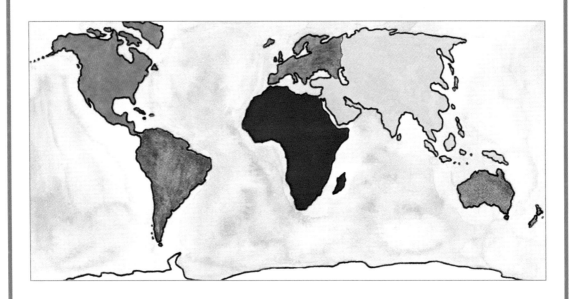

British History and Geography

PARENTS: Please read the World History and Geography section of this book with your child first, as the following section assumes some familiarity with terms introduced in World History and Geography.

Your Country

Do you live in the United Kingdom? Then that's your nation. Sometimes people call it Britain, or Great Britain, or the UK, or else they say they live in England, or Northern Ireland, Wales or Scotland, which are all parts of the United Kingdom. For a long time Ireland was part of the United Kingdom of Great Britain and Ireland. During this period the Kings and Queens of Britain were also the Kings and Queens of Ireland. Now only a small part – Northern Ireland – is part of the same nation. When we talk about England, Wales, Scotland and Northern Ireland altogether we call it the United Kingdom or UK.

Here is our 'flower' map of the British Isles again. Do you remember which countries the flowers represent? The list on page 123 will tell you.

PARENTS: Help your child to point to the approximate location where you live in the UK. Does your child know the name of where he or she lives?

The Union Jack

The British flag is called the Union Jack. The name reminds us of the time when England and Scotland became one nation instead of two under the Act of Union in 1707. To show that these two countries had really joined together, their flags were put together. The English flag was a red cross on a white background. It is called the Saint George's cross, after the patron saint of England, the Saint George we read about in Language and Literature who saved a princess from a dragon. The Scottish flag was a white Saint Andrew's cross on a blue background. So to make one flag, the two crosses were placed one on the top of the other and they made something very like the Union Jack – but not quite. Later, Ireland was also united with England and Scotland, so the flag changed again. The cross of Saint Patrick (which is the same as a Saint Andrew's cross, but is red on a white background) was combined with the cross of Saint George and the cross of Saint Andrew to create the Union Jack that has been flying ever since. The Southern part of Ireland became an independent country in 1921, but the Union Jack is still the flag of the United Kingdom of England, Scotland, Wales and Northern Ireland.

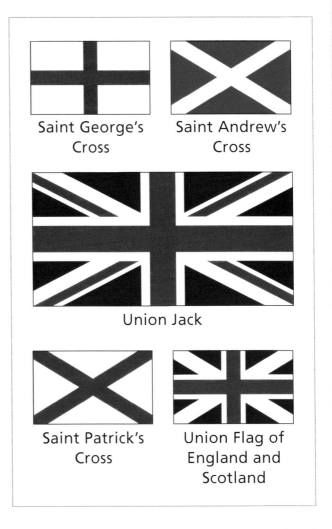

Saint George's Cross

Saint Andrew's Cross

Union Jack

Saint Patrick's Cross

Union Flag of England and Scotland

You know that your country, Great Britain, is part of a large group of countries called a continent. Do you remember which continent Great Britain is part of? It's the continent called Europe.

Looking Back

Britain is an island. That means it is an area of land surrounded by water. Ireland (can you find that on the map on page 135?) is also an island. This meant that for thousands of years, before aeroplanes were invented, people could only get to Britain and Ireland by sailing across the sea on a boat.

But long before that – so very long ago that it is difficult for us to think about how long ago it was – Britain and Ireland were not islands. They were joined together, and joined to the rest of Europe. You could have walked from one country to another!

Let's go back in our imaginations to that time, thousands and thousands of years ago. What would Britain have looked like then? You know all those homes and buildings you see today? All the school buildings, banks, shopping centres, railway stations, office blocks – well, imagine them all fading away. As they disappear, you see something taking their place and you are almost blinded by the glare, because for miles and miles, all you can see is ice!

The Ice Age

In those days, many thousands of years ago, it was so cold that we call that time the Ice Age. A large part of Europe was covered with thick sheets of ice called glaciers. It was so cold that it was hard for plants or animals to survive. It was certainly too cold for people.

This map shows Europe during the Ice Age, when Britain, Ireland and the rest of Europe were joined by ice. Do you see the big woolly creatures? They are called 'woolly mammoths' and lived during the Ice Age.

However, gradually the climate became warmer. More plants began to grow and animals arrived from parts of Europe that had not been covered in ice. They were followed by people who were so adventurous that they travelled to the land that is now Britain and Ireland. They were not the first people ever to live there: there had been people living there before the temperature dropped and great sheets of ice covered the land. But from this time onwards there have always been people living in what we now call Britain, so those men and women who arrived after the Ice Age are our very, very distant ancestors.

As the great sheets of ice began to melt, they turned into rivers of water that flowed into the sea. Can you guess what happened next? As more and more water poured into the sea, it started to rise. The water flooded some of the low-lying parts of the land and cut off the land we know as Britain from the rest of Europe. It also cut off Britain from Ireland. This is how Britain became an island, and being an island has been important in all sorts of ways. This is why the story of our country – its history – is sometimes called Our Island Story.

So what was life like for our very, very distant ancestors in the land we now call Britain? They lived in what we now call the Stone Age. This is not because everything they used was made of stone! It is because they lived very primitive lives, and didn't have many tools or things to make life comfortable.

To stay alive people hunted and gathered plants. At night they huddled around fires in damp caves to keep warm. They couldn't buy their clothes or food. They had to make or find everything. They made tools out of sticks and stones. They made needles out of bones, which they used to sew clothes made out of animal skin. Sometimes, they even found time to decorate their caves with paintings like the ones in this picture.

But their most important task was finding food. Just like you, they got hungry and they had to eat. Of course, way back then they couldn't go shopping at a supermarket! To get food, they sometimes picked the wild plants growing around them, but most of all they hunted for animals to eat.

Because the early humans were hunters, they were always on the move from place to place. Why did they have to keep moving? Can you think of a reason? They kept moving because they were following the animals they hunted. In those long-ago days, great herds of woolly mammoths and deer roamed the land. As the animal herds moved on, looking for greener grass and a warmer climate, the human beings followed because those animals were their breakfast, lunch and dinner!

'Stop! It's dinnertime.'

Having to follow the animals made life hard for our Stone Age ancestors, until they made a great discovery. They learned how to tame animals and grow crops like wheat. This meant that they could settle down and stay in one place, knowing that they had a regular supply of food.

Stonehenge

Although the people of those days had only very simple tools, they left something that has amazed people ever since. It is called Stonehenge and it is in Wiltshire, in the South-West of England.

Huge stones, some of which were brought over land from hundreds of miles away, were set up in a circle. Other stones were arranged inside this circle in a special pattern. These stones are very, very heavy. A lot of people would need to work together to move them around and raise them up. How did they do it, with only very simple tools made of sharp stones and animal bones? It is a great mystery, and people have tried for hundreds of years to understand it. Nobody knows what Stonehenge was built for. Perhaps it was to do with religious beliefs, as it is arranged so that the rising sun falls on the stones in a certain way. Perhaps it was a sort of calendar or a place people went to when they wanted to get well. One day you might visit Stonehenge, then you can try to think it out for yourself.

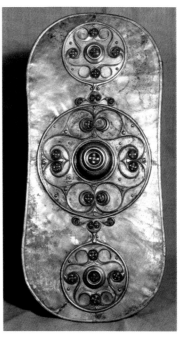

The Bronze Age

People still had only very simple things, made of flint or bone, to help themselves, until they made another great discovery: they learned how to make bronze. Bronze is a very hard metal, made from two other metals: tin and copper. Discovering how to make bronze meant that people could make themselves all sorts of new things like bowls and decorative ornaments, as well as swords and arrows.

The Iron Age

The Bronze Age was followed by the Iron Age when people learned how to make iron. This is an even harder metal than bronze. It can be hammered into all sorts of shapes when it is hot and put together with other metals like gold and silver to make beautiful and useful things.

This Iron Age shield is called the Battersea Shield because it was found on the bed of the River Thames near Battersea.

How did the Iron Age come to an end? It certainly wasn't because people stopped using iron! We are still using it today, thousands of years later. But something happened that changed everything, as far as history is concerned. The Romans, who had established a great empire that covered large parts of Europe, Africa and Asia, decided to invade our little island. They already ruled the land we now call France, so it wasn't a very long journey across the stretch of water we now call the English Channel to add this country to the great Roman Empire. We will find out more about the Romans in another book. The thing about them that you need to know

The Romans arriving in Britain

now is that they could read and write. Amongst other things they wrote – history! From the arrival of the Romans onwards, we have written accounts of what happened in our country, so we don't have to rely on digging up pots and spears and other things to try to work out what happened for ourselves. We call the time before the Romans arrived pre-history. Pre- means before, and this was before history was written down. History starts with the Romans!

Kings and Queens

What do you think people in other countries know about Britain? One thing that almost everyone knows about us is that we have a Queen and that she lives in Buckingham Palace. We have had kings and queens for hundreds of years, and the history of Britain is closely tied up with them. Some of them were good people who tried to rule wisely and do their best for their subjects. However some were not quite so good. Some kings were cruel and mistreated people who disagreed with them or would not do what they wanted. Some kings were greedy, and they took away so much of people's money and possessions that people felt they were being treated unfairly. But what could they do? The King was the King!

People began to feel that the king should not rule completely on his own. Even a very good king could not know everything he needed to know in order to make the best decisions. It was felt that the king should have some wise people to advise him, and that some of the great nobles, who owned a lot of land and had many people who were loyal to them, should play a part in the government of the country. Sometimes the king found it helpful to call together these groups of nobles and church leaders to advise him on what to do, because it made it easier for him to govern the country if he had supporters in different areas. However, it was up to the king to decide whom to ask to join his group of advisers and it was up to him to decide when they met and whether he took their advice or not. Sometimes he did and sometimes he didn't!

These gatherings came to be known as 'parliaments' [PAR-leeya-ment]. The word comes from the French word *parler* [par-LAY] which means 'to talk'. So a parliament is a place where you talk about things.

The Magna Carta

During the reign of King John something happened that made it harder for the King to do just as he liked. People thought King John was a very bad king – in fact, he was one of the most disliked kings we have ever had. He was greedy and cruel and only cared about himself. The noblemen, who were rich and powerful and were called barons, decided that he could not be allowed to go on behaving so badly. No one was safe from him, because he did just as he liked. So they drew up an agreement which was called Magna Carta (MAG-ner CAR-ter), or the Great Charter. A charter is an agreement which is written down and signed by the people who say they will do what it says. It is like making a very serious promise that you can't break. Have you ever had to promise to be good?

The Magna Carta protected the people of England from greedy kings. It said that:

- No one shall be punished a great deal for a very little fault. However bad they may have been, we will not take their tools or the other things they need to earn their living away from them.

- No one shall be put in prison or have his belongings and lands taken from him unless he has been brought before a judge and allowed to tell his side of the story.

There were lots of other promises that the barons wanted the King to make, saying that he would listen to the advice of his barons and follow it, but he became very angry and refused to sign the Magna Carta. He said he wouldn't be a proper king if other people could tell him what to do.

This just made the barons more determined that King John must sign the Magna Carta or no one would be safe. Agree he must. Yet he kept delaying, from Christmas till Easter, from Easter till midsummer. Friend after friend deserted him, until

King John signing the Magna Carta

he realised the whole country was against him. The barons forced the King to meet them at a little place beside the River Thames called Runnymede [runny-meed]. The barons and their army camped on one side of the river and the King on the other. On a little island in the river they met and talked and there, on 15 June 1215, King John signed the Magna Carta.

King John didn't keep his promises. He broke them over and over again. But the important thing was that he had admitted that the king can't do just as he likes. He needs to respect other people. So 15 June 1215 is a sort of birthday in our country's history – the birthday of the idea that kings and queens have to rule with the support of the people.

The Father of the English Parliament

Simon de Montfort calls a parliament

When King John died, his son Henry became king. Henry was not as bad as his father, but he was still not a very good man. The barons became so unhappy with the way he behaved that they tried to make him promise to call regular parliaments to discuss how to rule the country. They also wanted the King to promise to have other people besides the barons in his parliaments. They wanted men who came from the different parts of the country to represent their neighbours' views to the King.

The King refused, so the barons rose up to make war against him. The King lost, and the most powerful of the barons, called Simon de Montfort (mont-four), called a parliament to make new rules about governing the country. This was the first parliament to include men who represented the towns and counties of England, which is the way parliaments have been made up ever since. As a result, Simon de Montfort is called the Father of the English Parliament.

As the years went by, people got used to the idea of the king calling together groups of people from all over the country to advise him in parliament. It was up to the king to decide when to call them, and whether or not he was going to do as they advised, but there was one thing he really needed parliament to do. Sometimes the king would do something that cost a lot of money – more money than he had himself. Usually this was when he went to war. So how was he to raise the money to pay for a war? He had to do it by raising taxes. That means people had to pay a part of what they earned to the king. Nobody really likes doing this, so kings would only raise taxes when they were agreed by parliament. Every time parliament was asked to vote for taxes it gave them the chance to ask the king for something in return. Gradually, parliament became more and more powerful. The king was still in charge, and parliament wouldn't go against the king's wishes, but he had to talk to them if he needed a lot of money.

Some kings really didn't like this, but they put up with it. Then a king called Charles the First decided he really couldn't be a proper king if he had to depend on anyone else agreeing with him, because he thought that kings are chosen by God, which means they can never be wrong about anything. This

King Charles went into parliament to try to arrest people who disagreed with him

was called the Divine Right of Kings. The men who sat in the parliament tried to tell him what to do, but he just became more and more stubborn. Finally he decided to put a stop to this. He went to parliament with lots of soldiers and tried to have some of the men who wanted to tell him what to do arrested and thrown into prison. But he was too late. They had been told that he was coming and run away. King Charles looked around and said: 'I can see my birds have flown.'

Parliament and the King at war

The members of parliament were very angry that King Charles had dared to come right into the parliament building to try to arrest them. They were supposed to be free to say whatever they wanted in parliament, and he was trying to stop them. Things went from bad to worse, until a war broke out between King Charles and his supporters, who were called Cavaliers (cavver-leers), and the members of parliament and their supporters, who were called Roundheads. This was called a civil war. Usually wars are fought between people who live in different countries. A civil war is fought between people who live in the same country. This makes it much worse, as neighbours are fighting neighbours, and sometimes even members of the same family are fighting each other. This is what happened when some families were divided between those who supported King Charles and those who supported the parliament.

The Roundheads won the war, then they cut off the head of King Charles and said that Britain wasn't going to have a king any more. Instead, a man called Oliver Cromwell would rule the country. He would be called the Lord Protector. He was a very serious man and he wanted everyone to lead very strict lives like him.

When Oliver Cromwell died, his son became Lord Protector. He was not a very good ruler and people thought they would like to go back to having a king again. When kings die, their oldest sons become kings after them. So they asked the son of King Charles the First, who was also called Charles, if he would like to be king and he said yes. So he became King Charles the Second. He had to agree that he would listen to what the members of parliament had to say, and that he would not try to be a king like his father, thinking that whatever he believed must be right.

Charles the Second did not have any children who could become king after him, so, when he died, his brother, who was called James, became king. King James was more like his father than his brother. He thought kings were chosen by God and did not have to think about other people's opinions.

The people began to say: 'We decided a long time ago that we didn't want to have a king who doesn't listen to anyone else's opinions. We want a king who talks to us and lets us have some say in how the country is governed.'

King William and Queen Mary and the Declaration of Rights

So the people decided to have another change. They asked the daughter of King James, who was called the Princess Mary, if she would like to be Queen, with her husband, who was called William, as King. Princess Mary talked to her husband and they decided that they would like to become King and Queen and rule the country together by talking to people and listening to the advice they were given by members of parliament.

First of all they had to sign a piece of paper – and it was one of the most important pieces of paper in the history

King William and Queen Mary receive the Declaration of Rights.

of our country. It was called the Declaration of Rights. When the new King and Queen signed it on 23 February 1689, they were agreeing that parliament had the right to make laws and raise taxes. Ever since then, the laws in Britain have been made by parliament and not by the King or Queen on their own. Kings and Queens play a very important part in our government, but the final decisions are taken by the members of parliament who are elected by the ordinary people of the country. So 23 February 1689 is another great birthday for Britain – the day when it was agreed that parliament would make the laws.

Prime Ministers

When the members of parliament became responsible for passing laws and raising taxes, they still needed the King and Queen to agree to whatever they wanted to do. The King or Queen used to sit with the most important members of parliament, who are called ministers, to talk about what needed to be done. However, when George I became King, there was a problem – because he came from Hanover in Germany and didn't speak very much English! Also, he spent a lot of time in Hanover because he loved his home country so much, which meant someone else had to be in charge of the meetings when he was away.

The best idea seemed to be for one of the ministers to be in charge when the King wasn't there. A man called Robert Walpole was chosen to do this. He was called the First Lord of the Treasury. This is a big name, but what it really means is that he was in charge of all the government's money. This made him a very important person. He could usually get the other members of parliament to do what he wanted, so he was sometimes called the Prime Minister, because 'prime' means first. First of all people said it to tease him, but the name stuck, and after a while whoever was the First Lord of the Treasury came to be known as the Prime Minister.

So Robert Walpole became the person in charge of the meetings of ministers, and afterwards he would tell the King what they had been discussing. To this day the Prime Minister still goes to meet the Queen every week to talk to her about what the government is doing. The Queen listens and offers advice to her Prime Minister.

Robert Walpole was the first Prime Minister

Prime Minister David Cameron meeting the Queen

Not only was Robert Walpole the first Prime Minister, he was Prime Minister for longer than anyone else has ever been – over twenty years! Although he was a very powerful man for a long time, he never forgot that he came from a farming family in Norfolk. He used to munch little apples, sent from his Norfolk farm, while he was sitting in the House of Commons listening to the other members of parliament.

The King admired Robert Walpole so much he offered him a house in Downing Street, near to the Houses of Parliament. Robert said he could not accept such a valuable gift for himself, but he would accept it as First Lord of the Treasury. This meant that whoever was First Lord of the Treasury after him would be able to live in this house. The British Prime Minister still lives there, and it is called 10 Downing Street. It still has the words First Lord

The Prime Minister lives at 10 Downing Street

of the Treasury on the front door, to remind us of why the Prime Minister is living there. Number 10 Downing Street is not only the place where Prime Ministers live: they also work there and entertain important people from other countries. Living and working in the same building means that the Prime Minister can always be ready to do whatever needs to be done for the people of Britain.

Other Prime Ministers

There have been many more Prime Ministers of Britain since Robert Walpole. You'll learn about them later (in school and in the other books of this series). The important things to know now are, first, that the Prime Minister is the leader of the government of Britain; and second that we choose the people we want to lead us. They don't get the job just because they're born into a certain family, like kings or queens. Instead, every four or five years, grown-ups in Great Britain get to choose the people who will make up the government. That's called voting. We vote for members of parliament, and one of those members of parliament will become the Prime Minister.

Who is the Prime Minister now? Do you know? See if you can find out, because that person may change our country and your life!

Visual Arts

Introduction

Doing, making, creating!

For a child in Year 1, art should mostly take the form of doing: drawing, painting, cutting and sticking, working with clay and other materials. In this section, we suggest art activities your child can do. You can also find engaging activities in some of the books below.

While art is doing, it is also seeing and thinking

By reading this section aloud with your child, you can both learn some of the ways that we talk about art. By looking closely at art, and talking about it, your child will begin to develop a love of art and a habit of enjoying it in thoughtful, active ways. Let your child point to details they see and trace lines with their fingers. Sometimes we suggest questions to help direct your conversations, but you should also feel free to move beyond these and follow your child's curiosity. By helping your child to become comfortable talking about art, not just making it, you will be supporting their developing language skills and literacy, as well as their creativity.

PARENTS: We can't encourage you enough to provide your child with materials and opportunities to be a practising creative artist! If you are concerned about not having resources or space for art at home (although it need not be expensive or messy!), most galleries and museums offer creative sessions for parents and children free of charge. These sessions also enable you to interact with great works of art in the original. For suggestions, see overleaf.

Suggested Resources:

Art activity books:

N. Buchanan, *Amazing Art Attack* (Dorling Kindersley, London 2005)
C. Weidemann *et al.*, *A Year in Art: The Activity Book* (Prestel, London 2009)

Looking at and talking about art books:

L. Micklethwait, *I Spy Colours in Art* (Harper Collins, London 2007)
J. Richardson, *Looking at Pictures: An Introduction to Art for Young People Through the National Gallery Collection* (National Gallery Publications with A & C Black, London 2009)
J. Saxton, *Snail Trail: In Search of a Modern Masterpiece* (Frances Lincoln, London 2009)
G. Woolfe, *Look! Zoom in on Art* (Frances Lincoln, London 2003)

Art story books:

L. Anholt, *Degas and the Little Dancer* (Frances Lincoln, London 1996)
J. Mayhew, *Katie and the Sunflowers,* (Orchard Books, London 2001)
J. Mayhew, *Katie's Picture Show,* (Orchard Books, London 1991)
A. Sturgis and L. Child, *Dan's Angel: A Detective's Guide to the Language of Painting* (Frances Lincoln, London 2003)

Colouring/complete the masterpiece books:

All My Own Work: Adventures in Art (The National Gallery with Frances Lincoln, London 2005)
Art Masterpieces to Colour: 60 Great Paintings from Botticelli to Picasso (Dover, Mineola, New York 2004)

Free gallery/museum based art appreciation and creative art sessions:

Tate (London and other sites): http://www.tate.org.uk/families/
National Gallery, London: http://www.nationalgallery.org.uk/families/
Engage, an association of people involved with gallery education, can give you information about listings and events nationally, including Children's Art Day. Consult: http://www.engage.org/

Where to find the works of art in this chapter:

Lascaux cave paintings, near Montignac, Dordogne, France
Vincent van Gogh, *Sunflowers*, 1888 (National Gallery, London)
Henri Rousseau, *Surprised! A Tiger in a Tropical Storm,* 1891 (National Gallery, London)
Pieter Bruegel, *The Hunters in the Snow*, 1565 (Kunsthistorisches Museum, Vienna)
David Hockney, *A Bigger Splash*, 1967 (Tate Modern, London)
Joan Miró, *Painting (Peinture)*, 1925 (National Galleries of Scotland, Edinburgh)
Pierre Bonnard, *The Lunch (Le Déjeuner)*, 1923 (National Gallery of Ireland, Dublin)
William Hogarth, *The Graham Children*, 1742 (National Gallery, London)
John Singer Sargent, *Carnation, Lily, Lily, Rose*, 1885-6 (Tate Britain, London)
Paolo Uccello, *Saint George and the Dragon*, 1470 (National Gallery, London)
Jacopo Tintoretto, *Saint George and the Dragon*, 1555 (National Gallery, London)
Hubert Le Suer, *Equestrian Portrait of King Charles I* (Bronze) 1633 (Trafalgar Square, London)
Henry Moore, *Family Group* (Bronze sketch), 1944 (Fitzwilliam Museum, Cambridge)
Barbara Hepworth, *Infant* (Wood), 1929 (Tate, St Ives)
Edgar Degas, *Little Dancer Aged Fourteen*, 1880-81 (National Gallery of Art, Washington D.C.) (in England you can see a cast version made around 1922 at Tate, Liverpool)
Hamo Thornycroft, *Oliver Cromwell* (Bronze)1899 (Palace of Westminster, London)
Nelson's Column (1840-43), *William Railton with Statue of Lord Horatio Nelson* by E.H. Baily (Trafalgar Square, London)
Antony Gormley, *The Angel of the North* (Steel) 1998 (Gateshead)

What Do Artists Do?

Do you like using clay or blocks to make models, to draw pictures or cut and stick? When you do these things, you're creating art. People have been making art since the earliest times. Art is something that makes humans different from animals. Some of the oldest art we know can be found inside caves and on rocks in many different parts of the world. In France at the Lascaux caves, our ancestors painted over 900 large animals, as well as some human figures, using paint they made themselves from natural materials. These paintings are thought to be about 18,000 years old! There was no writing at that time, so we don't know exactly what the paintings were for. Perhaps they showed stories, or recorded great hunts. What do you think?

People who create art are called artists. Some artists draw with pencil on paper, some paint pictures. Some artists collage, arranging and sticking mixed materials. Others make statues. They have a special name; they're called sculptors. The materials an artist chooses can be very different, and so can the ways they work. Yet there is one thing all artists have in common: an imagination! You probably have plenty of imagination, so you could be a great artist!

Activity 1: Cave Painting

If you can find a really big cardboard box that no one is using (the kind of box a T.V. or a fridge comes in), you can pretend to make your own cave art, using the box for a cave. What animals will you draw on the inside? Horses, stags and bulls like at Lascaux? Or animals you know well, perhaps cats, dogs or birds? Do your 'cave' drawings have a tale to tell?

Lascaux cave paintings

Colour, Colour Everywhere

What colour are your eyes? What colours make up our Union Jack flag? What colour is the sky today?

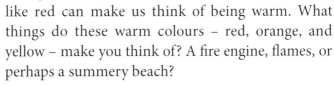

The world is alive with colour. How many colours can you name? Red, blue – which others?

When we think of some things, we think of their colours. When we think of the sun, we think of yellow. What colour does grass make you think of? Some colours, like reds and oranges, are called 'warm'. This doesn't mean that something painted red is actually warm to touch, but it does mean that colours like red can make us think of being warm. What things do these warm colours – red, orange, and yellow – make you think of? A fire engine, flames, or perhaps a summery beach?

Other colours, such as blues and greens, are known as 'cool' colours. They can make us think of icy water or dewy grass.

Warm colours are also considered to be 'strong', which means that in pictures they seem to jump forward; whereas cool colours are 'weak', appearing farther away.

As well as making us think of things and places, colours can give us feelings. Paintings made up of mostly cool colours usually create a different feeling to those made up with warm colours. Which feelings go with warm colours red and orange? Do you imagine 'hot' kinds of feelings, like you feel when you are cross, or after lots of laughing? What about cool colours; does green make you feel calm, does grey make you feel sad?

Artists choose their colours carefully, usually thinking about the atmosphere or mood their colours will create. For Vincent van Gogh (said 'fan-Hoch'), a Dutch painter living in the south of France in the nineteenth century, colour was the most important way of showing feeling. Yellow, to Vincent, was the colour which meant happiness. In 1888 Vincent painted this vase of sunflowers to welcome his friend Paul Gauguin (Go-Gan). Can you read the painting's colour to find out how Vincent felt about Paul's arrival? In a letter to his brother Theo, Vincent told how this painting was one of several from the same bunch of flowers, and that he worked very quickly to do the paintings, catching the flowers before they died. You can imagine how fast Vincent painted if you look at how thick and buttery his brush strokes are. How long do you think it took Vincent to paint his sunflowers? How long would it take you? What shape do you think Vincent's paint brush was? Was it a delicate pointed brush, or a rough and broad one?

Here is a collage made by a six year old girl. You can make a collage, too. The only things you need are paper, card and glue. You don't even need scissors, you can tear your shapes, creating interesting edges. Abby has chosen warm and cool colours for her collage. Which colours will you use and why?

Activity 1: Warm and cool colours

Separate your coloured drawing materials (crayons, felt tips) into 'warm' and 'cool' piles. Draw a picture of a tree using only warm colours. Draw the tree again but with cool colours this time. Do your pictures show different times of day or seasons? Do they make you feel differently? Can you start to link colours with feelings, like Vincent did?

Also working in France around the same time as Vincent was Henri Rousseau (said 'Roo-sew'). Vincent was very interested in the colour yellow but Henri was fascinated by green. Do you know which two colours you need to mix together to make green? How many different shades of green can you see in Henri's painting *Surprised!*? Henri made each and every one of these greens himself; he didn't get them ready-mixed from a tube! Are Henri's greens cool, or do you think he has managed to create

Surprised!

some which are warm? How do the greens help to tell a story by setting the scene in the painting? What sort of place is this and what is the weather like there? What has frightened the tiger – can you see the lightening bolt? Henri called this painting *Surprised!* Why do you think he chose this title?

Activity 2: Mixing colours

Make a painting based mostly around one colour, like Vincent and Henri did. Use a single ready-mixed colour, with water to make it pale, and thick undiluted strokes for bold patches. Alternatively, follow Henri's example and make a range of shades of one colour. Use a paper plate as your mixing palette and a cotton bud to stir. Start by mixing a drop of blue and a drop of yellow. Make a new mixture using more yellow. See what happens if you add spots of other colours – red, white, purple – to your greens.

Here are two paintings, one done with mostly cool colours and the other with mostly warm.

Hunters in the snow

In the first painting, *Hunters in the Snow*, which season is shown? What are the colours and clues you can see which helped you work out your answer? Have you ever noticed how there are fewer bright or strong colours in winter than in spring? Pieter Bruegel (said 'Broy-Gul'), the artist, used mainly white, with touches of black, brown and green to suggest the freezing winter weather of the Netherlands over 400 years ago. The trees are bare of leaves, and the icy grey-green of the frozen pond in the distance is matched in the muted colour of the sky. Pieter cleverly made sure people looking at his painting, even hundreds of years after he painted it, could imagine how cold the scene was. He did this by including details such as contrasting the thin clothing his hunters wear on their legs and arms with the bulky jackets they have layered over their bodies. He also arranged all of the figures with their heads down, as if they were too cold to look up and talk to each another. Even the hunting dogs seem cold; most carry their tales between their legs, too cold for wagging. Brrr!

A Bigger Splash

Hundreds of years after Pieter, in the 1960s, an English artist called David Hockney decided to leave behind the cold damp English winter and visit the warm west coast of America, near Los Angeles. David was impressed by the strong colours the Californian sunlight created. *A Bigger Splash* is a painting David made in Los Angeles. Its warm, vibrant colours make us feel the hot sun and show us the bright, clear skies he saw. Point to all the warm colours you can find in *A Bigger Splash*. Did you find red, yellow, and orange? What about blue? Is David's blue warm or cool? How has he managed to make this usually cool colour feel so warm and summery?

Follow That Line!

You may not have noticed, but if you look around you'll see you're surrounded by lines! Lines can be found in nature and in art. You make lines every time you write your name or draw. Lines on the road tell cars which side to drive on. Zebras are striped with lines. Bare tree branches make lines against the sky. Look at your hands: they're covered with thin lines. Lines come in all kinds: straight, curved, zigzag and wavy.

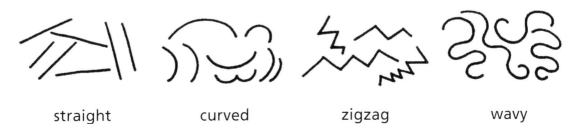

straight   curved   zigzag   wavy

Artists use lines in different ways. Here's a picture Joan Miró (said 'Me-row') made in the 1920s. His lines are easy to see. Most of them are strong, black and thin. Can you find others which are more tentative and pale? Let's look more carefully at Joan's lines and see if we can describe some of them. Can you see straight and curved lines, zigzags and dotted lines? There are even scribble lines in this picture.

But what is it a picture of? Do any of the lines form shapes which you recognise? Can you find lines which make a foot (or is it a paw?), lines for bows (or are they butterflies)? Did you find a seagull's head, a human face, what about winged birds? Does the title give us a clue? Joan called it simply *Peinture*, which is

Peinture

the French word for painting. It sounds like a name which tells us how he made the picture, but that's not quite right, because he used black chalk as well as paint to do it. Maybe Joan used painting and drawing to create a picture *about painting*. Joan believed in painting what he saw in his dreams; does that help you read the picture? Perhaps this work of art shows how Joan felt while he dreamed of painting. Have you ever painted one of your dreams? If you dream tonight, try to paint and draw it tomorrow, remembering Joan.

Now let's look at a painting by Pierre Bonnard (said Bon-R), also made in the 1920s. The first thing you might notice about *The Luncheon* is the bright, joyful colours, but for now let's look at the lines in the painting. It is painted using lines of colour. Unlike Joan's sharp, black lines, Pierre's are bright, fuzzy and thick. The bright colours, as well as the cut-off figures, mean that this painting doesn't seem like a dream, it looks more like a snap-shot memory of a special event. Do you ever have special lunches which you'd like to remember with a photo or picture? Perhaps for your birthday or Mother's Day? In *The Lunch,* look for lines which are like each other. Repeating lines like these are called patterns. Can you see a pattern of lines on the table cloth, and another on the woman's orange jumper? Are there other kinds of painted lines in the picture? Take your finger and trace all the lines you can see. Can you find some line patterns around you now; perhaps on your clothing or in your home? Are they colourful and thick in the style of Pierre, or thin and varied in the style of Joan?

The Luncheon

Looking at Pictures – Really Looking!

Paintings of Children

The Graham Children

An English artist, William Hogarth, painted the picture on the next page more than two hundred years ago. It shows the children of Daniel Graham, who worked for the King. Due to their father's success, the Graham children grew up with great wealth, lovely clothes, plenty of fresh food, toys, instruments and pets. In this portrait we see the children's play interrupted when an adult – perhaps their father – comes to find them. We can't see the adult, but we know they must be important because the girl in the middle of the picture is curtseying. Whoever it is, they must have arrived quietly, because one child carries on with his game – have you ever been caught out like this?

- Which child is being naughty and what is he doing? What's going to happen next: will the cat reach the bird?

- There are old fashioned toys, including one which makes music, in this painting. Can you find and name them?

- How can you tell the children are wealthy? Point to things in the painting which show that these children are from a rich family.

The Graham Children

- The children's clothes are quite different from the clothes you wear. Can you describe how their clothes might have felt to wear and play in (tight, heavy, hot)? Did you notice that the very youngest child (sitting in a wheeled cart) is wearing a boned dress? Does it surprise you to know that this child is actually a boy called Thomas? In William's day, boys were dressed as girls for several years!

Carnation, Lily, Lily, Rose

This painting was made by the American painter John Singer Sargent and it took him more than one year! He worked on it from the end of the summer of 1885 until the winter of 1886. One reason it took him so long was because he would only paint it at dusk – he wanted to capture a real light effect. Another reason could be that John worked with real children and they found it hard keeping still for him. On the left is Polly Barnard, who was 11, and on the right is her seven-year-old sister Dolly. They were the daughters of one of John's artist friends. John got the idea for this painting when he

Carnation, Lily, Lily, Rose

saw children lighting Chinese lanterns from a boat trip along the river Thames. He re-created the scene in a garden almost every evening afterwards, until his painting was done. The painting's title *Carnation, Lily, Lily, Rose* comes from a song that John and his friends enjoyed. One singer asks, 'Have you seen my Flora pass this way?' The others reply, 'Carnation, Lily, Lily, Rose'. What do you think this exchange means? Can you imagine how the song sounded? Judging by the painting, do you think it was a cheery or a melancholy tune?

- Can you identify and point out the three different flowers from the title within the painting? Could all three flowers bloom at once? What time of year would it need to be? (In fact, it took John so long to do this painting that the real flowers had died and he had to use artificial ones!)

- What are the girls doing?

- Can you describe the painting's setting: the time of day, the weather, the smells, the sounds? Can you imagine the tall grass crunching under Polly's foot as she steps forward? The girls' light clothes tell us it was a mild day. Are they feeling cold now?

- The girls don't look at us – they are concentrating on lighting their lanterns. Can you imagine what they are feeling?

Narrative Paintings

A painting by Jacopo Tintoretto

Here are two paintings showing the same story. Both were painted by Italians several hundred years ago. Can you be an art detective, and use looking to work out what the pictures show? You will probably know this story already, as it comes up in the Language and Literature chapter. It is a popular legend about a Christian hero called George. (That's a big clue!) Can you see a monster in the paintings? What other characters can you see? Who is the young lady? It is easiest to identify her by looking at the painting in upright – so-called 'portrait' – format. This one, from 1555, was painted in Venice by Jacopo Tintoretto (said 'Tin-tour-et-Toe'). You can find details which explain who she is if you look carefully; there is a crown on her head, she wears precious pearl jewellery, her gown is made of expensive satin, her cloak of velvet, and there is a castle in the background. She is a princess! George is rescuing her from the dragon. Now compare her with the princess in the painting by Paolo Uccello [You-Cello], made in 1470.

- Start by comparing the colours of the clothes. Do the outfits reveal character? Is Paolo's princess as sharp as her pointy shoes? Why is Jacopo's princess bare-footed? Perhaps to show her reactions are more natural; she is understandably terrified and lost them running away!

- What about George: look at his costume and accessories. How do they add to the story? Do both artists have the same idea about George as a character? Is he brave and fearless or would you choose other words to describe him?

- One of the paintings is made in a 'portrait' format (remember this means it is upright) and the other is landscape (meaning it is like a television screen, with action moving from one side to the other instead of from the back forwards). Are there other differences to the settings? What is the weather like, what times of day and what sort of places are shown?

● Paolo painted in a very careful style, achieving a smooth finish, making it hard to see his brushstrokes unless you are right in front of the original painting. Jacopo preferred a looser style, working with a broader brush and thicker paint. What moods do these different styles create?

We can use a special word to describe the story in a painting; the 'narrative'. This is a word which comes from literature. An artist telling a story in a painting, or in pictures, has to do some of the same things that a writer telling a story does. You could say the only real difference is that where the writer uses words to tell his stories, the artist starts with colour and line. Paintings like these two are especially close to literature because their source was a famous book called *The Golden Legend*. Look up the text on page 103 the Literature chapter of this book, and compare it with the paintings. What have the artists used from the written narrative and what have they imagined?

A painting by Paolo Uccello

Activity 1: George and the Dragon – Beginning, Middle or Ending.

Design, then paint or colour, a part of the George legend which you have read in 'Two Tall Tales' on page 103, but that Paolo or Jacopo missed out in their paintings. Include as many details in your work as you can. Is your scene a beginning, middle or ending?

Sculpture: All Around Art

King Charles

Look at these pictures. The first one shows a statue of one of our kings, King Charles the First, who ruled from 1625 until 1649 (when he was charged with treason and beheaded – you can find out more about this in the History and Geography chapter). The second shows a family, and was made by an English artist of the twentieth century called Henry Moore. One is very large, over six feet tall. The other is small, less tall than a regular ruler. Yet they have something important in common; they are both artworks you can see from all sides. They are sculptures.

Sculpture isn't flat like a painting, you can walk around it! We say that it has 'three dimensions'.

An artist who creates sculpture is called a sculptor. There are lots of reasons why an artist becomes a sculptor. Some artists prefer working in three dimensions. Others prefer the solid materials of sculpture; the most usual ones are clay, wood, stone and metal.

The English sculptor Barbara Hepworth worked by carving her sculptures out from solid pieces of stone

Family Group

or wood. *Infant*, from 1929 and pictured here, is one of the artworks she made like this. Can you believe the baby is really made from wood! Barbara has chiselled, carved, polished and varnished the wood so lovingly that it looks like polished metal. How do you think *Infant* would feel if you touched it? What about if you picked it up? Do you think it would be light or heavy?

Infant

Edgar Degas (said 'D-ga'), a French artist, turned to sculpture as an older man when his eyesight weakened. It suited him to be able to use his hands to feel his art, so he started modelling in wax or clay. Unlike Barbara who carved *into* a block of wood to make her Infant, Edgar made his *Little Dancer* by *building up* his material, adding soft wax on to a simple wooden skeleton.

A sculpture in wax or clay can then be 'cast', or copied, in bronze, a strong attractive metal. Many bronze casts have been made from Edgar's wax original. The warm tone of bronze matches the colour of Edgar's wax. If you live in England you can see a bronze cast of *Little Dancer* in Liverpool. The first *Little*

Little Dancer

Dancer Aged Fourteen was made in 1880-81 and is now in America. Edgar modelled it from a real dancer he knew, called Marie van Goethen. Can you see how hard Marie worked while she posed, by using your careful looking? She can barely keep her eyes open because she's so tired. Her fists are tightly clenched; her arms seem too long, as if they were stretched by posing. Have you noticed her real skirt and hair ribbon?

You can make a hedgehog like this one out of some clay, a few cocktail sticks, cloves and string. By adding everyday materials to your sculpture to bring it to life you are showing the influence of Edgar and his Little Dancer.

Like *Little Dancer*, sculptures often have interesting stories to tell, even if they are not 'narrative' art works. After Charles I was beheaded, for example, Oliver Cromwell decided Hubert Le Suer's (said 'l-Sewer') Charles I statue should be destroyed. It was sold to a man named John Rivet who was supposed to break it up, but he hid it instead! When Charles's son was asked to be a king of England again, the secret of the sculpture's survival leaked out. Rivet was forced to give it up and by 1675 Charles I had a public home in the place we now call Trafalgar Square. You can see it there today, looking down Whitehall towards the Palace of Westminster.

Charles (he is the one sitting on his horse on page 166) gazes ahead; what do you imagine he is thinking about? Perhaps Whitehall's Banqueting House, which had been his favourite palace building – but was also the site of his execution. Or maybe he is looking out for the statue of his enemy, Oliver Cromwell. Hamo Thornycroft's Cromwell of 1899 stands outside the Palace of Westminster. Inside, in parliament, a great argument broke out over whether a statue of Cromwell should even be put there. Cromwell, as Hamo sculpted him, looks suitably humble with downcast eyes. He faces away from Whitehall, and so avoids Charles' gaze.

Oliver Cromwell

Towering above Charles I, back in Trafalgar Square, is the best known large sculpture in England. In fact, it is one of the biggest sculptures in the world! Have you heard of Baily's *Lord Horatio Nelson*. Probably not, but I expect you recognise it from postcards and films of London, even if you don't know its proper name. Nelson's Column (as Baily's statue and the pillar it stands on are usually called), has become a symbol of England, like Buckingham Palace and the Union Jack. Nelson's Column was raised to mark the death of Nelson. He died at the battle of Trafalgar in 1805, after beating England's French and Spanish enemies.

Nelson's Column stands 52 metres tall.

This makes it six metres taller than New York's Statue of Liberty, and twenty-two metres taller than Rio's Christ Redeemer. While it is certainly England's tallest sculpture, there is another which is wider... Antony Gormley's *Angel of the North* (1996). Antony's Angel (shown on the next page) watches over Gateshead as Nelson surveys London. It is only 20 metres to Nelson's 52, but its width is much greater. The distance between its outstretched wings is 54 metres! The football pitch at Wembley is 105 metres long, so that gives you an idea of

Lord Nelson

what a 'monumental' sculpture Antony's Angel is. Can you see the tiny people in the picture standing underneath the Angel? They look like dots of paint compared to its great size!

Angel of the North

Now that you know some of the elements of art and some of the language of art, you will be able to 'really look' and talk about paintings and sculptures wherever you see them. Let's go over some starting points:

- What is the art work made of? Can you walk around it or is it flat on a wall? (This will help you work out what kind of art it is.)

- What colour or colours can you see? Are they warm or cool colours, and how do they set the scene or create a mood?

- Find and describe some of the lines in the painting. Are they straight, curved, zigzag or wavy? Are they thick or thin, clear or blurry? Is there a pattern? Can you read the lines or brushstrokes to understand how quickly or carefully the artist worked.

- If there are people in the art work, who are they, what are they doing and can you read their expressions? If you could give the characters words, what would they be saying, or thinking?

- Are you looking at a portrait – an art work showing a real person – a narrative art work, or something else?

Music

Introduction

We encourage you to give your child a wide range of musical experiences – singing songs, listening to all kinds of music, dancing around at home, attending local musical performances.

One of the best and easiest activities is singing with your child. We suggest some favourite songs in this section (see pages 182–191). If you don't feel confident about your own singing voice, remember that in your own home, you're the star! It's fine to play recordings for your child (see the Suggested Resources, below), but the more you sing with your child, the more comfortable you'll feel, and the more you'll both enjoy music together.

Some families will choose to provide their children with lessons that will take the children to a level of musical competence beyond what we describe in the following pages. Of course, different children will develop musical appreciation and skills at different rates and to different degrees. What's important is for you and your child to enjoy music and have fun with it.

You can help develop your child's knowledge and appreciation of music through the activities suggested in this section. Some of the activities ask your child to play with the basic elements of music, such as rhythm, pitch and tempo. Others involve moving and listening to music. Repetition is fine: children love to hear, sing or dance to the same song over and over again.

Have fun and enjoy these activities and songs with your child.

Suggested Resources:

Singing Games and Rhymes for Tiny Tots, Early Years and Middle Year by Lucinda Geoghegan (National Youth Choir of Scotland, 2000). These books are full of traditional songs and rhymes adapted into age-appropriate games. *Singing Games and Rhymes for Early Years* is a collection of tried and tested material for use in the nursery and infant classroom. Each singing game/rhyme has step-by-step instructions, and the accompanying CD provides everything you need to run a successful programme of music for your children. Ninety singing games and rhymes with CD, ideal for specialist and non-specialist teachers, support school curricula for Years 1 to 3 in England, Wales and Northern Ireland and suit the vocal range of young children perfectly.

Seasonal books: It Must be Spring, Happy Sun High, It's Autumn Time and It's Winter Time, Niki Davies (International Music Publications, 2005). These books are full of lovely songs, complete with a backing track.

The Singing Storycloth by Helen East *et al.* (A & C Black) is one of a series of excellent books for young children which offer activities as well as music.

www.singup.org Sing Up! A national singing programme for primary school-aged children includes databases of songs arranged by Key Stage, year group and subject, helpful resources and suggested activities. Sing Up! also produce a termly magazine packed full of singing stories, advice and tips for parents, teachers and children.

Do You Like Music?

Do you like music? Do you like to sing and dance? Do you have a favourite song or a favourite kind of music?

You can make music by drumming on a pot, or humming through a paper-towel tube, or shaking a plastic container half-full of dry beans, or plucking rubber bands stretched over a small open box. With a little imagination, you can be a one-man band, with all sorts of homemade instruments! Would you like to play an instrument someday? With practice, maybe you'll learn to play one of the instruments pictured here.

PARENTS: If you have recordings that feature the instruments pictured here, play them and point out the sound of the specific instruments to your child. If you and your child get a chance to see, hear, and touch the actual instruments, that's even better!

flute

trumpet

drum

guitar   piano   violin

What instrument is this girl playing?

Musical Activities for Parents and Children

Activity 1:
Moving responsively to music

You and your child can have fun moving to music. When you play music, talk about how the music makes you feel, and encourage your child to be comfortable and creative: there is no right or wrong way to move to the music. At times, get up and move with your child; it's fun!

Get Ready: Go to a room in which you can move around comfortably. There, you'll need to have the equipment necessary to play a recording of one of the following selections or some other music that encourages steady, rhythmic movement.

Suggested Music: recordings of Tchaikovsky's *Nutcracker* ballet; or 'The March of the Siamese Children' from the Rodgers and Hammerstein musical *The King and I*; or 'The March of the Toys' from Victor Herbert's *Babes in Toyland*.

Go: Play the music and talk with your child about the way the music makes him feel. Ask him, 'How does this part of the music make you feel like moving?'

For *The Nutcracker*, you can play music from different scenes, and move in different ways as suggested by the music. Some contrasting scenes you might want to try include: from Act I, 'March'; and, from Act II, 'Tea (Chinese Dance),' 'Trepak (Russian Dance),' and 'Dance of the Sugar Plum Fairy.'

Go a Little Further: Listen with your child to Camille Saint-Saëns's *Carnival of the Animals*, which uses different instruments of the orchestra to paint musical portraits of animals. (Many recordings of this work are available; some include a narrator reading amusing poems written by Ogden Nash to go along with the music.) You and your child can 'act out' the animals by using different movements while listening to the music, such as hopping, skipping, bucking, short steps or high steps.

Activity 2: 'Beat it!'

Get Ready: Talk with your child about steady sounds, that is, sounds that you hear over and over again, such as the ticking of a clock, or the sound made by windscreen wipers or a washing machine.

Tell your child that a steady sound has a steady beat, like her own heartbeat. Have her place her hand over her heart and ask her, 'Do you feel the steady beat?' (If she can't feel it, have her run around or jump up and down, then try to feel it.)

Now tell your child that you're going to say a rhyme with a steady beat. Tell her to listen to the following rhyme:

March together keep a beat
Feel that movement in your feet.
Stand together in a row
Marching forward off we go!

Left, right, left, right...

After you repeat the rhyme a few times, begin stamping your feet to its steady beat, and ask your child to join you in 'marching to the beat,' as follows:

March to**geth**er **keep** a **beat**
Feel that **move**ment **in** your **feet.**
Stand to**geth**er **in** a **row**
Marching **for**ward **off** we **go!**

Left, right, left, right...

Go: Tell your child that you're going to play a game called Beat It! You're going to use your hands and feet to make different steady beats. Ask her to watch and listen as you do the following:

clap, clap, stomp
clap, clap, stomp
clap, clap, stomp

Ask your child to join in with the beat. Then let her continue clapping and stomping the beat on her own a few more times.

Continue the game with other steady beats. Follow the pattern: you clap and stomp, she joins in, then she finishes on her own. You can make up your own steady beat, but keep it simple at first, such as:

- *clap, stomp, clap, stomp*
- *clap, clap, clap, stomp*
- *stomp, stomp, clap*

You can also ask your child to make up a steady beat for you to follow.

Go a Little Further: You and your child can clap to the beat in poems with strong cadences, including many Mother Goose rhymes (see pages 22–38), such as:

Pat-a-cake, **pat**-a-cake, **bak**er's man!
Bake me a **cake** as **fast** as you **can**.

You can also clap to the beat in many children's songs. For example:

Old MacDonald **had** a **farm**,
E-I-E-I-**O.**

Activity 3: LOUD and quiet

This activity has several parts. It begins with everyday sounds, then uses a familiar song, then drumming, and finally recorded music.

Which baby is loud?
Which baby is quiet?

Get Ready: Ask your child to talk with you about loud sounds and quiet sounds (you can raise your voice on 'LOUD' and whisper the word '*quiet*'). A baby crying is LOUD; a baby sleeping is quiet. Ask your child to point to various objects in the room that make a sound: a telephone, a squeaky door, a fan, a smoke alarm, a fridge. Ask if the sound they make is loud or quiet. Then talk about sounds your child is familiar with (not necessarily in the room but anywhere) that are usually loud (for example, a siren or a bus engine) or usually quiet (for example, a whisper or a cat's purr).

Now ask your child to sing with you a song that has some LOUD parts and some *quiet* parts. One such song is an old favourite, 'The Wheels on the Bus.' Here are some of the words:

[Loudly]

The babies on the bus say, 'WAA, WAA, WAA'
'WAA, WAA, WAA, WAA, WAA, WAA'
The babies on the bus say 'WAA, WAA, WAA'
All day long.

[Quietly]

The mummies on the bus say, 'Shhh, shhh, shh'
'Shhh, shhh, shh, shhh, shhh, shh'
The mummies on the bus say 'Shhh, shhh, shh'
All day long.

Repeat it three times. Sing the first verse and make sure you cry really loudly, just as a baby would do, when you sing the words 'WAA, WAA, WAA'. Sing the second verse quietly, as if you were trying to calm a crying baby.

Go: Now you need a toy drum – or if you don't have a drum, you can use an upside-down kitchen pot, bucket or a recycled ice-cream tub. You also need something to use as a drumstick, such as a pencil or wooden spoon.

Say the following lines with your child several times, making your voice sound LOUD on the first two lines and quiet on the second two lines. Then ask him to say the lines with you and play the drums as the words direct. (You can show him how to use his fingertips to rub the drum for a quiet sound.)

MY DRUM CAN SOUND LOUD,
WITH A LOUD SOUND, A LOUD SOUND.

My drum can sound quiet,
With a quiet sound, a quiet sound.

Talk with your child about what he does differently to make the drum sound loud or quiet.

Go a Little Further: Listen to music with dramatic contrasts between loud and quiet passages. Talk with your child about how the loud and quiet sounds change the way the music feels, and what kind of different movements he could do to go along with the loud and quiet parts. For example, a favourite work that builds dramatically from quiet to loud is Grieg's 'In the Hall of the Mountain King' from *Peer Gynt*. Have your child tiptoe during the quiet parts, and jump up and down during the loud parts.

Activity 4: Fast and slow

Get Ready: Talk with your child about animals that usually move slowly, such as turtles and cows. Then talk about animals that can move *very* quickly, such as birds and mice. Ask your child to think of other animals that we think of as usually moving slowly or quickly.

Go: Sing 'Old MacDonald' with your child, then choose one of the animals you discussed earlier that move slowly. Sing a verse of 'Old MacDonald' in which you name this slow animal, and sing at a slow tempo (you'll have to use your imagination when you sing the sound the animal makes). Encourage your child to choose another slow moving animal and sing the next verse by herself, again singing at a slow tempo. For example:

Old … Mac … Don … ald … had … a … farm …
E … I … E … I … O.
And … on … this … farm … he … had … a … turtle …
E … I … E … I … O.
With … a … ho … hum … here
and … a … ho … hum … there, etc.

Then ask:

● 'What animal can move fast?'

● 'At what speed should we sing the verse for this animal?'

For example, you could sing at a brisk tempo:

Old MacDonald had a farm,
E-I-E-I-O.
And on this farm he had a rabbit,
E-I-E-I-O.
With a zip-zip here and a zip-zip there, etc.

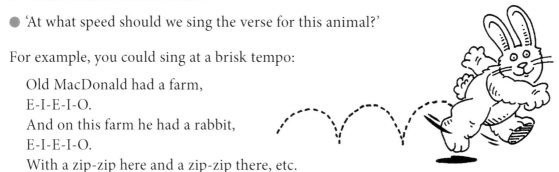

Go a Little Further: Listen to music that is sometimes slow and sometimes fast. For example, 'In the Hall of the Mountain King' from Grieg's *Peer Gynt* starts out moderately slow and turns furiously fast by the end. Then ask your child:

● 'What movement would you like to do when the music is slow?'

● 'What movement would you like to do when the music is fast?'

Play the music again and have your child move to the music. If you're feeling up to it, join in!

Activity 5: High and low

Get Ready: You'll need a simple xylophone for this activity. If your child has never played a xylophone before, begin by letting him play freely with the instrument. (Although this activity assumes the use of a xylophone, you can adapt the suggestions to a keyboard instrument, such as a piano, toy or real, or a small electronic keyboard.)

Tell your child that you're going to play a game with *high* and **low** sounds (change the pitch of your voice to illustrate high and low.) Help him think of high and low sounds in nature. For example, you could say:

● 'A bird high in the sky makes a high sound: *tweet, tweet.*'

● 'A toad down in a pond makes a low sound: **croak, croak.**'

Go: Use a book or similar object to prop up the end of the xylophone with the shortest key (this can help visually reinforce the concept of high and low). Tap the longest bar on the xylophone. Then tap the shortest bar. Repeat this a couple of times, then tell your child which sound is high and which is low (remember to change the pitch of your own voice to illustrate high and low):

● [as you tap the shortest bar] 'This is like the bird: *tweet, tweet*. This is a *high* sound.'

● [as you tap the longest bar] 'This is like the toad: **croak, croak**. This is a **low** sound.'

Here's how to arrange the xylophone

Now, tap the longest bar, then tap the shortest bar and ask your child:

● 'Which sound was *higher* – the first or the second?'

Again, tap the longest bar, then tap the shortest bar and ask your child:

● 'Which sound was **lower** – the first or the second?'

Continue by asking your child to identify which sound is higher or lower as you tap two more bars near the ends of the xylophone. Now switch roles: have your child tap two bars and ask you which sound is higher or lower.

If they are available, bells of different sizes also provide a good way to illustrate high and low. With two bells, one big and one small, you can show that big things make low sounds, and little things make high sounds.

Favourite Songs

PARENTS: At home, in the car, in the bathtub, walking along: there are many good times and places for singing, and many wonderful songs to sing. Here are some to share with your child. (See also page 173 for some suggested song recordings.)

Hush, Little Baby

Hush, little baby, don't say a word,
Papa's gonna buy you a mocking bird.
And if that mocking bird won't sing,
Papa's gonna buy you a diamond ring.
And if that diamond ring turns brass,
Papa's gonna buy you a looking glass.
And if that looking glass gets broke,
Papa's gonna buy you a billy goat.
And if that billy goat won't pull,
Papa's gonna buy you a cart and bull.
And if that cart and bull turn over,
Papa's gonna buy you a dog named Rover.
And if that dog named Rover won't bark,
Papa's gonna buy you a horse and cart.
And if that horse and cart fall down,
You'll still be the sweetest little baby in town.

Bingo

There was a man who had a dog,
And Bingo was his name-o.
B-I-N-G-O, B-I-N-G-O, B-I-N-G-O
And Bingo was his name-o.

London Bridge
Is Falling Down

London Bridge is falling down,
Falling down, falling down,
London Bridge is falling down,
My fair lady.

How shall we build it up again,
Up again, up again,
How shall we build it up again,
My fair lady?

Build it up with iron bars,
Iron bars, iron bars,
Build it up with iron bars,
My fair lady.

Iron bars will bend and bow,
Bend and bow, bend and bow,
Iron bars will bend and bow,
My fair lady.

Build it up with wood and clay...
Wood and clay will wash away....

Build it up with silver and gold...
Silver and gold will be stolen away...
[*Repeat first verse.*]

Here We Go Round
the Mulberry Bush

Here we go round the mulberry bush,
The mulberry bush, the mulberry bush,
Here we go round the mulberry bush,
On a cold and frosty morning.

This is the way we wash our face...

This is the way we brush our teeth...

This is the way we put on our clothes...

This is the way we clap our hands...

[*Sing other verses about other things you do.*]

My Bonnie Lies over the Ocean

My bonnie lies over the ocean,

My bonnie lies over the sea,

My bonnie lies over the ocean,

Please bring back my bonnie to me.

Bring back, bring back,

Oh bring back my bonnie to me, to me.

Bring back, bring back,

Oh bring back my bonnie to me.

Old MacDonald

Old MacDonald had a farm, E-I-E-I-O.

And on this farm he had some chicks,
E-I-E-I-O.

With a chick-chick here and a chick-
chick there,

Here a chick, there a chick, everywhere
a chick-chick,
Old MacDonald had a farm, E-I-E-l-O.

Old MacDonald had a farm, E-I-E-l-O.

And on this farm he had some ducks,
E-I-E-I-O.

With a quack-quack here and a quack-
quack there,

Here a quack, there a quack, everywhere
a quack quack....

[*Continue in the same manner with:*

cow: moo-moo

sheep: baa-baa

pig: oink-oink, etc.]

Twinkle, Twinkle

Twinkle, twinkle, little star,
How I wonder what you are.
Up above the world so high
Like a diamond in the sky.
Twinkle, twinkle, little star,
How I wonder what you are!

Pop! Goes the Weasel

Half a pound of tuppenny rice,
Half a pound of treacle.
That's the way the money goes,
Pop! goes the weasel.

Up and down the City Road,
In and out the Eagle.
That's the way the money goes,
Pop! goes the weasel.

Every night when I get home
The monkey's on the table,
Take a stick and knock it off,
Pop! goes the weasel.

Head, Shoulders, Knees and Toes

Head, shoulders, knees and toes,
Knees and toes.
Head, shoulders, knees and toes,
Knees and toes.
And eyes and ears and mouth and nose,
Head, shoulders, knees and toes,
Knees and toes.
[*Repeat, getting faster each time.*]

One Man Went To Mow

One man went to mow,
went to mow a meadow,
One man and his dog [*woof, woof*]
Went to mow a meadow.

Two men went to mow,
went to mow a meadow,
One man, two men and their dog
[*woof, woof*]
Went to mow a meadow.

Three men went to mow,
went to mow a meadow,
One man, two men, three men
and their dog [*woof, woof*]
Went to mow a meadow.

Four men went to mow,
went to mow a meadow,
One man, two men, three men, four
men and their dog [*woof, woof*]
Went to mow a meadow.

Five men went to mow,
went to mow a meadow,
One man, two men, three men,
four men, five men and their dog
[*woof, woof*]
Went to mow a meadow.

Six men went to mow,
went to mow a meadow,
One man, two men, three men,
four men, five men, six men
and their dog [*woof, woof*]
Went to mow a meadow.

Seven men went to mow,
went to mow a meadow,
One man, two men, three men,
four men, five men, six men, seven men
and their dog [*woof, woof*]
Went to mow a meadow.

Eight men went to mow,
went to mow a meadow,
One man, two men, three men, four
men, five men, six men, seven men,
eight men and their dog [*woof, woof*]
Went to mow a meadow.

Nine men went to mow,
went to mow a meadow,
One man, two men, three men,
four men, five men, six men,
seven men, eight men, nine men
and their dog [*woof, woof*]
Went to mow a meadow.

Ten men went to mow,
went to mow a meadow,
One man, two men, three men,
four men, five men, six men,
seven men, eight men, nine men,
ten men and their dog [*woof, woof*]
Went to mow a meadow.

The Bear Went over the Mountain

The bear went over the mountain,
The bear went over the mountain,
The bear went over the mountain,
To see what he could see.
And all that he could see,
And all that he could see,
Was the other side of the mountain,
The other side of the mountain,
The other side of the mountain,
Was all that he could see!

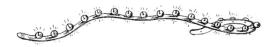

Jingle Bells

Dashing through the snow,
In a one-horse open sleigh,
O'er the fields we go,
Laughing all the way.
Bells on Bobtail ring,
Making spirits bright,
What fun it is to ride and sing
A sleighing song tonight!

Jingle bells, jingle bells, jingle all the way,
Oh, what fun it is to ride in a one-horse open sleigh!
Jingle bells, jingle bells, jingle all the way,
Oh, what fun it is to ride in a one-horse open sleigh!

The Farmer in His Den

The Farmer's in his den,
The Farmer's in his den,
Heigh-ho, the derry-o,
The Farmer's in his den.

The Farmer wants a wife,
The Farmer wants a wife,
Heigh-ho, the derry-o,
The Farmer wants a wife.

The wife wants a child,
The wife wants a child,
Heigh-ho, the derry-o,
The wife wants a child.

The child wants a nurse,
The child wants a nurse,
Heigh-ho, the derry-o,
The child wants a nurse.

The nurse wants a dog,
The nurse wants a dog,
Heigh-ho, the derry-o,
The nurse wants a dog.

Everyone pats the dog,
Everyone pats the dog,
Heigh-ho, the derry-o,
Everyone pats the dog.

Kum Ba Yah

Chorus:
Kum ba yah, my lord, kum ba yah,
Kum ba yah, my lord, kum ba yah,
Kum ba yah, my lord, kum ba yah,
O, lord, kum ba yah

Verse:
Someone's sleeping, lord, kum ba yah,
Someone's sleeping, lord, kum ba yah,
Someone's sleeping, lord, kum ba yah,
O lord, kum ba yah.

[*Sing other verses with 'laughing', 'dreaming', 'crying,' 'singing,'; then repeat chorus.*]

This Old Man

This old man, he played one,

He played knick-knack on my thumb,

With a knick-knack, paddy-wack, give a dog a bone,

This old man came rolling home.

This old man, he played two,

He played knick-knack on my shoe...

This old man, he played three,

He played knick-knack on my knee...

This old man, he played four,

He played knick-knack on my door...

This old man, he played five,

He played knick-knack on my hive...

This old man, he played six,

He played knick-knack on my sticks...

This old man, he played seven,

He played knick-knack up in heaven...

This old man, he played eight,

He played knick-knack on my gate...

This old man, he played nine,

He played knick-knack on my spine...

This old man, he played ten,

He played knick-knack over again ...

Row, Row, Row Your Boat

Row, row, row your boat
Gently down the stream,
Merrily, merrily, merrily, merrily,
Life is but a dream.

The Wheels on the Bus

The wheels on the bus go round and round,
Round and round, round and round,
The wheels on the bus go round and round,
All day long.
The wipers on the bus go swish, swish, swish...
The doors on the bus go open and close...
The driver on the bus says, 'Move on back!'...
The babies on the bus say, 'Waa, waa, waa' ...
The mummies on the bus say, 'Shhh, shhh, shh' ...
The kids on the bus go up and down ...

[*Repeat first verse*]

The Muffin Man

Do you know the muffin man,
The muffin man, the muffin man,
Do you know the muffin man,
Who lives in Drury Lane?

Yes, I know the muffin man,
The muffin man, the muffin man,
Yes, I know the muffin man,
Who lives in Drury Lane.

The Hokey Cokey

You put your right foot in,
You put your right foot out,
In, out, in, out,
Shake it all about,
You do the Hokey Cokey
And you turn around,
That's what it's all about.

You put your left foot in...

You put your right hand in...

You put your left hand in...

You put your whole self in...

If You're Happy and You Know It

If you're happy and you know it, clap your hands. [*clap, clap*]
If you're happy and you know it, clap your hands. [*clap, clap*]
If you're happy and you know it,
And you really want to show it,
If you're happy and you know it, clap your hands. [*clap, clap*]

If you're happy and you know it, stamp your feet. [*stamp, stamp*]

If you're happy and you know it, shout hooray. [*hooray!*]

If you're happy and you know it, do all three. [*clap, clap; stamp, stamp; hooray!*]

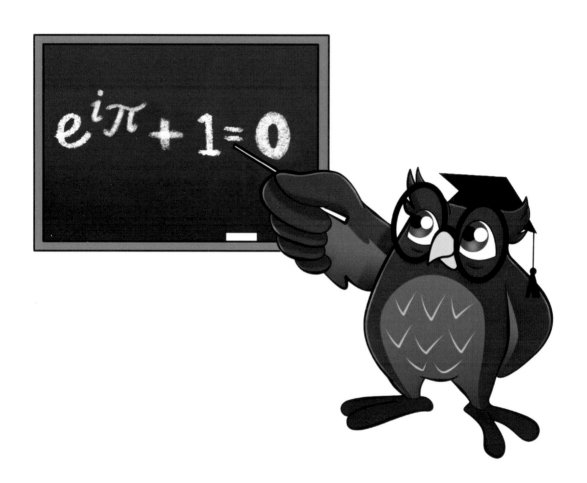

Mathematics

Introduction

We hope that parents will place a special emphasis on the activities in this section. The most effective Year 1 programmes in the world provide youngsters with lively and almost daily exposure to age-appropriate maths concepts and operations, thus giving the children a comfortable familiarity with the elements of maths, as well as a firm foundation for later mastery.

Among grown-ups, mastery of maths has been shown to be a reliable road to getting a good job in the modern world. Yet the greatest barrier to mastery – 'maths anxiety' – usually arises in the early years, because children have not been made to feel at home with the conventions and procedures of maths. The only good way for them to gain the needed familiarity, and avoid the widespread symptoms of maths anxiety, is to provide them with a lot of lively exposure and practice at an early age.

Practice does not mean mindless repetition but, rather, varied practice, including the use of countable objects and also some paper-and-pencil work. Regular practice and review in the early years will make the basic ideas and operations of maths interesting and familiar, and eventually lead children to the effortless, automatic performance of basic operations upon which later problem solving depends.

If we adults have 'maths anxiety' ourselves, our duty is to avoid conveying to our children the idea that we 'don't like maths' or 'aren't good at maths.' By engaging our children in the kinds of activities suggested in this section, we can let them know that maths is important and interesting to us. Keep in mind, however, that the activities suggested here are supplementary ways for parents to reinforce their children's learning at home. They are not sufficient for teaching maths in school, where children need more extensive opportunities for practice and review.

Suggested Resources

Ten Monkey Jamboree by Dianne Ochiltree (Simon and Schuster, 2003). In this cheerful, whimsical romp, readers explore just how many combinations of monkeys will add up to ten. Accompanying the amusing and captivating illustrations, the rhythmic text twirls and spins as much as the monkeys, and makes a perfect read-aloud for the very young. Dianne Ochiltree teaches writing in schools, and has written several mathematical-orientated picture books including 'Bart's Amazing Charts' and 'Cats Add Up'.

How Many Sharks in the Bath? by Bill Gillham (Frances Lincoln) is a great interactive number book which incorporates the concept of zero.

Five Little Monkeys by Zita Newcome (Walker) is packed full of number rhymes and games with lots of opportunities for joining in.

The Real Princess, a mathemagical tale by Brenda Williams (Barefoot) mixes number learning and fairy tales in a very entertaining way.

Number Rhymes by Opal Dunn (Frances Lincoln Children's Books). This entertaining collection of rhymes explores counting backwards, counting in twos and counting numbers beyond 10. From 'Five Little Monkeys' and 'Ten in a Bed' to 'One, two, buckle my shoe' and 'One hundred bees round a hive', these rhymes provide a rich range of enjoyable opportunities to familiarise children with ways of manipulating numbers. Collected by a highly reputable early years educationalist with the clear aim of developing early number skills, these rhymes are vividly illustrated.

Read and Learn: Finding Shapes is an extensive collection that helps young readers discover and understand the world around them. These books are packed full of fascinating facts and intriguing, labelled photographs that will really grab their attention. Using questions to focus learning, each title will prompt discussion, encourage information gathering and truly involve children in the topics they are studying. 'Finding Shapes' investigates the shapes that can be found at home, in school, in the park and those that can be found in nature. It develops simple mathematical skills as readers are invited to count the number of shapes they can spot, and includes a quiz to help with classifying objects in terms of their shape.

Reading Roundabout: My Money by Paul Humphrey (Franklin Watts) complements practical money work. See also the 'Money Books' (Easylearn) which are useful for consolidating material when pupils are learning to solve problems involving money. There is a wide range of interesting tasks to achieve understanding.

Patterns and Classifications

PARENTS: When you recall your earliest experiences with maths, you may think of counting on your fingers, or perhaps adding and subtracting: 2 + 2 = 4, 3 - 1 = 2. Besides such familiar operations, early maths also involves some fundamental concepts and ways of thinking.

Children need to learn how to sort and classify, and many start to learn these skills well before Year 1. By their first years, they are ready to recognise similarity and difference, to see patterns, and to sort objects according to specific attributes, such as size, colour, or function. You can help your child reinforce these concepts through some activities.

Activity 1: Collecting things by likeness

Get Ready: Tell your child you're going on a 'similarity hunt.' Get a paper bag and tell your child that you're going to collect objects that are alike in some way and put them in the bag. Talk about what sorts of things you will collect and how they will be alike. You may want to collect things that are all one colour or things that are all used in the same way (things to eat with, things to draw with, etc.).

Go: With your child, label the bag with the attribute or characteristic you've selected, such as 'red things' or 'things used to eat with'. Now it's time to collect. Together look for objects in and around where you live. If necessary, you can model the selection of the first object or two by finding an object and saying, 'Look, here's a red crayon. We can put it in our bag because it's red.'

Talk and Think: Guide your child to comment on each object as it goes in the bag, by asking:

● 'Why does this one go in the bag?' (If he says, 'It's red', you can reinforce the idea of similarity by saying, 'Yes, like all the other things'.)

● What else can you find that's red [or used for eating, etc.]?'

On another day, repeat this activity with a new bag and a new quality that makes the things alike. This is, by the way, a good activity to begin in the morning because you'll find that as you go through your day, you and your child will find objects for your collection even when you aren't thinking about the game.

Activity 2: Sorting everyday objects

Get Ready: You will need an assortment of familiar items from around the house. Choose items that can be sorted into two to four groups according to a specific attribute, such as size, colour, or function. For example, collect a bunch of socks, some white, some with stripes and others with spots. Or gather some books of varying sizes. For more groupings you could choose toys of different colours or four different kitchen utensils.

Go: With the pile of mixed-up items in front of you, tell your child you're going to separate the objects into two groups. Ask her to guess the rule you're using to separate the objects. Then start to put items into two groups: for example, the white socks in one pile, the socks with designs in another. Next try sorting into three, then four different groups.

Talk and Think: To help your child focus on the concepts of similarity and difference, ask:

● 'How are all the items in each group alike?'

● 'How are the items in these two groups different?'

- 'Here's one more item. Where would you put it? Why?'

- 'What do you think is the rule for sorting these items?'

Go a Little Further: Give your child an item that doesn't belong in either group; for example, if you're sorting big and small books, give her a spoon. Then talk about why the item is different and why it can't be sorted into either group.

Activity 3: Similar and different

Get Ready: Put a variety of different objects in a bag. Choose items that can be grouped in different ways – by colour, shape, texture, or function: for example, crayons, buttons, or blocks in different colours and shapes. Be sure to include at least one set of items that share the same function, such as three different drinking cups.

It's easier to see some qualities of things than others, so it may help to examine some of the objects with your child in order to help him see both the obvious characteristics of an object, such as colour, and the less obvious qualities, such as function. For example, if you examine a common pencil, you can ask such questions as: 'What colour is it?' (Yellow.) 'What do we use it for?' (To write with.)

Go: Place the objects on the floor and spread them around if necessary. To model the activity for your child, pick up two items that are similar in some way and tell your child how they are similar and how they are different. For example: 'Here are two cups. They are similar in the way that we use them; we use them both to drink with. They are different in their colour: one is red, but the other is blue.' Then tell your child to pick two other items that are similar in some way. Discuss the items by asking:

- 'How are the items similar?'

- 'How are they different?'

- 'Can you find another item that belongs with these?'

- 'How is it like the other items?'

As your child answers the questions, occasionally give him words that help him categorise. For example, if your child picks two red blocks and says that they are similar because 'they're both red,' you might say, 'Yes, they're both red; the way they're similar is their colour.' With two writing implements – for example, a pen and a pencil – if your child says they're similar because 'they're both long,' you might add, 'Yes, and another way they're similar is the way we use them: we use them both to write with.'

Activity 4: **Shape sort**

Get Ready: To do this activity, your child needs to be familiar with the six basic shapes pictured here and with their names. If she is not yet familiar with these shapes and their names, we suggest that first you do Activities 1-2 in the Geometry section of this chapter (see pages 234–238).

You will need:

sturdy paper such as stiff card, crayons, scissors

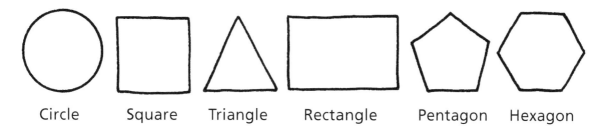

Circle　　Square　　Triangle　　Rectangle　　Pentagon　Hexagon

Review with your child the shapes pictured here and tell her their names several times. You might want to have her touch each shape and say or sing its name. You can point out that a square and a rectangle are similar: they both have four sides. But in a square, the sides are all the same.

Draw some circles, squares, triangles, rectangles, pentagons and hexagons of different sizes on sturdy paper. As you draw, talk with your child about the shape names. Let her join in the preparation by colouring the shapes before you cut them.

Go: Spread the cut-outs on a flat surface. Ask your child to pick one and help her examine the shape by asking:

● 'How many sides does this shape have?'

● 'Are the sides straight or round?'

● 'How many corners does this shape have?'

● 'Does the shape look the same if I turn it this way? How does it change?'

● 'Can you tell me the name of this shape?' (If your child correctly names the shape, you can reinforce the name by repeating it: 'That's right, it's a [name of shape].')

Talk and Think: Pick another shape that's different from the first one. To help your child focus on the differences, put the shapes side by side and ask:

- 'How are the shapes different from each other?'
- 'Do both shapes have sides?'
- 'Do they both have corners?'
- 'Do they have the same number of corners?'
- 'Does each shape have the same number of sides?'
- 'If we turn the shapes this way, do they still look different?' Then ask her to sort the rest of the shapes and tell which shapes belong together and why.

Go a Little Further: Have a scavenger hunt for shapes. For example, your child may compare a rectangle and a tabletop; an ice-cream cone and a triangle; or a tyre and a circle. The hunt can take place at home, in the park, in the car, or anywhere else that shapes exist – that's everywhere!

Activity 5: Shape train

Get Ready: This activity will help your child learn how to identify and describe patterns of alternating shapes.

You will need a set of blocks with geometric shapes. Make sure there are at least twelve blocks of three different shapes, such as four blocks with square faces, four blocks with triangular faces and four blocks with rectangular faces.

After you collect the blocks, discuss the names of the block faces with your child and give him some time to examine and touch the three kinds of shapes.

Go: Tell your child that you're going to build a 'shape train'. To get started lay six blocks in a row, alternating the shapes. To help your child understand the pattern, point to each block face and ask:

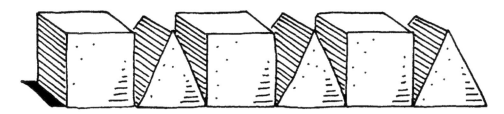

A shape train.

- 'What shape is the first carriage? And the next? And the next?' Talk about the pattern with your child; for example: 'Do you see the pattern? There is a triangle carriage, then a square carriage, then a triangle carriage, then a square carriage.' Then tell your child that you want to continue the pattern, and ask him to add another carriage. Ask:

- 'What shape should the next carriage be? Why?'

Talk and Think: To help your child focus on different patterns, use the same blocks to form a different pattern, such as two squares and two triangles. Ask:

- 'How many squares are there?'

- 'How many triangles?'

- 'What pattern can you see in this shape train?' Ask your child to add more blocks to the train and describe the pattern.

Go a Little Further: Introduce another shape, such as a sphere. Work with your child to make and describe other shape trains. Encourage him to name the shapes he uses to build the train and then describe the pattern he has made.

Activity 6: Potato prints

Get Ready:

You will need: 2 large potatoes, a paring knife, newspaper, poster paint in several colours, some big sheets of paper, paper towels.

WARNING: The adult must do all the cutting in this activity. Explain that you are going to cut the potatoes so that they can be used to print shapes: a square, a rectangle, a circle, and a triangle. First, cut the potatoes in half and draw an outline of one shape on each half. Next, cut down around each outline, which will leave a raised shape that you can use to print with.

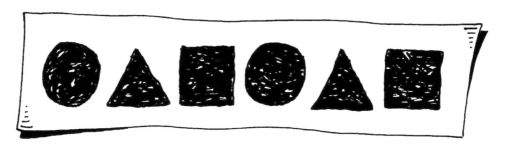

Cover your work surface with newspaper; this activity can get messy! Put about two tablespoons of paint on a small plate or in a shallow plastic lid. Show your child how to dip the potato stamp into the paint to coat only the raised shape. Then show your child how to make a print by pushing the potato stamp firmly and evenly on a piece of paper.

Go: To get started, let your child make any prints he wants on a big sheet of paper. Children love to print and will enjoy just printing before you begin to work on patterns. (You'll need to rinse the potato stamp and dry it on a paper towel if your child wants to dip the same potato stamp into different colours.)

When your child is ready, get a new piece of paper and stamp out a pattern on it. Begin with a pattern of two shapes, for example, a triangle and a circle. Alternate the shapes but use only one colour. Repeat the pattern three times. Ask your child to copy the pattern. It's O.K. if your child makes mistakes doing this – it's all part of learning. While your child is stamping the pattern, ask:

- 'What are the names of the two shapes we're using?'
- 'Which shape comes first?'
- 'Which shape comes next?'
- 'Which shape comes after that?'
- 'What pattern do you see?'

Ask your child to continue the pattern.

Go a Little Further: Add another shape to the pattern so that you're using three different shapes: for example, a triangle, a circle, and a square.

Activity 7: More play with patterns

Get Ready:

You will need:

coloured sugar paper

scissors

Using three different colours of paper, cut out 18 of each shape (circle, triangle, rectangle, square, pentagon, hexagon), each about three by 10 centimetres. In other words, when you're finished you'll have, for example, 18 triangles: 6 blue, 6 yellow, and 6 red.

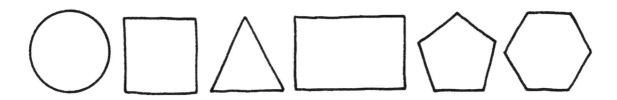

Go: To help your child focus on colour patterns, choose one shape and create a colour pattern, such as blue triangle/red triangle/yellow triangle. Repeat the pattern several times. Then point to the pattern and ask:

● 'What is the name of this shape?'

● 'What is the colour of this shape?'

● 'Are the colours of the shapes similar or different?'

● 'What pattern do you see?' Ask your child to continue the pattern. Then have him explain his choices.

Go a Little Further: Ask your child to make up his own pattern. To make the activity more challenging, guide him in creating a pattern that repeats both shape and colour, such as blue square/yellow triangle/blue square/yellow triangle.

Numbers and Number Sense

PARENTS: We encourage you to read this introduction, which is addressed to you, before proceeding with the activities for your child that begin on page 206.

At home and during nursery and Reception, your child will no doubt have experienced some familiar counting rhymes, such as 'One, two, buckle my shoe' (page 25) or:

> One, two, three, four, five,
> Once I caught a fish alive;
> Six, seven, eight, nine, ten,
> Then I let it go again.

Through such counting rhymes and games, many children, even before Reception, learn to recite numbers aloud ('one, two, three, four, five...') in the same way they sometimes recite the alphabet song, without really understanding what the numbers (or letters) represent, except that they are said in a certain order. Reciting the numbers aloud in order, quickly and without missing a number, is an important first step towards using numbers in a meaningful way.

Next, children can begin to combine their recitation of the number sequence with the act of counting objects. Counting aloud a group of objects then becomes the foundation for learning addition, subtraction, and later, place value.

Children also need to become aware that written numerals (1, 2, 3...) correspond to what they have been saying when they recite the number sequence aloud. They need to learn to put these written numerals in order, to match the written numerals to groups of objects having the same quantity, and to write the numerals themselves.

During Reception, your child may have begun learning these keys skills, but it is important that they continue practising them as they move into Year 1. Regular and continued practice is especially important with numeral writing. They will have been introduced to writing numbers in Reception but most children need continued practice to form their numbers clearly and the correct way round. Do not worry if they reverse their numbers at this stage, with lots of practice through Year 1, this will improve. You can help at home

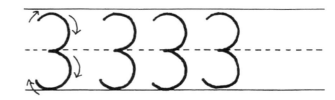

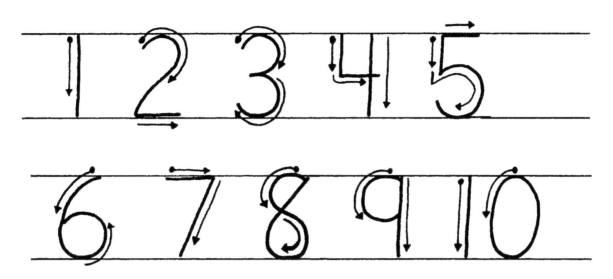

Handwriting chart for numerals. Start at the dot.

by having your child practise writing one numeral at a time. You can use workbooks available at bookshops and toy shops, or you can provide paper with broadly spaced lines, on which (as illustrated opposite) you lightly write the numeral a few times for your child to trace over, to be followed by writing the numeral several times without tracing it.

Your child should write the numerals as directed by the arrows in the chart above.

To begin with, focus on getting your child to practise until he can write all of the numerals from 1 to 10 without help.

Later, as your child works with quantities greater than 10, he can practise writing the numerals for those quantities. You might want to pay special attention to the differences between potentially confusing numerals, such as: 6 and 9; 1 and 7; 12 and 21; 13 and 31; etc.

To summarise, the first step is for your child to learn to count from 1 to 10 fast without making any mistakes, and to write the numbers up to 10. He may need to review the numbers many times in order to learn them. By the end of the Year 1, your child should be comfortable counting to higher numbers (a reasonable goal is counting by ones up to 51, and counting by fives and tens up to 50), as well as writing the corresponding numerals.

There are some excellent counting books that can make learning about numbers enjoyable for both you and your child in the list of Suggested Resources on pages 195–196.

Activity 1: The size of 10

Get Ready:

You will need:

15 small objects like buttons, raisins or pasta shapes

2 small clear plastic bags

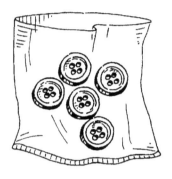

Go: Put 5 of the small objects you have selected in one of the plastic bags and 10 in the other. Put the bag with 5 items on a table in front of your child. Ask her to guess, without counting, if the bag has 5 or 10 items.

Then ask:

- 'How can you tell?'
- 'How can you find out if there are that many in the bag?'

Have her count to find out how many are in the bag.

Talk and Think: To help your child think about the size of 10, put the bag with 10 items in front of her and ask:

- 'What about this bag? Do you think there are five buttons or ten buttons?'
- 'How can you tell?'

Then have your child count to find out how many are in the bag.

Go a Little Further: Later, when your child is comfortable with counting larger quantities, you can put 20 buttons in a clear plastic bag. Ask her to guess if there are 20 or 50 buttons in the bag. Then she can count to find how many are in the bag.

Activity 2: Counting game

Get Ready:

You will need:

paper markers,

pencils, or crayons

small objects to be used as markers, like buttons or pebbles

a dice

Tell your child you're going to play a number game. Make up a game board like the one below, with a path of squares numbered in order. Have your child help you write the numbers in the squares.

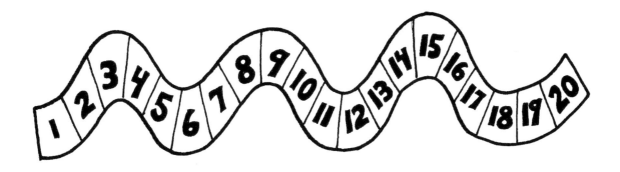

Go: Tell your child to put a button (or pebble) on square 1. Then tell her to say each number as she moves the button from one space to the next. When she gets to the last number on the board, have her turn around and move the button back to number 1, saying the numbers backward. Next tell your child she is going to play a game to see how quickly she can get to number 20. She should roll the dice and move that many spaces. This can also be played with two players. Who can make it to twenty first? Ask your child:

- 'What is the first number on the board?'
- 'What is the last?'
- 'Can you say every number that you put your button on?'
- 'Can you say the numbers backward?'

- 'Which number have you landed on?'
- 'How many spaces left until you reach the last number?'

Talk and Think: To help your child focus on counting numbers, place her button on a number on the board. Then ask:

- 'Which number is the button on?'
- 'Which number comes before it? After it?'
- 'Can you count forward from where the button is to 20?'
- 'Can you count backward from where the button is to one?'
- 'How many spaces until you reach the last number?'

You can have fun counting backward by singing this favourite song with your child. As your child becomes confident with higher numbers, increase the number of monkeys jumping on the bed.

TEN LITTLE MONKEYS

Ten little monkeys jumping on the bed,
One fell off and bumped his head.
Mama called the doctor, and the doctor said,
"No more monkeys jumping on the bed."

Nine little monkeys jumping on the bed,
One fell off and bumped his head.
Mama called the doctor, and the doctor said,
"No more monkeys jumping on the bed."

Eight little monkeys jumping on the bed,
One fell off and bumped his head...

Go a Little Further: You can challenge your child by extending the game board to higher numbers. A reasonable goal is to reach the number 51 by the end of the year. It is sensible to increase the final number by ten at a time, as your child is confident with the numbers they have already been working with. You may want to ask your child's teacher when their class will begin working on those higher numbers.

If your child experiences difficulty with this counting activity, or any others that go beyond the number 10, revise the activity with numbers from 1 to 10 before gradually introducing higher numbers. Your child may need a little extra help when he first works with numbers greater than 10, since the English names for numbers do not always give a clue to the actual quantity. That is, in some languages, the numbers after 10 are logically called 'ten-one,' 'ten-two' and 'ten-three' but in English we say 'eleven', 'twelve' and 'thirteen'. This may cause some initial confusion for your child, but encouragement and gentle review will lead to understanding.

Activity 3: How many?

Get Ready: This activity helps children develop number sense. You will need at least 30 pennies.

Go: Arrange 6 pennies in a row and another 6 pennies in a cluster. Ask your child which group has more pennies. Then take the cluster of pennies and line them up coin-for-coin under the row of pennies. Have your child count along with you as you point to the pennies in each line. Ask:

- 'How many pennies are in this group?'
- 'How many are in the other group?'
- 'Are there the same number of pennies? How do you know?'

Talk and Think: For more practice with number sense, arrange 5 pennies in a row and 5 in a stack. Point to the stack and ask:

● 'Do you think this group has more pennies?'

● 'How can you find out?'

Go a Little Further: Make three groups of pennies of equal amounts up to 10. Arrange one group in a row. Put the second group in a cluster, and stack the third group. Talk with your child about which group she thinks has the most pennies. Then ask her to arrange the other two groups coin-for-coin under the row of pennies.

Activity 4: Number match

Get Ready:

You will need:

a pack of 10-by-15-centimetre unlined index cards

crayons, markers, or pencils

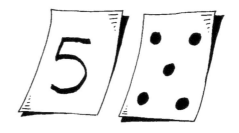

Tell your child that you are going to prepare some cards so you can play a kind of matching game.

On twenty of the index cards, draw large dots for the numbers from 1 to 20. Your child can colour in the dots. Next, have your child count the dots on each card and draw a numeral on a blank card to match the number of dots. When he's finished, you'll have one set of twenty dot cards and one set of twenty numeral cards.

Go: Tell your child to mix up each pile of cards and place the piles face down on a table. Then take turns turning up a card in each pile until someone finds a dot card and a numeral card that match. Keep playing by reshuffling the unmatched cards and putting them back into two piles until you've matched all the pairs.

Talk and Think: As you play, ask:

● 'How many dots are on this card? What number does the other card show?'

● 'Do they match? How can you tell?'

Go a Little Further: Ask your child to put the number cards in order, laying them out flat on a table from left to right. You might need to help by putting the first two or three cards on the table to show him what you mean. Then ask him to put the matching dot cards in order under the number cards. As your child becomes more confident, increase the numbers to fifty over time, ten at a time.

Activity 5: More and less

Get Ready: To give your child practice with the concepts of more and less.

You will need:

at least 20 blocks or 20 large beads

a string or a shoelace

Tell him that you're going to play a game in which you say a number and he shows that number by lining up that many blocks or putting that many beads on the string or the shoelace.

Go: Say any number between 1 and 20, such as 17, and ask your child to show that number of blocks. To focus on the concept of one more, say:

● 'Now show me one more than seven.'

● 'How many is that?'

Then start again and have your child show a different number. This time, ask him to show one less and to tell how many that is. Repeat this asking him to show '2, 3, 4 or 5 more or less.'

Talk and Think: Continue choosing new numbers for your child to show. For the fourth or fifth number that you choose, have him predict without counting what will be 2, 3, 4 or 5 more and 2, 3, 4 or 5 less. Then have him make more or less and count to be sure. Ask:

● 'How can you tell what is more [or less]?'

● 'Can you tell without counting the blocks?'

Activity 6: **Most and fewest**

Get Ready: Tell your child that you're going to play a counting game together using the names of family members. If your family is small, include the names of family friends or pets.

You will need: a sheet of paper, a marker or a pencil

Go: Ask your child to name four or five family members. As she names each person, use the marker to write the names in big letters on a sheet of paper. When you complete each name, point to the name and read it with your child. Then ask:

● 'Which name has the most letters?'

● 'Why do you think this name has the most letters?'

● 'How can you tell?'

● 'How many letters does it have?'

Then ask your child to count to find out how many letters there are.

Talk and Think: To focus on the concept of fewest, ask her which name has the fewest letters:

● 'How can you tell this name has the fewest letters?'

● 'How many letters does it have?'

Have your child count to find out.

Activity 7: **Counting more than 10 objects**

Get Ready: Children find it easier to count objects when they can touch objects that are lined up in an organised way. With practice, your Year 1 child will find it easier to keep track of items that aren't organised or touchable. To start out, let your child help you gather between 10 and 31 small items, such as paper clips, pasta shapes, or small toys.

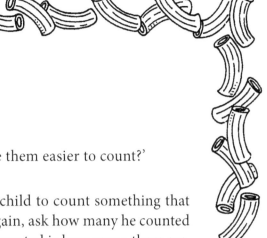

Go: Arrange the items in a row and ask your child to count them. Ask:

- 'How many [paper clips, pasta shapes, etc.] are there?'

Then spread the items around and ask your child to count them. Ask:

- 'How many did you count this time?'
- 'Which way that you counted is easier?'
- 'Is there a way you can organise these to make them easier to count?'

Go a Little Further: Go outside and ask your child to count something that cannot be touched, such as a row of windows. Again, ask how many he counted to be sure he understands that the last number counted is how many there are.

Activity 8: Things that come in pairs

Get Ready: To get started, have your child look at a stuffed animal or doll. Ask her to name parts of the stuffed animal or doll that come in twos:

- 'What do you see that your animal [or doll] has two of?'

Then tell your child that 'a pair is two of something that go together,' and that the animal (or doll) has a pair of eyes, and a pair of arms, etc.

Go: Arrange several groups of like objects, including some pairs of objects, such as a pair of shoes, a pair of gloves or socks, etc. Other groups should contain three objects. Say:

- 'Here is a pair of shoes; there are two shoes, and they go together. Can you show me some other pairs of things here?'
- 'How do you know this is a pair?'
- 'Why isn't this group a pair?'

Activity 9: **Counting by twos**

Get Ready: Tell your child that you're going on a shoe hunt. Try to find at least five pairs of shoes and line them up in pairs next to each other. Then tell your child that you're going to find out how many shoes there are by counting them two ways.

Go: First, ask your child to count the shoes one by one. Tell him he is 'counting by ones.' Then, tell him there is another way to count the shoes called 'counting by twos.' Ask him to listen as you point and count the shoes. Put the emphasis on every second number. For example, you could whisper the numbers 1, 3, 5, 7, 9 and say the numbers 2, 4, 6, 8, 10 in a loud voice. After this, count the shoes by twos: 2, 4, 6, 8, 10. Repeat and then ask your child to follow along. Then give him an opportunity to count the shoes by twos on his own. Ask:

● 'How many shoes are there? Can you count them by twos?'

Go a Little Further: Use other items, such as spoons or crayons, and gradually use more than ten items. Start with a review of counting by twos up to 10, then ask:

● 'What number comes next if we keep counting by twos?'

Activity 10: Counting by fives and tens

Get Ready:

You will need: a big sheet of sturdy paper, finger paints

Tell your child that you are going to make a handprint poster. You're using finger paints, so do this where it's okay to make a mess! (Note: Your child should already have practised counting by ones to 30 before you do this activity.)

Go: Use the finger paints to make colourful handprints all over the paper. If possible, have family members or friends make handprints, too. At first, start with six handprints; later, you can work up to ten handprints. When the poster is finished, point to it and ask:

● 'How many fingers are there?'

● 'How could you find out?'

Point to one handprint, and ask:

● 'How many fingers are on this one hand?'

Point to the next handprint and ask your child to continue to count. Continue until your child has counted all the fingers on the poster. Ask:

● 'How many fingers are there in all?'

Talk and Think: Explain to your child that there is a faster way to count in twos, threes, fours and so on. Explain that you're going to learn to count in fives. Say:

● 'We're going to count five fingers at a time, like this: five, ten, fifteen, twenty...'

(As you count, move your finger from one hand on the poster to another.)

Have your child listen as you count in fives. After repeating the pattern, ask her to join in. Repeat the same procedure as you count in tens. Then ask:

● 'Did you end up with the same number when you counted by ones? How about fives?'

● 'Which way is faster?'

Go a Little Further: The next time the family is having dinner, ask how many toes are under the table.

Activity 11: Halves and quarters

Get Ready:

You will need:

10 items of one kind that are of particular interest to your child, such as stickers, biscuits, or small toy cars, 8 pennies, a slice of bread

Go: Spread the 10 items out on a table. Ask your child to show a fair way to share the items between the two of you. When your child has made two equal shares of the 10 items, explain that each share is half of the whole group of items: you have one half, and he has the other half. Now, show your child the 8 pennies; allow him to count them. Then put all 8 pennies in a pile between you. Give 2 pennies to your child. Ask:

● 'Do you have half?'

● 'Can you show me how to share them fairly, half for you and half for me?'

Then repeat the activity, this time sharing fairly between four. Explain that each share is a quarter.

Talk and Think: Many children in Year 1 do not yet understand that two halves are equal in size, and one quarter is the same size as another quarter. To focus on the concept of halves and quarters as equal shares, ask:

● 'Do we each have the same number of toy cars [or other items]?'

● 'How could you find out?'

Go a Little Further: Put the piece of bread on the table, and ask your child to show a fair way to break it into 2 pieces to share, half for you and half for him. After he has broken it (in roughly two equal pieces), ask:

● 'Is my half of the bread the same size as yours, or is it a different size?'

● 'If two more people needed to share the bread, what could you do?'

● 'Does everyone have the same size piece of bread? Are all the quarters the same size?'

Reinforce what he has done by saying: 'You have half of the whole piece of bread, and I have half of the whole piece of bread, and both halves are equal.' Similarly reinforce sharing into quarters.

Activity 12: A good-job graph

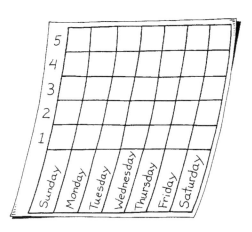

Get Ready:

You will need:

a sheet of paper

crayons or markers

Tell your child that the two of you are going to make a Good-Job Graph, which will show some of the good things she does in a week. You can talk together about what sort of jobs to include: picking up toys, brushing teeth, washing hands before dinner, helping Mum or Dad, etc.

Write the days of the week along the bottom of a sheet of paper and numbers up to 5 along the side edge. Post this chart in an easy-to-reach spot and explain that every day she can colour a square on the graph for each of the 'good jobs' she does. Try to help her record from 1 to 5 'good jobs' a day.

Go: At the end of the first day, look at the graph with your child. Point to the name of the day and ask:

● 'How many 'good jobs' did you do today?'

● 'How do you know?'

At the end of each day, look at the graph together and make some comparisons by asking:

● 'How many squares did you colour today?'

● 'Was that more or less than yesterday?'

Talk and Think: To help your child think about graphs, at the end of the week, ask:

● 'On which day did you colour the most squares? How many did you colour?'

Go a Little Further: Ask your child:

● 'How many good jobs did you do in all this week?' To help her answer this question, ask her how she could find the answer to that question. You might need to coach her that one way to find out would be to count all the squares on the graph. Then ask her to count all the squares.

Activity 13: **Block train**

Get Ready: This activity provides practice with order words – 'first,' 'second,' 'third,' etc. Let your child help you gather:

10 blocks

10 different small objects (such as a button, a pasta shape, a pebble, etc.)

Go: Tell your child to build a block train by arranging the blocks in a row. Then have her put one of the small objects on top of each block. Identify one carriage for your child by using an order word such as 'first' or 'second' in a sentence, like this: 'The button is on the second block.' Then have your child identify the other cars, using an order word. Ask:

● 'Which block is carrying the pasta shape?'

● 'Which block is carrying the pebble?' Continue until you and your child have identified all the blocks by their order words.

If your child has trouble using these words, say them all aloud in order as you point to each car. Have her repeat them as you point to blocks first in order and then at random. Then repeat the questioning activity.

Money

PARENTS: Even before children know what money is for, they are fascinated by the shape and appearance of coins and notes. By Year 1, your child probably also realises that money is important.

Year 1 children need to know that money is used to buy things, and that different kinds of coins and notes have different values. The following activities will help children start to recognise coins and to understand what each is worth. At this point, don't expect your child to be able to trade coins for other coin combinations of the same value. Exchanging money is a skill that will come later.

Activity 1: Identifying money

Get Ready:

You will need:

8 small containers such as margarine tubs

a way to label your containers (masking tape and pen or marker)

coins: at least 2 of each type of coin

Label the containers 1p, 2p, 5p, 10p, 20p, 50p, £1, £2. Pile the coins in front of the containers. Tell your child that together you are going to separate the coins into different groups.

Go: Spread out the coins. To get started, pick up one of each kind of coin and tell your child what it is. Give him an opportunity to look at the coins and say their names to you. Ask him to watch as you put one coin of each type in a container. Then ask him to sort the rest of the coins. Depending on your child's experience with money, you can explain what each coin is worth as you sort, or simply have him tell you in which container to put the coins. Ask your child to find the number written on pence coins to find their value.

One Penny

Two pence

Five pence

Ten pence

Twenty pence

Fifty pence

Two pounds

One pound

Talk and Think: To help your child become familiar with coins and their value, have him look over the coins pictured below in order of their value. Read through the text about what each coin is worth and what the pence and pound signs mean.

- The sign 'p' means penny or pence. Only the 1 pence coin is called a penny. Values higher than this are called 'pence'.

- The sign '£' means pound or pounds.

Explain that the pictures show both sides of each coin. Tell him that the side with a head on it is called the heads side of the coin. Point out that the face on the heads side of the coin is the head of the Queen. And tell him that the other side is called the tails side. Then have him look again at real coins and ask him to show you their heads and tails sides. Ask:

- 'Are all the kinds of coins the same shape? Are they all the same size and colour?'

- 'How is the penny different from all the other coins?'

- 'Which coin looks smallest? Is this coin worth less than a penny?'

- 'Which coin looks largest? Is this coin worth more than the other coins?'

Go a Little Further: The next time you go shopping, give your child a change purse with some coins. Ask for his help in picking out coins to give the cashier. (But don't expect him to know which coins add up to a certain amount. That skill comes later.)

Activity 2: Money bingo

Get Ready: Tell your child that you are going to play Money Bing
remind your child of the different coins and what they are worth. Sho
and the pounds sign, and show how these denominations are written:
50p, £1, £2.

You will need:

stiff paper or card

scissors

a ruler

crayons or markers

buttons or other small
items for markers

a supply of coins

a box or hat

1p	5p	10p	20p	£1.00
2p	£1.00	1p	5p	£2.00
£2.00	10p	50p	£1.00	1p
20p	5p	2p	10p	20p
£2.00	50p	£1.00	1p	5p

Make at least two bingo cards. Each card should have five squares across and five squares down. Instead of numbers, use these labels: 1p, 2p, 5p, 10p, 20p, 50p, £1, £2 in the squares. Let your child help you write the numbers and pounds and pennies signs on each card.

If your child has never played bingo, explain that you are going to cover the rows on the cards with markers and that the first person to cover a whole row – across, up and down, or diagonally – calls out 'Bingo!'

Go: Put the coins in the box or hat, then give each player a bingo card and about a dozen markers. To play the game, choose a coin and hold it up. As you hold each denomination of money, ask these three questions:

● 'What am I holding up?'
● 'How much is it worth?'

Then each player puts a marker in every box on the card that says the amount just held up. When one of you calls out 'Bingo!' ask your child to remove each marker and read out the money values underneath. Now you're ready to play again.

...nputation

PARENTS: You probably don't remember a time when you didn't know that adding two groups of things gives you one larger group, while taking away something from one group leaves you with a smaller group. But these fundamental mathematical concepts are likely to have only been introduced to your child in Reception. It is important, especially during the early stages of Year 1, that the concepts of addition and subtraction continue to be practised with concrete objects in order to secure your child's understanding.

The activities that follow use concrete objects to help your child understand what happens when groups of things are added together or taken away. By working with concrete objects, your child will learn that addition requires counting forward, while subtraction requires counting backward. The activities also introduce the + and - symbols. Some children can make an immediate connection between joining or separating groups and using symbols to describe what happens. Other children need a little more time to see this connection. Also, while some children might memorise specific addition and subtraction facts such as 2 + 2 = 4, don't expect or demand it of all Year 1 children. That ability will come after your child understands the basic concepts.

Activity 1: Addition

PARENTS: Before you begin this activity, it may help to read aloud the following introduction to addition with your child:

When two groups of things are put together, it's called addition. There are 3 flowers in a vase. If you pick 2 more flowers and put them in the vase, how many flowers are in the vase now? This is an addition problem, because you start with 3 flowers and add 2 more. After the flowers are added, there are 5 flowers. To show what happens, you can write

3 + 2 = 5

The sign + means 'plus'. It shows that you are adding.

The sign = means 'equals'. It shows that two amounts are the same:

3 + 2 is the same as 5

3 + 2 = 5

Get Ready: Gather 10 objects of the same kind, such as crayons, blocks, pebbles, or pennies. Put some of the objects in one pile and some in another pile. (When you start out, you do not have to use all the objects.) Draw a large plus sign on a slip of paper and place it between the two piles. Tell your child that the two of you are going to play an addition game.

Go: Have your child count how many crayons are in each pile and tell you how many. Tell him that you are going to add the two piles to make one new pile. Point to the plus sign between the piles to show what you will do. Then put the piles together. Ask your child to count the crayons and tell how many there are now.

Talk and Think: After you make the new pile, ask:

- 'How did we make the new pile?'

- 'How many crayons are in the new pile?'

- 'Were the other piles bigger than this pile?'

- 'Is this the biggest pile?'

Repeat this activity several times with different-size piles so your child can practise adding various combinations up to 10.

Go a Little Further: Ask your child to do some simple addition mentally. Here's how: display two groups that each contain just one or two items. Have your child count the items in each pile. Ask him to put both groups into a bag. Close the bag. Ask him to tell you how many objects are in the bag. Then he can open the bag and count the new group. Repeat this several times with different-size piles.

Activity 2: Subtraction – the take-away game

Get Ready:

You will need:

a small group of no more than 5 objects of the same kind, such as buttons or pebbles

Go: Tell your child that you're going to play a number game. Put the buttons on a table and ask your child to count them. While she watches, cover some of the buttons with your hand and slide them a few centimetres away (keeping them under your hand). Then ask:

● 'How many buttons did you count before?'

● 'How many buttons do you see now?'

● 'Can you tell how many were taken away?'

Talk and Think: After she tells you, lift your hand to show the missing buttons. Tell her that when you took away some of the buttons, you were subtracting. Ask:

● 'How did you know how many buttons I took away?' If your child has trouble with these questions, put all the buttons back on the table. Have her count them again. Then take one button away while she watches. Ask:

● 'How many buttons am I taking away?'

● 'How many are left?'

Go a Little Further: As your child begins to understand subtraction, you can use more than five objects in the group. You can also try reversing roles, and let her take away the items. For fun, you can occasionally 'guess wrong' and have her tell you how many items she removed.

As your child repeats this activity, remind her that when you take away buttons, you are subtracting a number.

Activity 3: Addition and subtraction stories

Get Ready:

You will need:

5 to 10 index cards, a pencil or marker

Write a plus sign on one of the index cards, a minus sign on one, and an equals sign on another.

Tell your Year 1 child that you're going to tell some number stories. Show each sign to your child and remind him what each symbol means.

Go: As your child listens, tell a number story about a family event. For example, you might tell him about the time that Uncle Ralph was a boy and ordered five hot dogs but could eat only four.

PARENTS: Put your hand over 4 of the hot dogs to show 'taking away' the hot dogs that Uncle Ralph ate.

Talk and Think: Use the plus, minus and equals signs as you tell the story. Ask:

- 'How many hot dogs did Uncle Ralph order?' (Put a 5 on one card.)

- 'How many did he eat?' (Put a 4 on a card.)

- 'How many were left?' (Put a 1 on a card.)

- 'How could you use a plus sign [+] or a minus sign [-] to tell the story?'

Using the index cards, help your child write an addition or subtraction sentence that tells his story, for example, 5 - 4 = 1. Have him read the numbers and symbols aloud: 'Five minus four equals one,' as he points to each card.

Go a Little Further: Have your child tell another story using the same addition or subtraction sentence. The story can be about something that really happened or something he makes up.

Measurement

PARENTS: Your Year 1 child probably uses words that describe size such as 'big', 'smaller', 'long', 'tall' and 'taller.' These words show that she recognises size relationships. This important skill is fundamental not just to mathematics but to science, geography, and even story telling.

Children need to learn that measuring is one way of describing something—for example, how big, hot, heavy, or tall something is, or how long something takes to do. Children also need to learn that measuring is a way to compare objects in terms of such qualities as size, weight, and capacity.

Year 1 children generally have little trouble comparing things by placing them next to each other, but they are only beginning to understand measurement. The activities that follow will help your child recognise the standard measuring tools. Don't expect your child to be able to use the tools to measure. Your child should, however, be given opportunities to use arbitrary units, such as paper clips or footsteps, to measure length.

Activity 1: Measurement tools

Get Ready: Let your child help you gather some household measurement tools such as a ruler, tape measure, thermometer, clock, and bathroom scale.

Go: Tell her that these are all tools used to measure things. For each tool, ask:

- 'Do you know the name of this one?'
- 'Do you know what we use this for?'

Talk and Think: To help her focus on how these tools are used, ask:

- 'Which tool tells us what time it is?'
- 'Which tool tells us how hot or cold it is?'
- 'Which tool tells us how heavy something is?'
- 'Which tools tell us how long something is?'

Activity 2: Measuring with paper clips

PARENTS: When children first learn to measure, many of them have difficulty measuring with rulers that use standard units such as centimetres or inches. To help a child understand concepts of measurement and why we measure using units like centimetres, it is generally helpful to begin by asking your child to use a set of identical objects, such as paper clips, to measure the length of an object.

Get Ready: Get together a few pairs of similar items to measure, such as two books, two cereal boxes or two toy trucks. The items in each pair should be of different sizes. Also have ready a bunch of paper clips (all the same size) to use as measuring tools.

Go: Tell your child that the two of you are going to measure some items. Show him the pair of books and ask:

● 'Which book looks bigger?'

● 'How can you find out which is bigger?' Your child may say that one book looks bigger, or he may hold the books next to each other to compare. Give your child some paper clips. Help him measure the book. Line up the clips one by one along the binding side of one book until you reach the end of the book. Do the same with the other book. Ask:

● 'How many paper clips long is this book?'

● 'How many paper clips long is that book?'

● 'How can you tell which book is longer?'

Go a Little Further: Have your child hook the paper clips together after measuring each of several items. Then ask him to arrange the paper clip chains in order from shortest to longest.

You can also have your child make a paper ruler by tracing a paper clip several times, end to end. Have him use his new ruler to measure length. As he becomes familiar with using the paper ruler, provide a centimetre ruler and help him investigate how to measure small objects with this tool.

Activity 3: Measuring with hands and feet

Get Ready: Tell your child that you're going to measure some items using your hands.

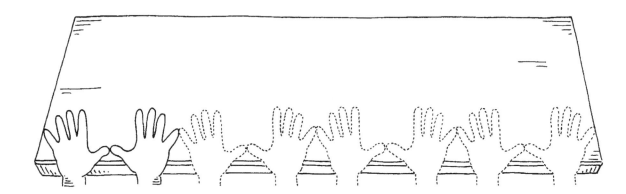

Go: Spread out your hand and have your child do the same. As your child watches, measure a table by alternating hands the length of the table. Ask her to count the number of hands it takes to measure the table. Ask:

- 'How many hands long is the table?'

- 'Will the table still be [number of] hands long if I measure it again?'

- 'How long is the table if we use *your* hand?'

- 'Why does it take more of your hands to measure the table than mine?'

- 'What about our feet? Do you think it takes more hands or more feet to measure the table?'

Go a Little Further: Show your child how you can use your feet to measure an item, like a small rug, by counting as you place one foot in front of the other. Then have your child use the length of her foot to measure the table by cutting out a paper foot length, using your child's foot as a model. Show her how to use this paper foot to measure the length of the table. She can also measure other furniture and spaces using this paper tool.

Activity 4: Full, half-full, and empty

Get Ready: You will need four identical glasses and a jug of water.

Go: Arrange the glasses in a row and fill up one glass with water. Fill another glass half-full. After that, pour a small amount of water into the glass next to the half-full glass. This glass should be less than one-quarter full. The glasses should not be in order from full to empty.

Talk and Think: Have your child compare the water levels. Ask:

- 'Which glass is full?'
- 'Which glass is half-full?'
- 'Which glass is empty?'
- 'Are the glasses in order from full to empty?'
- 'Can you put them in order?'

Go a Little Further: Add another glass that is half-full. Have your child decide which glass is 'as full as' the new one.

Activity 5: Heavy and light

Get Ready: Ask your child to help you pick out several different items of different weights, such as books, pebbles, and blocks. You can also use grocery items of different weights.

Go: Put all the items on a table. Ask her to pick something heavy from the group.

Talk and Think: To help your child recognise the difference between heavy and light ask:

Which child is holding something light?
Which child is holding something heavy?

- 'Why did you pick this [name of item]?'
- 'Is it hard to lift? Can you find something that is harder to lift?'
- 'Can you find something that is easier to lift?'
- 'Can you find something that is light? Is it very easy to lift?'

If your child has difficulty understanding which object is light, you can pick up a light object and say, 'This is not very heavy at all – it's light; it's very easy to lift.' This will help her recognise that heavy things are hard to lift, while light things are easy to lift.

Then ask your child to choose two items. Ask:

- 'Which item is heavier? Why?'

Go a Little Further: Choose three items of obviously different weights. Ask your child to arrange the three items in order of weight, from heavy to light.

Activity 6: Long and short events

Get Ready: Gather some photos or picture books that convey the idea of things that take a long time. For example, they might involve a car or train trip that takes all day or the growth of a pet or plant.

Go: Ask your child to listen as you tell him about something that takes a long time. Show the pictures you've gathered as you tell your story. Then, ask your child to tell you about something that he thinks takes a long time. Next, give one or two examples of things that take a short time, such as snapping your fingers, clapping, or eating a biscuit. Ask your child to tell you about some other things that take a short time.

Talk and Think: To help him become more familiar with long and short events, you can ask questions like:

- 'Which would take longer: combing your hair or going from our home to school?'
- 'Which would take longer: pouring a glass of water or reading a whole story?'

Activity 7: Before and after; morning, afternoon, and evening

Get Ready: A good time to begin this activity is in the evening, before your child's bedtime. Ask your child to tell you about some of the things she did today.

● 'Did you play today?'

● 'Did you eat lunch?'

● 'Did you brush your teeth?'

Go: Tell your child you want to talk about the parts of the day – morning, afternoon, and evening. Then ask:

● 'What do we do in the morning?'

● 'What do we do in the afternoon?'

● 'What do we do in the evening?'

Talk and Think: To follow up, you can ask:

● 'Did you eat breakfast in the morning, the afternoon, or the evening?'

● 'Did you eat breakfast before or after you got dressed?'

● 'Did you come home from school in the morning, the afternoon, or the evening?'

● 'Did you eat supper before or after you came home from school?'

● 'What part of the day is it now? Is this the morning, the afternoon, or the evening?'

Activity 8: **What time is it?**

Get Ready:

You will need:
a sheet of coloured paper
scissors
a paper plate
a marker or a crayon
a split pin

To make clock hands, cut two narrow strips from the coloured paper: one strip should be longer than the other. Then, have your child help you turn the paper plate into a clock face by numbering around the rim from 1 to 12. Finally, use the split pin to attach the ends of both strips to the centre of the clock face. Your child can use this homemade clock face to show different times.

Go: Put a real clock on a table. Use a clock with two hands and twelve numbers rather than a digital clock. Discuss the clock with your child. Point out the twelve numerals. Tell him that the short hand is the hour hand. It indicates what hour it is. The long hand is the minute hand. It shows the minutes.

Set the clock to show 4 o'clock. Point out how the short hand points to the hour and the long hand points straight up, to 12. Tell your child you can see what hour it is by looking at the short hand. Go over another example, such as 5 o'clock: point out that the long hand points straight up, to 12, while the short hand points to the 5.

When your child confidently recognises the o' clock times, introduce her to half past the hour. Move the long hand down to six – making sure she sees this happen. Tell your child this means 'half past', point to the number that the short hand has just travelled past and say 'half-past [hour]'.

Then ask:

● 'Where is the short hand pointed?'

● 'Where is the long hand pointed?'

● 'Can you say what time it is?'

● 'Can you show the same time on your clock?'

Talk and Think: Set the clock to show 8 o'clock and then 9 o'clock. Each time, ask:

● 'Where is the short hand pointed now?'

● 'Can you say what time it is?'

● 'Can you show the same time on your clock?'

You can continue the activity by having her name the time shown as you move the short hand to other numerals on the clock. Show only whole and half hours. Don't expect your child to recognise parts of an hour, such as 5, 10, or 20 minutes before or after the hour.

Go a Little Further: Have your child help you keep track of the time until it's time for a snack or a story. About ten or twenty minutes before the hour of the activity, tell him that you will have a snack at (the next hour) o'clock. Several times before the hour, ask your child if it's time yet. You can also tell your child to let you know when it's time.

Activity 9: The calendar

Get Ready: You will need a calendar, preferably one with big, easy-to-see numbers.

Go: Show your child the calendar. Remind her that a calendar is a way of keeping track of time and of showing what day today is. Explain that every day is part of a week and also part of a month. Have her touch the line of days that make up a week. With your help, have her point to and say the names of the days of the week, starting with Monday. Then have her touch all the weeks that make up the month.

Show her today's date on the calendar. Identify today by the day of the week, the date, and the month; for example: 'This is Wednesday, the fifth of October.' Have her mark an 'X' in the box for today's date on the calendar. Explain that tomorrow you will mark tomorrow's date. Set aside a regular time each morning to mark the calendar.

Talk and Think: When you and your child mark the calendar every day, have her tell you what day of the week it is. When she answers, follow up by telling her the more complete date: 'Yes, today is Wednesday. Today is Wednesday, the fifth of October.' Then say:

- 'Today is Wednesday. Do you know what day it will be tomorrow? What day was it yesterday?'

- (On a Friday) 'Today is Friday. What things do we usually do on Friday? Tomorrow is Saturday. What things do we usually do on Saturday?'

Most Year 1 children don't have a good sense of long-term time, so ask about events that happen on a single day or on the same day every week.

Go a Little Further: As your child becomes familiar with the calendar, ask:

- 'Can you name the days of the week in order, starting with Monday?'

- 'How many days are there in a week? How can you find out?'

- 'How many days are in this month? How can you find out?'

Geometry

PARENTS: Year 1 children are likely to already recognise and name the first four basic 2D shapes – squares, circles, triangles and rectangles – and may be able to use words of position and direction to tell you where things are. The activities in this section will help you introduce more basic shapes and words of position and direction to your child and describe the properties of shapes. Beyond these activities, you can use lots of everyday opportunities to give your child practice with shapes and words of position and direction. For example, you might ask, 'What shape is that piece of pizza? That's right, it's a triangle. Can you point to its corners?' Or, while reading aloud, you can point to a picture and ask, 'Can you tell me where the troll is? That's right, he's under the bridge.'

Activity 1: What's that shape?

Get Ready:

You will need: cardboard, scissors, markers or crayons, a brown paper bag

With your child, look at these pictures of the six basic shapes. Say their names aloud as you point to them and run your finger around their outline. As you run your finger around the shapes, explain their properties, for example, 'This is a side and this is a corner.' Show your child how to count sides by running your finger along each one. Show your child how to count corners by pointing to each one.

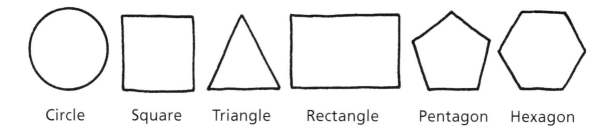

| Circle | Square | Triangle | Rectangle | Pentagon | Hexagon |

You can point out that a square and a rectangle are alike: they both have four sides. But in a square, the sides are all the same.

Now tell your child that you are going to make shapes like these and play a game. Cut from cardboard several of each of the six basic shapes. They should be about 10 centimetres by 10 centimetres. Your child can colour or decorate the shapes as you cut them.

Go: Let your child put the shapes in the bag. Then hold the bag so your child cannot see into it. Ask him to reach into the bag (with one or both hands) and, without looking, to pull out a circle. If he brings out one of the other shapes, show him the picture of a circle and try again. Repeat this game with all the shapes.

Talk and Think: After playing with all the shapes, ask your child, when he pulls out a correct shape, how he knew it was a (shape name). Ask your child:

● 'How many sides does it have?'

● 'Can you count the corners?'

Activity 2: Shape and size

Get Ready:

To make twenty-four shape cut-outs, you will need:

stiff paper or cardboard

scissors

markers, crayons, or other decorations like stamps or stickers

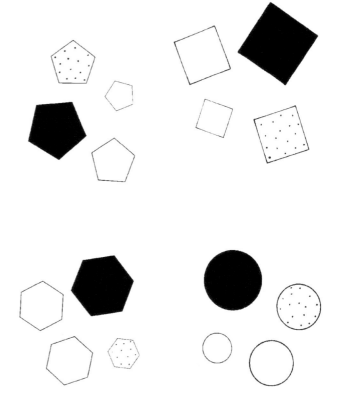

Cut out four of each shape. Two of the cut-outs of each shape should be the same size, a third should be smaller than the others, and a fourth should be larger than the others. As you make the shapes, ask your child to tell you the name of each shape. Your child can colour or decorate the shapes as you cut them.

Go: Put the shapes on a table and mix them up, turning some at different angles. Choose one and ask your child to find another cut-out that has the same shape.

Talk and Think: To help her compare the shapes, ask:

● 'Are the two shapes the same size?'

● 'Is the shape you chose larger or smaller than the first one?'

Go a Little Further: You can extend the game by picking up a shape and asking your child:

● 'Can you find another piece that's the same shape and size as this?'

● 'Can you find another piece that's the same shape as this but [bigger or smaller]?'

● 'What is the name of this shape? Can you pick out all the other pieces that are the same shape?'

Activity 3: Where is it?
Using words of position and direction

PARENTS: Direct your child's attention to the pictures below. Ask questions that will encourage your child to use position words in his answers. You can model the use of position words by answering the first two or three questions yourself.

- 'Where is the lamp?' (The lamp is on the table.)

- 'Where is the cat?' (The cat is under the table.)

- 'Where is the balloon?' (The balloon is over the table or next to the lamp.)

- 'Where is the girl?' (The girl is next to the table.)

- 'Is the door open or closed?' (The door is open.)

- 'Is the window open or closed?' (The window is closed.)

- 'Is the girl in front of the house or behind the house?' (The girl is in front of the house.)

- 'Is the boy in front of the girl, or is he behind the girl?' (The boy is behind the girl.)

- Are the children inside the house, or are they outside the house?' (The children are outside the house.)

- 'Do you see where the path goes?' (It goes around the house.)

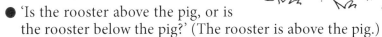
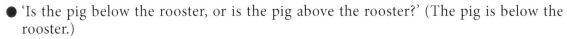

- 'Do you see the cow?' (The cow is between the pig and the sheep.)
- 'Is the pig to the left of the cow, or is the pig to the right of the cow?' (The pig is to the left of the cow.)
- 'Is the sheep to the left of the cow, or is the sheep to the right of the cow?' (The sheep is to the right of the cow.)
- 'Is the rooster above the pig, or is the rooster below the pig?' (The rooster is above the pig.)
- 'Is the pig below the rooster, or is the pig above the rooster?' (The pig is below the rooster.)
- 'Does the tree look like it is near the animals or far from the animals?' (The tree looks like it's far from the animals.)
- 'Is the pig near the fence, or is the pig far from the fence?' (The pig is near the fence.)

Activity 4: Simon Says

Get Ready: This game emphasises right and left, but you can also use other directional words, such as 'behind', 'beside', 'between', 'above', 'below', 'under', 'far from', 'near', 'inside', 'here' and 'there'.

Go: Tell your child that you are going to play a game of Simon Says. If she does not know the game, explain that she is to do what you say only if you use the words 'Simon says'. If you tell her to do something without saying 'Simon says', she should not do it.

Play the game by giving commands that use directional words, especially 'left' and 'right', such as:

- 'Simon says: Put your right hand on your hip.'
- 'Simon says: Put your left hand on your chin.'
- 'Simon says: Put your left hand on your tummy.' Occasionally give commands that do not begin with 'Simon says'.

Talk and Think: To get your child to focus on directional words, after playing for a while, ask:

- 'Which commands were hard to follow?'
- 'Which were easy?'

Go a Little Further: If your child has no difficulty with left and right, make the commands harder by using more directional words. For example, instead of saying 'Put your right hand on your neck', say 'Put your right hand behind your neck'. Or, 'Put your right hand beside your left knee.'

Science

Introduction

Children gain knowledge about the world around them in part from observation and experience. To understand the world of plants and animals, or of seasons and the weather, or of physical forces like magnetism, a child needs firsthand experience with many opportunities to observe, experiment and get her hands dirty. In the words of the Association for Science Education, a good primary and early years science education:

● Acknowledges that children come to science education with ideas, observations and questions about the world around them and uses these as the foundations for their learning

● Nurtures children's curiosity and inspires them, in a rich learning environment, to discover more and to develop positive attitudes and an appreciation of the nature of science

● Challenges children to develop and use scientific skills; acquire and apply scientific knowledge, understanding and language; investigate through playing, exploring and experimenting; communicate and collaborate effectively with others; challenge scientific evidence

● Enables children to make connections between scientific ideas and to see how they are developed and applied in other disciplines and beyond the classroom

While experience counts for much, book learning is also important, for it helps bring coherence and order to a child's scientific knowledge. Only when topics are presented systematically and clearly can children make steady and secure progress in their scientific learning. The child's development of scientific knowledge and understanding is in some ways a very disorderly and complex process, different for each child. But a systematic approach to the exploration of science, one that combines experience with book learning, can help provide essential building blocks for deeper understanding at a later time. It can also provide the kind of knowledge that one is not likely to gain from observation: consider, for example, how people long believed that the earth stands still while the sun orbits around it, a misconception that 'direct experience' presented as fact.

In this section, we introduce Year 1 children to a variety of scientific topics, consistent with the early study of science in countries that have had outstanding results in teaching science at the elementary level. The text is meant to be read aloud to your child, and it offers questions for you and your child to discuss as well as activities for you to do together.

Where the Forest Meets the Sea by Jeannie Baker (Walker 1998). In this prize-winning tale, a young Australian boy's father takes him by boat to a tropical rainforest. The boy explores, musing about the nature of the forest, its history and future until it's time to go and eat the fish his father has caught and cooked. Beautifully illustrated with colourful and textured collages, and featuring a rainforest modelled on a real wilderness in North Queensland, *Where the Forest Meets the Sea* is sure to stimulate thought and debate, and encourage even the youngest reader to develop an interest in the environment.

The Lighthouse Keeper's Lunch by Rhonda and David Armitage (Puffin) tells the story of the Lighthouse Keeper's wife and her attempts to get a meal to her husband way out at sea. While enjoying the story, children can learn about the science of pulleys.

There are many children's stories which celebrate the natural and animal world. In particular, the illustrator Jackie Morris captures the spirit of animals in her splendid books published by Frances Lincoln. *Ice Bear* and *Snow Leopard* are two beautiful examples, while *Can you See a Little Bear?* offers children the opportunity to explore sumptuous pictures.

Where do plants grow? by Louise Spilsbury and Richard Spilsbury (Heinemann Library).

Plants and Plant Growth

Plants Are All Around Us

I'm going to say a word and you tell me what you think of. Ready? Here's the word: 'plants'.

Did you think of something like a green bush or blooming flower or tall tree? Can you tell me two more things about plants?

We live in a world full of plants. Some plants grow big, like the California redwood trees. Some redwoods stand over three hundred feet tall – that means almost one hundred children your size would have to stand on each other's shoulders to reach the top!

Other plants stay tiny. A plant called duckweed grows in lake water. It's so tiny that it just looks like a green speck.

Thousands of different kinds of plants grow all around the world. Some plants, like tropical orchids, grow only in

This orchid grows in a hot, wet place.

This cactus grows in a hot, dry place.

steamy jungles. Some plants, like cactuses, grow where it's hot and dry. Some plants can grow just about anywhere: the dandelion grows in the cracks of city pavements just as easily as in fields and gardens.

Some plants smell wonderful, like a rose in bloom. Some plants stink, like the plant with a name that says a lot about its smell: skunk cabbage! Have you ever smelled a sweet-smelling flower, or a plant you didn't like at all?

All the food that you eat comes from plants. Peas and potatoes, carrots and cucumbers, the wheat that gets ground into flour and baked into bread – they all come from plants. But wait a minute. What about meat – like sausages or roast chicken? And what about fish? Cows, chickens and fish are not plants – they're animals! That's right – but all those animals eat plants.

And that's not all: without plants we would have no paper for writing and drawing, no timber for building houses and no cotton cloth for clothes. We couldn't live without the plants in our world.

Look at the pictures and put your finger on each part of the plant as you say the name of the part.

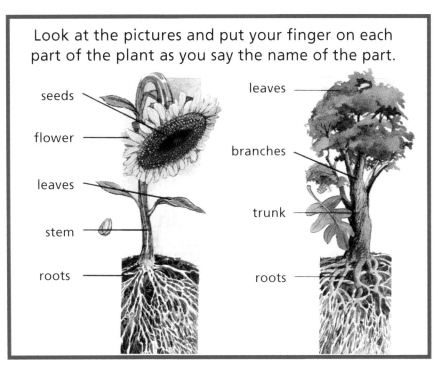

Seeds Grow into Plants

Many plants grow from seeds. Have you ever seen the little seeds inside an apple? Or have you eaten a slice of watermelon and had to spit out a lot of seeds? Have you eaten a peach, which has one big seed in it? (Don't eat the seed!)

Many plants have flowers, and these flowers make seeds. Flowers bloom in all the colours of the rainbow: yellow tulips, orange marigolds, red roses, purple lilacs, blue forget-me-nots. A bouquet of colourful, sweet-smelling flowers is one of the nicest presents a person can give.

A little seed can turn into a giant plant. Even big trees start from little seeds. Have you ever found an acorn, then looked up to see the big oak tree that dropped it? That little acorn has all it needs to start growing another oak tree.

'Great oaks from little acorns grow'

An acorn is the seed of an oak tree: only an oak tree can grow from an acorn. Do you think a peach tree can grow from an apple seed? No—only an apple tree can grow from an apple seed. And only a sunflower can grow from a sunflower seed. What can grow from a pumpkin seed? That's right: only a pumpkin.

If you put a seed in soil and water it, it will usually sprout into a baby plant.

This bean is a seed. Let's look at what happens when it's planted and watered. After a little while, a small root pokes out and grows down into the ground. Then a tiny shoot with leaves grows up in the other direction.

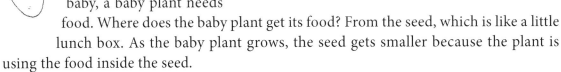

Just like a human baby, a baby plant needs food. Where does the baby plant get its food? From the seed, which is like a little lunch box. As the baby plant grows, the seed gets smaller because the plant is using the food inside the seed.

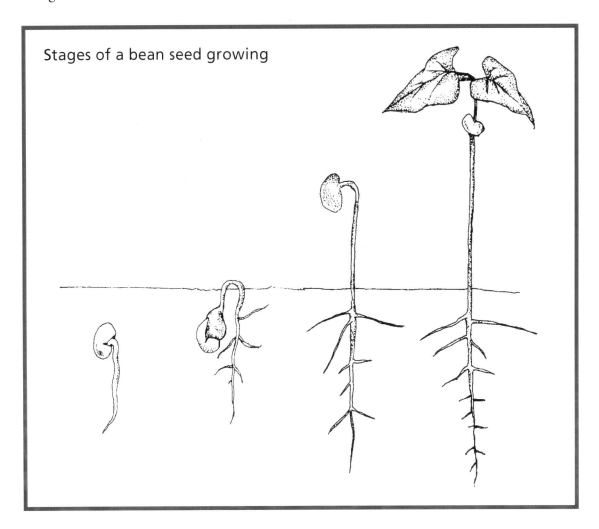

Stages of a bean seed growing

Activity 1: Watch a Seed Grow in a 'See-Through' Planter

PARENTS: Here's an activity you can do with your child that will let you see a seed grow into a plant. Tell your child that you're going to make a 'see-through' planter. Have your child do as much as you and he are comfortable with. You'll need to be in charge of the first steps of making the planter, which require cutting a plastic milk bottle with strong scissors or a utility knife.

Get Ready:

You will need:

a 2-pint plastic milk bottle

scissors or a utility knife

clear plastic wrap, e.g. cling film

sticky tape (masking tape or transparent tape)

a big rubber band

potting soil

some bean seeds (not beans to cook and eat from the supermarket but the kind that come in a sealed package for growing)

a plate

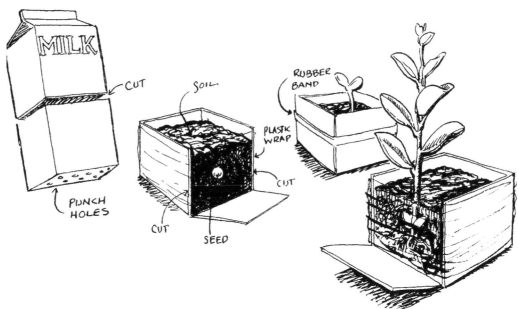

Go: First, cut the plastic milk bottle to about one half of its height. Now you have a bottle with no top. Poke some holes in the bottom, for drainage.

Now cut straight down along two corners of the plastic milk bottle. This will allow one side of the bottle to fold down, like a flap, while remaining hinged at the bottom.

Leave the flap down so that you have an open side. Cover this side with a sheet of clear plastic wrap or several layers of cling film. Pull the wrap taut and tape it securely to the outside of the plastic milk bottle. Now raise the flap and slide a big rubber band around the plastic milk bottle to hold the flap in place.

Fill the plastic milk bottle about three-quarters full of soil. Now take some of the bean seeds and put them in the soil, next to the see-through side. Cover these seeds with just a little more soil (about two centimetres).

Put the plastic milk bottle on a plate and sprinkle in just enough water to make the soil moist, not dripping wet. Put the plate and plastic milk bottle in a warm place. Check the soil daily and add water as necessary to keep the soil moist. Every day, remove the rubber band and let down the flap. This will let you look through the window of clear plastic wrap and see how your seeds are growing 'underground'! Pretty soon you should see roots poking down, and sprouts growing up through the soil.

What Plants Need to Grow

What's the difference between a plant and a person like you? Well, both you and a plant start out small and then keep on growing. But you can walk around. Most plants stay put. As a plant grows, its roots sink deep down into the soil and hold on tight. A plant may sway in the wind, but it stays rooted, growing in one place for all its life. Another big difference between you and a plant is how you eat your breakfast, lunch and dinner. Have you ever seen a plant eat breakfast? Plants don't sit down for a meal, but they do need food. In fact, plants make their own food.

To make their food, plants need air, light and water and also minerals from the soil. The plant's leaves take in air and sunlight. The plant soaks up water and minerals through its roots. (These minerals are dissolved in the water, the way you can dissolve sugar in a cup of water.) The plant uses the air, light, water and minerals to make its own food. Don't you wish you could do that when you're hungry?

You can grow a plant in a pot of soil if you give it enough water, air and light. What do you think would happen to a plant if it doesn't get enough water or light? Let's find out.

Activity 2: What Do Plants Need? An Experiment

PARENTS: Here is a simple experiment you can do with your child to show what a plant needs to live. Have your child do as much as you and she are comfortable with.

Get Ready:

You will need:

3 paper cups

a sharpened pencil

potting soil

9 bean seeds (not beans to cook and eat from the supermarket but the kind that come in a sealed package for growing)

a baking tray

Go: Tell your child that you're going to do an experiment together that will take several days. In this experiment, you're going to plant some seeds and see what they need to grow.

Poke a tiny hole (you can use a sharp pencil point) in the bottom of each paper cup. Let your child fill each cup with potting soil to about two centimetres from the top. Then show her how to plant the seeds: have her use her finger to poke three holes in the soil in each cup, half a finger deep. Then put one seed in each hole and cover them all with soil. (You need only three bean plants for this experiment, but you're planting more in case some of the seeds don't germinate.)

Put the cups, once planted, on the baking tray. Water the plants sparingly, so that the soil is damp but not muddy. Take the tray to a spot near a sunny window. Help your child water the seeds (just a bit) every day until the seeds sprout and the first leaves begin to spread. If more than one plant has sprouted in a cup, then carefully pull out the other plants and leave only one plant per cup in order to proceed with the experiment.

When you have a plant growing well in each cup, write numbers on the cups: 1, 2, and 3. Now explain to your child that you're going to do something different with each of these plants.

Plant 1: Leave this plant where it is and continue to water it every day. Talk with your child so that she can see that this plant is getting everything it needs to live: water, air, light, and minerals from the soil.

Plant 2: Leave this plant where it is but do not water it anymore. Ask your child what this plant won't be getting. Help her see that it won't be getting water but that it will be getting air and light.

Plant 3: Have your child put this plant in a dark place, such as in a kitchen cupboard. Tell her to keep giving this plant a little water daily. Ask your child what this plant will not be getting. Help her see that the plant will be getting air, water and minerals but no light.

Check the plants with your child every day. As changes in the plants become noticeable, you can ask your child:

● 'What is happening to each plant?'

● 'Which plant seems to be doing best?'

● 'What does a plant need for healthy growing?'

Seeds to Eat

You've learned that a baby plant sprouts from a seed and then uses the seed for food as it grows. Did you know that you get food from seeds, too? Here are some seeds you might eat.

Corn is the seed of the corn plant that grows tall in the farmer's field. When you eat corn on the cob, you are eating rows of seeds.

Wheat is the seed of the wheat plant. Wheat seeds are so hard that if you tried to eat them, they would almost break your teeth. So we grind wheat seeds into flour to use in baking bread.

Peas are the seeds of the pea plant. Peas grow in long green pods.

Green beans are the seed pods of the bean plant. When you eat a green bean, you are eating a pod and a seed. If you pull one apart very carefully, you can see the little seeds inside.

Peanuts are the seeds of the peanut plant. Next time you eat a peanut, pull it apart very carefully. You can see the start of a tiny new peanut plant inside.

We Eat Many Plant Parts

Seeds aren't the only part of plants that we like to eat. We eat roots like onions, carrots and radishes. We eat stems like celery. We eat leaves like lettuce and cabbage. We even eat some flowers. For example, when we eat broccoli, we're eating the flower of the broccoli plant just before it blooms.

And of course, we eat the fruit of many plants. Apples, pears and oranges are fruits. For us, these fruits are food. For a plant, the fruit protect the seeds that grow inside the fruit. In the plant world, by the way, tomatoes, green peppers, and pumpkins are also fruits, even though most of us call them vegetables. They are fruits because they hold seeds inside them as they grow.

Growing Food Plants

You may think that fruits and vegetables come from the supermarket. But that's just where we go to buy them. Somebody has to grow most of the fruits we eat. Many of the fruits and vegetables at the supermarket grew on plants at farms and orchards.

The food you buy at supermarkets often comes from really big farms. There are different kinds of big farms. There are poultry farms (where they raise chickens). There are dairy farms (where they raise cattle and where your milk comes from). There are grain farms (where they grow big fields of wheat, corn, barley and other grains). There are farms that grow all kinds of fruit and vegetables like apples and pears, lettuce and broccoli.

Other farms grow important crops, but not for eating. For example, cotton comes from farms. You may be wearing something made of cotton.

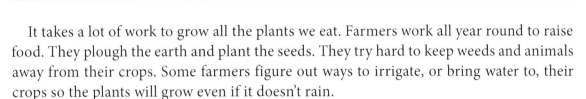

Look what plants provide us with!

Many of your favourite foods come from plants. Can you add to this list?

Chips	come from	potatoes.
Sugar	comes from	sugarcane plants.
Cereal	comes from	wheat, oats, corn and rice.
Maple syrup	comes from	maple trees.
Baked beans	come from	bean plants.
Chocolate	comes from	cocoa trees.
Bananas	come from	banana trees.

It takes a lot of work to grow all the plants we eat. Farmers work all year round to raise food. They plough the earth and plant the seeds. They try hard to keep weeds and animals away from their crops. Some farmers figure out ways to irrigate, or bring water to, their crops so the plants will grow even if it doesn't rain.

Each farm or orchard packs its vegetable or fruits into crates and boxes so lorries can carry them to supermarkets across the country. Some lorries have refrigerators inside so the food stays fresh until it reaches the supermarket. Some fruits or vegetable are cooked in factories, then canned or frozen to keep even longer.

Seasons and Weather

The Four Seasons

A year is divided into four parts, called the four seasons. Do you know the names of the seasons? They're spring, summer, autumn and winter.

What is each season like? That depends on where you live. In many places, spring is warm, and flowers bloom. Then comes a hot summer. Then comes a cool autumn, when the days get shorter. Then comes a cold winter, and maybe lots of snow.

In other places, the seasons change in other ways. Some children live in places where it never snows. In some neighbourhoods, the leaves stay green all year round.

But no matter what the weather does where you live, the year still cycles through four seasons – spring, summer, autumn, winter – over and over, every year.

What are the seasons like where you live? When you think of each season, what do you hear or see or smell? What different things do you like to do during the different seasons?

Two Kinds of Trees

In many parts of our country, the leaves on many trees and bushes turn from green to red, gold and brown, and then fall off. This happens in the season called – you guessed it – autumn.

Trees and bushes whose leaves fall in the autumn have a special name. It's a big word so hold on: deciduous [dee-SIJ-oo-us]. It's almost a tongue twister: try saying 'deciduous' four times very fast! 'Deciduous' means 'falling off'. Even though deciduous plants lose their leaves in the autumn, they grow new leaves in the spring. Maples, oaks, and apple trees are all deciduous trees.

But you may have noticed that some trees and bushes stay green all through the winter. They lose some of their leaves every year, but because they seem to stay green forever, we call this kind of plant evergreen. Pine trees and holly bushes are evergreens.

The tree in the middle of this picture is a deciduous tree. Look at all the leaves it has in the summer!

Here's a similar tree in the winter, after its leaves have fallen.

Talking about the Weather

I'm going to ask you the same question in two different ways. Here's the first way: 'What's it like outside?' Here's the second way: 'What's the weather?'

The weather is what it's like outside. Did you think about the weather today? Maybe you did, without even realising it. What kind of clothes did you wear today? The weather had a lot to do with your choice.

No matter where people live, they talk about the weather. It's something everybody shares. When it's cold outside, we shiver. When it's pouring rain, we need raincoats or umbrellas. When it's hot and humid ('humid' means the air is moist and sticky), we sweat and want a cold, icy drink.

What do we talk about when we talk about the weather?

Temperature

Is it hot or cold, cool or warm? The temperature goes up and down. When the sun comes up, it warms the air and the temperature goes up. When the sun goes down, the air gets cooler and the temperature goes down.

The temperature changes with the seasons. In many places, summer days are usually warm or hot. In most places, the temperature in summer is much higher than in the winter. Winter days are usually cool or cold.

> To tell what the temperature is, people use a thermometer. Many thermometers, like the ones in the picture here, have a coloured liquid inside a tube. As the temperature goes higher, the liquid rises in the tube. As the temperature goes lower, the liquid goes down in the tube.

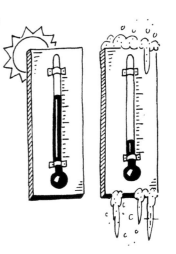

Clear or cloudy?

Look up in the sky. Is it a clear day? On a clear day, the sun shines in a bright blue sky. Or is it a cloudy day? Or a 'partly cloudy' day – which means that there are some clouds but also some blue sky?

Clouds are made of very tiny drops of water or tiny bits of ice. Clouds come in different shapes, sizes, and colours. Are there any clouds in the sky now? Are they big, white and puffy? Or are they white streaks. Or dark grey stripes? Or is the sky covered over with a blanket of grey clouds so thick that you can't see through to the sun? A thick blanket of grey clouds sometimes means that rain is coming.

The Wind

Is the air calm and still, or is the wind blowing? The wind is moving air. You can't see the wind, but you can see the way the wind moves the branches of trees or carries a kite higher and higher, or blows your hat off your head. Sometimes the wind blows gently and feels good. Sometimes the wind blows hard and brings stormy weather.

I Do Not Mind You, Winter Wind *by Jack Prelutsky*

I do not mind you, Winter Wind
When you come whirling by,
To tickle me with snowflakes
Drifting softly from the sky.

I do not even mind you
When you nibble at my skin,
Scrambling over all of me
attempting to get in.

But when you bowl me over
And I land on my behind,
Then I must tell you, Winter Wind,
I mind... I really mind!

Activity 1: The Wind Blows in Many Directions

PARENTS: This activity can help your child see which way the wind is blowing and understand that the wind blows in different directions. The activity requires some cutting and stapling. Have your child do as much as you and she are comfortable with.

Get Ready:

Tell your child that together you are going to make a weather vane that she can use to see which way the wind is blowing.

You will need:
an empty plastic carton
scissors and a stapler
a plastic straw
a pen or marker
a pin
a pencil with a rubber

Go: The weather vane will look like an arrow. Cut two small squares out of a side of the plastic carton. Staple one square to one end of the straw. Cut a triangle out of the other square, then staple the triangle to the other end of the straw.

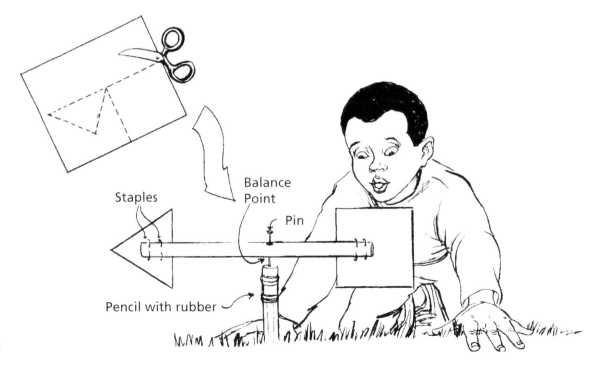

Now, hold out your index finger and put the straw across it. Move until it balances on your finger. With a pen or marker, mark this balancing point. Push a pin through the straw just at the balancing point.

Now take the straw with the pin through it and carefully push the pin into the rubber of the pencil. Push the pencil into the ground, straight up and down.

The weather vane will point in the direction the wind is blowing from. Check your weather vane everyday for a few days or more. Does the wind change directions?

Rain and Snow

Rain can pour down hard.

> # Rain
>
> *by Robert Louis Stevenson*
>
> The rain is raining all around,
> It falls on field and tree,
> It rains on the umbrellas here,
> And on the ships at sea.

Rain

Rain falls from clouds and soaks into the earth, filling up the lakes and streams and helping the plants grow. Sometimes you may not welcome the rain: you know the poem, 'Rain, rain go away, come again another day'. But without enough rain, the ground becomes dry and hard. When that happens then the roots of plants cannot soak up enough water and the plants can die.

Rain can fall in fine, tickly droplets, called mist or drizzle. It can come down in a short, friendly shower. Or it can pour down hard. Have you heard the funny expression people sometimes use to describe a really heavy rain? They say, 'It's raining cats and dogs!'

Have you ever seen a rainbow?

If it rains too much for a long time, then that can cause a flood.

If you're lucky, then sometimes, when it's raining, or just after rain, you'll see a rainbow. Rainbows look like magic, but they appear naturally, when sunlight shines through raindrops in the sky. Have you ever held a prism up to sunlight and seen how it breaks the light coming through it into bands of colour? Raindrops do the same thing to sunlight – they break it into bands of colour – and that's why you see a rainbow.

Snow

In winter, if the temperature drops low enough, then instead of rain we get snow. When just a little snow falls, we call it a snow flurry. If a big snowstorm dumps lots and lots of snow, we call it a blizzard.

When snowflakes fall, they may look like little bits of white, all of them the same.

But did you know that every snowflake is different? Each snowflake is its own beautiful design of tiny icy crystals.

It's snowing!

Almost every snowflake is different, but they're all six-sided. Can you count the sides?

Activity 2: Make a Snowflake

PARENTS: Children like the lovely snowflake designs they can cut out of folded paper. The folding is a bit complicated, and some cutting is required.

Get Ready:

You will need:
white paper
scissors

Go: Tell your child that, though almost every snowflake has a different design, all snowflakes have six sides, and that you're going to cut some six-sided snowflake designs out of white paper. Proceed as follows:

1. Begin with a square sheet of paper.

2. Fold your square in half diagonally.

3. Fold your triangle in half – again diagonally.

4. Fold your paper in thirds – this is tricky, so follow the diagrams carefully.

5. Trim the extra pieces of paper off the end of your small triangle.

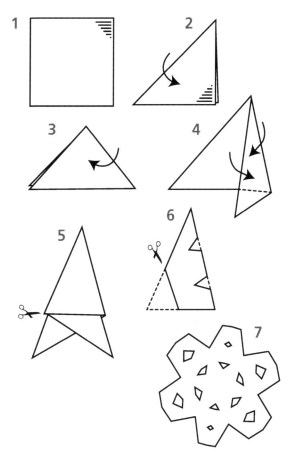

6. Now, each time you clip through your folded piece of paper, you are making six cuts. Snip here, snip there.

7. Open it up – you've got a six-sided snowflake.

Storms

On any day, the weather can change quickly. You might be playing outside on a sunny day and then suddenly a storm will blow in.

What's the sound of a thunderstorm? Rumble! Boom! Snap! Crack! Boom again! You hear the thunder roaring. You see the bright, jagged streaks of lightning in the sky. Thunder and lightning might scare you, but they're part of nature during a thunderstorm.

You don't have to be scared of lightning if you follow some simple rules. If you're outside when you hear thunder and see lightning, go inside quickly. Never stand under a tree during a lightning storm. Never stay in a swimming pool or lake during a lightning storm. Find your way to a dry shelter and wait for the storm to pass by. Lightning storms usually don't last long.

During a thunderstorm, rain can fall fiercely. Sometimes the rain can even freeze before it comes down. Then it becomes hail – balls of ice that can be as small as peas or as big as golf balls!

Bolts of lightning light up the sky.

Animals and Their Needs

What's your favourite animal?

Is it a wild animal, like an owl or a bunny?

Is it an animal at the zoo, like a monkey or a hippopotamus?

Is it an animal on the farm, like a cow or a horse or a goat or a chicken?

Or maybe your favourite animal is one that lives at home – a pet dog or a cat, a goldfish or a hamster.

We share the world with many different animals. Some are wild like lions, wolves and bears. Can you name some wild animals that live near you? Have you seen squirrels in the park or the woods? Have you seen the robins or blackbirds in the trees?

This is a badger.
Is he wild or tame?

Some animals are tame, like pet dogs and cats. Whether animals are wild or tame, they need certain things to live. Do you remember that plants can make their own food (from water, minerals, air and sunshine)? But animals can't do that. Some animals, like rabbits, eat plants. Some animals, like lions, eat meat.

Animals also need safe homes. Wild animals find or make their own homes. Some rabbits make their homes in holes in the ground. Bald eagles build their nests way up high, on mountain ridges or in the tops of tall trees.

PARENTS: Wherever you live, you can find evidence of animal life all around you. Go on an Animal Search with your child. Look for different animals and the evidence of animal life: birds, feathers, caterpillars and other bugs, webs, footprints, even droppings!

Taking Care of Pets

Wild animals can take care of themselves. But pets need special care. You can learn a lot about animals by taking care of a pet. Owning a pet is almost like being a parent. Think about what your pet needs. You provide food and water and a safe home. You teach your pet and you love your pet. If you do all these things well, you'll have a healthy pet.

Some people like dogs best. They give them food and water and a place to sleep. Dogs love to take walks. Some dogs can learn tricks like fetching a ball, rolling over or catching a frisbee in midair!

These children are taking care of their hamster

Some people like cats best. They give them food and water and a place to sleep. Cats curl up on the sofa or at the foot of the bed. When cats feel content, they purr. When they're frightened, they arch their backs, their hair stands on end, and their tails puff out like a big brush!

Some people like birds best. They give them food and water and a clean, dry cage. Some birds sing. Some birds even 'talk'. People teach parrots to say funny things like 'Hello, Sugar!' and 'What's up, Doc?'.

Some people like to keep more unusual animals as pets, like tropical fish, snakes, iguanas, ferrets or monkeys. No matter what kind of pet a person chooses, the animals will always need food, water, a safe home and loving care.

Animals Care for Their Babies

Have you ever held a kitten? It's so tiny, it fits inside your hands. It's soft and furry, just like its mother. It has two eyes, four paws and one tail, just like its mother.

How is a kitten different from its mother? Well, it's smaller. It may have the same colour and markings as its mother, or it may have very different colour and markings. An orange-striped mother cat could have a kitten with grey stripes or black and white spots. Or she could have orange-striped kittens. Even though the kittens may not have the same colour or markings as their mother, the kittens are definitely cats! Can a mother cat have a puppy? No way!

If you've ever seen a mother cat with kittens, you know how much attention she pays to her babies. She washes them by licking them clean (imagine if you took your bath that way!). She plays with them. She makes sure they get enough food, by letting them drink her milk. She even teaches them how to hunt when they get bigger.

Many animal parents take special care of their babies. Mother robins bring insects and worms back to the nest, and then they help their babies learn to fly. Mother whales help their babies learn to swim down deep and come up for air above the water. Baby animals need these special lessons because one day they will have to take care of themselves.

Just like baby animals, human babies also need special care and attention from their parents.

Think of all the ways adults help a newborn baby. Babies can't feed themselves. Babies need adults to help them learn how to walk and talk. Sometimes you still need help from adults, right? But you're not a baby any longer and there's a lot you can do for yourself.

This mother bird is feeding her babies a caterpillar. Yum!

The Human Body

Your Five Senses

Look up. Look down. What part of your body do you use? Your eyes.

Listen very carefully. What part of your body do you use? Your ears.

Sniff. What do you smell? What part of your body do you use? Your nose.

Lick your lips. Can you taste anything? What part of your body do you use? Your tongue.

Rub the top of your head. Use your fingertips to feel your hair.

Your body can sense, using your five senses:

sight   hearing   smell   taste   touch

You can see with your eyes. With your eyes you can see how big things are, and what colours things are. Did you know that some animals can't see colours? Cats, for example, can't see colours. But their eyes can see better in the dark than your eyes can.

You hear with your ears. You hear pleasant sounds, like a bird singing or someone reading to you. You hear loud sounds, like the siren of a fire engine. You hear quiet sounds, like a whisper. You can hear a lot, though some animals can hear more than you: a dog, for example, can hear a special whistle that puts out a very high-pitched squealing sound that you may not be able to hear. Some animals can't hear at all: you may hear a bee buzz, but the bees never hear their own buzzing, because they don't hear anything.

You smell with your nose. Smells can be pleasant, like the scent of a rose or the aroma of bread baking in the oven. What smells good to you? Smells can be unpleasant, like the smoke from a car's exhaust or the odour of a rotten piece of fruit. What smells bad to you? You can smell a lot, but dogs can smell even more. Have you noticed how dogs like to sniff, sniff, sniff, around almost everything? Have you ever heard of dogs who can help find people who've become lost in the woods or the snow? The dogs do this by using their sense of smell.

Your sense of smell also helps you taste things. Have you noticed that it's hard to taste things when you have a bad cold? Why do you think that happens? What's your nose like when you have a bad cold?

You taste with your tongue. Look in a mirror and stick out your tongue. See how it's covered with little bumps? Those little bumps have tiny parts that tell you what things taste like. They tell you whether things are sweet, like ice cream; sour, like a lemon; salty, like crisps or bitter, like some medicine you might have to take when you're sick.

You touch things and feel them. What do you feel if you pick up an ice cube? If you pet a cat or dog? If you rub a piece of sandpaper? If you step barefoot on the grass? You feel by touching with your hands, and with the skin all over the rest of your body.

Taking Care of Your Body

Okay, get ready to use your body. Ready? Then...

Put your arms over your head and reach way up to the sky. Stretch!

Jump up and down!

Bend at your waist and touch your toes.

Curl up in a little tiny ball.

Lie down and be absolutely still. Close your eyes. Shh! Don't move!

Your body can do so many things. It can bend and jump and run and sleep. It can see and hear and smell and taste and touch. It can talk and sing. It can draw and paint.

It's important to take good care of your body. Your body needs special care. You need to keep clean by washing your hands before eating and after going to the bathroom, by taking baths regularly and by brushing your teeth. You need to help your body grow stronger by eating good foods, by getting plenty of exercise, and by getting a good sleep every night.

Taking Care of the Earth

The Forests and the Trees

Imagine that you're climbing a high tower. When you reach the top, you look out over a great forest. You see trees stretching for miles, like a big blanket of green – so many trees that it might seem as though we could never run out of them.

Think about the forest and the trees. Why are they important? If you were an animal in the forest – a fox, a badger, an owl or a deer – the forest would be important to you because it's your home!

Many people like to hike through forests and camp out in the woods, where the air is fresh and clean. Those are some reasons why forests are important: because they are homes for many animals; because people enjoy hiking and camping in the woods and because the trees help keep the air we breathe fresh and clean.

But people cut down trees. Think how many ways we use the wood from trees. We burn wood in fireplaces. We use wood to build houses. We use it to build furniture: chairs, tables, sideboards and more. Paper comes from wood. Twenty million people read a Sunday newspaper in Britain, and all those papers started life as trees. Think of all the other paper we use: paper towels, cardboard, the paper you use for writing and drawing and the paper that makes up the pages of this book.

These toys are made of wood

So, trees are important to us when we cut them down and use them to make things we need: houses, furniture, paper and more. But trees are also important to us when they're standing tall in the forests. We have to be very careful not to cut down too many trees. And we should grow new trees to take the place of the ones we've cut down. Some logging companies – companies that cut down trees – are careful to plant new trees after they have cut down the old ones.

Conservation: Saving and Protecting the Earth

It's not just trees that we have to be careful about. We have to be careful about how we use other riches of the earth, too.

For example, the earth has only so much fresh water for us to drink and use. So it's important not to waste water. You can help save water if you don't let the water run in the sink when you're not using it, and if you turn off the tap firmly whenever you're finished.

When you don't let the tap run and you make sure to turn it firmly, you're helping to conserve water. To 'conserve' means to use something carefully. It means to save and not to waste. There's an old saying that people use: 'Waste not, want not.'

That means, if we're careful not to waste what nature gives us, then we will have enough of what we need. But if we waste what nature gives us, then someday we may want something – like trees or fresh water – but be unable to find it.

It's Smart to Recycle

One good way to waste less is to recycle. Recycling means using things over and over instead of throwing them away. Lots of families already recycle clothing: when one child grows up and gets too big for a shirt or a pair of trousers, then the clothes are passed on to a smaller child – maybe a

You can recycle, too

brother or sister, cousin or neighbour – to be worn again.

By reusing things instead of throwing them away, we help conserve what the earth has given us. 'Waste not, want not!'

Many cities and towns have recycling centres to collect materials that can be used over and over. You can recycle, too.

Is there a recycling centre in your town or city? Do you know where it is? Here are some things that you shouldn't throw away: instead, take them to a recycling centre.

Paper

Factories can recycle newspapers and lots of other kinds of paper with writing on it. They grind it up and make it into new paper. You can recycle paper, too. How? You can take a piece of paper that you or someone else has already used, turn it over, and draw or write on the back.

Cans

Factories can recycle most metal cans. They clean them and melt them and use them to make new cans. Recycling centres will ask you to separate two different kinds of cans. One kind is made of aluminium, like the cans that fizzy drinks come in. The other cans are often called tin cans: these can hold fruits and vegetables, dog food and cat food, beans and spaghetti with sauce and lots more.

Glass

Factories recycle glass jars and bottles. They wash them, then grind them up and use them to make new glass. If you want to save your glass jars and bottles to recycle, you should separate them into colours: clear glass, green glass, brown glass. Most recycling centres have different bins for the different colours.

Plastics

Factories recycle plastic, like milk bottles and fizzy-drink bottles. They melt the plastic and reshape it into other things, like chairs and picnic tables. You can recycle plastic bottles at home or at school. You can use them for all kinds of things: as paint jars, as pots to grow plants in, even as musical instruments.

Keep Our Earth Clean

It's hard to live without making a mess. When you paint a picture, you make a mess. When you cook dinner, you make a mess. When people work in factories, making cars or clothes or televisions, they make a mess too. But we all have to learn to clean up our messes.

People who work in factories today are studying the problem. They are trying to figure out how to make the things we need without making messes. They are trying to keep dangerous chemicals from going into the streams and polluting the water.

We can help, too. There's a place to put our rubbish. Not on the floor. Not on the pavement. Not in the street. Not in the woods.

You know where rubbish belongs, right? Rubbish goes in the rubbish bin. People who throw rubbish wherever they want are littering. Don't litter: that's one way to help clean up the earth.

> Here are three things you can do to help conserve.
> Can you add to this list?
> 1. **Turn off water taps firmly.**
> 2. **Recycle paper, metal cans, glass and plastic.**
> 3. **Turn off the lights when you don't need them.**

An Invisible Force: Magnetism

PARENTS: We recommend that you obtain a simple magnet and some paper clips to use with your child as you read this section. (But keep magnets away from computers.)

This is a paper clip. It's made of metal. Can you pick it up without touching it? Don't use tweezers or pliers – you're not allowed to touch it with anything. So, can you pick it up?

Yes! How? With a magnet. If you hold a magnet close to the paper clip—which is made of metal—the clip will come flying up to the magnet.

Now, if you pull the paper clip off your magnet, what do you feel? You feel the magnet pull back. Hold your magnet close to a fridge door: can you feel the pull? Let the magnet touch the fridge and it won't fall. It sticks to the door. Put a pencil or shoe up against the fridge, and what happens? It just drops to the ground. But the magnet sticks.

It seems almost like magic, but it's not: it's magnetism that pulls the paper clip to the magnet and makes the magnet stick to the fridge door.

We cannot see magnetism, but we can see what magnetism does. We can see the magnetic force attract a paper clip. We can see how a magnet holds a note or picture on the fridge door. In some cabinets you can see how little magnets keep the cabinet doors closed. And if you were to visit a scrapyard, you could see how huge magnets pick up things as big as a whole car.

Activity 1: Can Magnetic Force Pass Through an Object?

PARENTS: Here is an experiment you can do with your child to find out whether the invisible force of magnetism can pass through another object.

Get Ready:

You will need:
a piece of paper
a paper clip
a magnet
a piece of sugar paper
a book

Go: Have your child start with the plain piece of paper. Show him how to hold it flat in front of him, with one hand. Put the paper clip on top. Now have your child put the magnet under the piece of paper. Tell him to move the magnet under the paper clip and to keep moving the magnet while he watches the paper clip move. Talk with your child about what's happening. The magnetic force is passing right through the piece of paper. See if it will pass though thicker objects. Try the same experiment with a piece of sugar paper and with a book.

Hold the paper thumb-up like this

Activity 2: What Do Magnets Attract?

A magnet is made of metal. It feels cold and hard, like a doorknob or a spoon. A doorknob and spoon are also made of metal, but they're not magnets. Only magnets have that special magnetic attraction. Let's do an experiment.

PARENTS: Tell your child that she's the scientist and she can do an experiment to figure out what materials magnets will attract.

Get Ready:

You will need:
a crayon or marker
2 boxes
a magnet
a variety of objects and materials, such
as: a sheet of paper, a piece of wood,
a safety pin, a plastic toy, a key chain,
an apple, a ruler, a staple, a pencil, an aluminium
drinks can, a penny, a drawing pin, a small rubber ball, a nail, a feather

Go: Use your crayon or marker to label the two boxes. On one write 'Yes' – this means, 'Yes, a magnet attracts these materials.' On the other write 'No' – this means, 'No, a magnet does not attract these materials.'

Now have your child hold the magnet close to a variety of materials. Does it attract? Does she feel a pull? As she tries each material, have her put it in the appropriate box. (Be careful with sharp objects, like the drawing pin and staple.)

You can also have your child try the magnet on some objects too large to put in one of the boxes. Does the magnet attract a car door? A tree trunk? A tabletop?

So, what has your scientific experiment shown? Do magnets attract paper, wood or plastic?

No. But magnets do attract safety pins, drawing pins, staples, nails, paper clips, the car door and the fridge door. What are all these different things made of? They're made of metal. So, magnets attract things made of metal.

But not everything made of metal. Some metals are not attracted by magnets. If you try to make your magnet stick to a drinks can, it won't. Drinks cans are made of a metal called aluminium. Try to pick up a penny with a magnet: it won't work. Pennies are made of a metal called copper. Magnets attract some metals, but not aluminium and copper.

The most common metal that magnets do attract is called iron. All the things your magnet picked up before – the paper clip, safety pin, nail, and other things – they all have some iron in them.

Sometimes people say that a person has a 'magnetic personality'. Can you figure out what that means?

Stories about Scientists

Joseph Banks

Joseph Banks was born in 1743. He was a particular type of scientist known as a 'botanist', one who studies plants.

Joseph Banks's love of plants began at school and he always dreamed of travelling the world in search of new and different types of plants that no one had ever seen before. Banks was particularly interested in plants that could be used for practical purposes. Did you know that plants are not only used as food but can also be used in medicines and to make clothes?

It was not very easy to travel around in those days, however. Transport was very limited and it took a very long time to get anywhere – there were no aeroplanes and not

Joseph Banks

even any cars! Most people never left the town in which they were born.

But, after he finished his studies at Oxford University, the opportunity arose for Banks to travel with one of the most famous explorers of the day, Captain James Cook.

So in 1766, they set off in a great sailing ship, not knowing if they were ever to return. The three-year journey had already taken the adventurers to Madeira, Rio de Janeiro and New Zealand, where many new and exciting plants had been collected before the ship even reached the yet unexplored land of Australia.

Banks collected an enormous number of plants on the way. He discovered many new types. In New Zealand he saw that the local people used a particular type of plant called 'flax' to make their clothes, so he brought some back to England and it is now

This picture of flax was painted in New Zealand when Joseph Banks was sailing with Captain Cook.

commonly found in people's gardens. Why don't you have a look outside to see if you can find some?

In Australia, Banks collected over 1,000 different types of plants, in what must have been a thrilling 70 days – with new discoveries being made at every turn. Much of what he found had never been heard of before.

On his return to England, he became president of the Royal Society. The Royal Society is a group of the world's most important and famous scientists and is the oldest scientific academy still in existence. So this was indeed a very great honour.

By this time, Joseph Banks was held in such high regard that he even advised the King of England on which plants would be best for the new gardens the King was creating at Kew. You can still visit Kew Gardens in London today and see different types of plants from all over the world.

The plants Banks discovered, like the one in the picture, can still be seen in the Natural History Museum in London.

Jane Goodall

Did you ever try to sit very, very still and watch an animal? Maybe you looked out the window and saw a bluejay at a bird feeder, or you watched a mother dog lick her puppies clean. Or maybe you sat very quietly and looked at a fly as it landed on your arm. You can learn a lot about animals by watching closely, especially if you take care not to scare them.

When she was a little girl, Jane Goodall loved watching animals. She crouched in a hen house quietly for hours, hoping to see how a chicken lays eggs. She brought earthworms into her bed to see how they move. When she read *The Story of Dr. Dolittle* about an imaginary doctor who goes to Africa and learns to talk with the animals, she decided, 'That's what I want to do!'

When she grew up, Jane Goodall went to Africa. She was especially interested in the apes and chimpanzees. Since their bodies are so much like human bodies, she thought that we could learn a lot from the chimpanzees.

Goodall went to the African country of Tanzania (tan-zuh-NEE-uh). She lived in a part of the country where hunters were not allowed and where a group of a hundred chimpanzees lived. She was very patient. Every morning at five-thirty, she would climb a hill and look through her binoculars, trying to see how the chimpanzees lived. For months the chimpanzees were scared of her, but they slowly came to trust her.

After a year, the chimps let Jane Goodall come close to them, but not close enough to touch. After two years they knew her well enough that they would eat the bananas she put out for them near her house.

The more the chimpanzees trusted Jane Goodall, the more she saw how they really lived. She learned a lot about chimpanzees that people didn't know before.

She saw chimpanzees holding hands, hugging, and kissing. She saw them fighting. She learned the sounds and the facial expressions they used to communicate with one another.

Roots & Shoots is the Jane Goodall Institute's international environmental and humanitarian programme for youth of all ages. If you would like to know more about them and the work that they do, go to www.rootsandshoots.org

Perhaps most important of all, she saw chimpanzees making tools. For example, chimpanzees know how to make tools to catch red termites, which they love to eat.

They break off long, thin twigs or pieces of grass and poke them down into the holes where the termites live. The termites climb on, then the chimpanzees pull the twigs or grass out of the holes and lick off the termites. The chimps had invented something like a fishing pole for termites! Before Jane Goodall saw this, no one believed that chimpanzees made tools.

Jane Goodall has now spent almost forty years living in Africa and watching the chimpanzees. She recognizes the chimps, and even calls many by name, like David, Greybeard, Goliath and Honey Bee!

Wilbur and Orville Wright

Nowadays, thousands of aeroplanes and jets fly across the country and around the world every day. But it wasn't very long ago that people thought that human beings would never fly. They thought that flying was something that birds, bats, and some insects could do – but people? No, they said, that won't happen. But it has happened; and it took two brothers, Wilbur and Orville Wright, to prove that human beings could build a machine to fly.

When they were young, Wilbur and Orville Wright were known by their friends as boys who could build and fix things. Together they opened a bicycle shop. They built, sold and rented bicycles. In the 1890s, many people wanted one of those new two-wheeled travelling machines.

At night the Wright brothers used their brains and tools to study the possibilities of flying. They heard about a German engineer who had built a glider. A glider is a plane with no engine; it's carried by the wind, like a kite. Even when the Wright brothers heard the sad news that the German engineer had been killed when his glider crashed, they kept on trying to find a way to fly.

They built their own glider. It had two big wings, one on top and one on the bottom, and a place for a person to lie down in the middle. They found a special place to test it, on the windy sand dunes near the Atlantic Ocean at Kitty Hawk, North Carolina.

That first glider flew low to the ground, but then it crashed. Wilbur was discouraged: 'Man will not fly in a thousand years,' he said. But he was wrong. He and his brother kept working and kept coming up with new ideas. Soon they had built another plane, but not a glider: this plane had an engine, to turn the propellers.

On December 17, 1903, the Wright brothers stood on the Kitty Hawk sand dunes and tossed a coin to see which one of them would fly their new plane first. Orville won.

Wilbur helped him climb into Flyer I, as they had named their new machine. The engine started. The plane rolled along the dune. Then it lifted into the air! Orville flew Flyer I a total of 120 feet, staying in the air 12 seconds.

That doesn't sound like a very long flight to us today, but to the Wright brothers, 12 seconds meant success! They flew Flyer I three more times that day, and on the fourth flight the plane stayed in the air 59 seconds – almost a minute – and flew 852 feet – almost the length of three football fields. The Wright brothers had proved it: human beings could fly in a flying machine!

The Wright brothers making their first powered flight

Only five other people saw them fly that December day at Kitty Hawk. Only a few newspapers even wrote about it. No one seemed to understand how important the aeroplane would be. But the Wright brothers kept on flying. They built new airplanes and flew them for audiences in France and the United States. Once Orville flew circles around the Statue of Liberty.

In five years of practice flying, they had only one accident, but it was a bad one. Orville was hurt, and a friend flying with him died. It reminded the Wright brothers how dangerous flying could be, but it didn't stop them from continuing to build and fly aeroplanes. By 1908 they were famous around the world for their flying machine.

Illustration and Photo Credits

From The Bridgeman Art Library

The Battersea Shield, c.350-50 BC (bronze with red glass). British Museum, London, UK/ The Bridgeman Art Library: **140 (a)**

Pieter Bruegel the Elder, (c.1525-69) *Hunters in the Snow* – January, 1565. Kunsthistorisches Museum, Vienna, Austria/ The Bridgeman Art Library: **158 (b)**

Edgar Degas, (1834-1917) *Little Dancer*, Aged 14 (polychrome bronze, muslin, satin and wood). Private Collection/ Photo © Christie's Images/ The Bridgeman Art Library: **167 (b)**

William Hogarth, (1697-1764) *The Graham Children*, 1742 (oil on canvas). National Gallery, London, UK/ The Bridgeman Art Library: **162**

Peter Jackson, (1922-2003), *The Wonderful Story of Britain: The Barons' War*, Private Collection/ © Look and Learn/ The Bridgeman Art Library: **143**

Charles Jervas, (1675-1739) *Portrait of Sir Robert Walpole* (1676-1745) (oil on canvas). Private Collection/ The Bridgeman Art Library: **147 (a)**

Henry Spencer Moore, (1898-1986) *Sketch Model for a Family Group*, 1944 (bronze), Fitzwilliam Museum, University of Cambridge, UK/ © Henry Moore Foundation/ The Bridgeman Art Library. Reproduced by permission of the Henry Moore Foundation: **166**

Rock painting of a bull and horses, c.17000 BC (cave painting), by Prehistoric Caves of Lascaux, Dordogne, France/ The Bridgeman Art Library: **138, 154 (b)**

Sir Joshua Reynolds (1723-92), *Portrait of Sir Joseph Banks* (1743-1820), 1771-72 (oil on canvas). Private Collection/ Photo © Agnew's, London, UK/ The Bridgeman Art Library: **272**

Henri J.F. Rousseau, (Le Douanier) (1844-1910) *Tiger in a Tropical Storm (Surprised!)* 1891 (oil on canvas). National Gallery, London, UK/ The Bridgeman Art Library: **157 (b)**

John Singer Sargent, (1856-1925) *Carnation, Lily, Lily, Rose.* Private Collection/ The Bridgeman Art Library: **163**

Jacopo Robusti Tintoretto, (1518-94), *St. George and the Dragon* (oil on canvas) National Gallery, London, UK/ The Bridgeman Art Library: **164**

Paolo Uccello, (1397-1475) *St. George and the Dragon*, c.1470 (oil on canvas). National Gallery, London, UK/ The Bridgeman Art Library: **165**

Presentation of the Bill of Rights to William III (1650-1702) of Orange and Mary II (1662-94) (engraving) (b/w photo). British Museum, London, UK/ The Bridgeman Art Library: **146**

Vincent van Gogh, (1853-90), *Sunflowers*, 1888 (oil on canvas), National Gallery, London, UK/ The Bridgeman Art Library: **156 (a)**

The Wright Brothers making their first powered flight, 17th December, 1903 (b/w photo). Private Collection/ Peter Newark American Pictures/ The Bridgeman Art Library: **276**

From other sources:

Pierre Bonnard (1867-1947), *Le Déjeuner* (The Luncheon), Oil on canvas, National Gallery of Ireland Collection. © ADAGP, Paris and DACS, London 2011 Photo. © National Gallery of Ireland: **161**

Quentin Blake from 'Boat' by Michael Rosen from *Mustard, Custard, Grumble Belly and Gravy*, illustrated by Quentin Blake text copyright © Michael Rosen 2006, image copyright © Quentin Blake, 2006 reprinted with permission from Bloomsbury Publishing Plc.: **28, 29**

C.C.I: **8 (b, c)**

Laurence Cendrowicz: **91**

Charles West Cope (1811–1890) *Speaker Lenthall asserting the privileges of the House of Commons when Charles I came to arrest the five members,* 1866 (waterglass painting). (c) Palace of Westminster Collection, **144**

Paul Collicut: **141**

Chuck Fishman/The Image Bank/ Getty Images: **129 (a)**

A.S Forrest from '*Our Island Story*' by H.E. Marshall, first published 1905; republished Civitas/Galore Park 2005: **108, 140 (b), 142**

Antony Gormley, *Angel of the North*, 1998 (photo), Gateshead, Tyne and Wear, UK / © the artist. Photo: Colin Cuthbert, Newcastle. Courtesy White Cube: **170**

Julie Grant: **244 (a), 245 (a, c)**

Steve Henry: **11, 122 (b), 139 (a), 157 (a), 158 (a), 159 (b), 174 (a), 178, 180 (a, b), 181, 187 (a), 197, 199, 200, 201 (a, b), 202, 203 (b), 204, 205, 206, 207, 208, 209, 210 (a, b), 211, 212, 213 (a, b), 214 (a, b), 216, 217, 219, 220, 221, 223 (a, b), 224, 225 (a), 226, 227, 228, 229 (a, b), 230, 233, 235, 236, 237 (a, b), 238, 248, 251, 254 (b), 269 (a, b)**

Barbara Hepworth, '*Infant*' (wood) © Bowness, Hepworth Estate; image © Tate, London, 2011: **167 (a)**

David Hockney, *A Bigger Splash,* 1967, Acrylic on canvas 96 x 96 © David Hockney Collection, Tate Gallery, London. Image © Tate, London, 2011: **159 (a)**

Luke Jefford: **7, 8 (a), 259**

Bob Kirchman: **119, 120, 121 (b), 122 (a), 124 (a), 125 (a), 126, 128 (a), 130, 132 (b), 133 (b), 134.**

Bob Kirchman and Kristina Riley: **123, 135, 137**

Vaim Kozlovsky/Shutterstock, **270**

Kenneth G. Libbrecht: **258 (b)**

Richard McGuire Photo, **129**

Gail McIntosh: **24 (b), 25 (a), 30 (c), 31 (a), 38 (b), 39, 40, 42, 43, 44 (a, b), 45, 46, 47, 51, 53, 54 (a, b), 56, 57, 59, 66, 68, 71, 73, 82, 83, 84, 86, 88, 97, 102, 105, 114, 118, 154 (a), 196, 225 (b), 231, 243 (a, b), 244 (b), 245 (b), 246, 249, 250 (a), 252, 254 (a), 255 (b), 256 (b), 257 (a), 264, 265, 270 (b), 271**

Joan Miro, *Peinture* [Painting], Scottish National Gallery of Modern Art. © Succession Miro/ADAGP, Paris and DACS, London 2011: **160**

Mark Otton, **i, iii, 1, 115, 149, 171, 193, 239**

Phormium tenax, New Zealand flax © Natural History Museum, London: **273**

Photos.com: **119 (a), 121 (a), 124 (b), 125 (b, c), 127 (a, b), 128 (b), 129 (c), 131 (a, b), 132 (a), 133 (a, c), 139 (b), 155 (b), 169 (b), 175 (b), 176, 242 (a, b), 250 (b), 253 (a, b), 255 (a), 256 (a), 257 (b), 258 (a), 260, 261 (d), 262, 266 (a, b), 267**

Hedgehog by Abby, Robin and Aurora Cox 2011 © Jo Saxton: **168**

Snail Collage, Image reproduced by permission of Abby Cox, 2009 © Jo Saxton: **156 (b)**

Jo Saxton (with thanks to the children of St. Matthew's School, Westminster): **151**

John Stillwell/PA Wire: **147 (b)**

E.H. Shepard from 'Pooh Goes Visiting and Gets into a Tight Place' from *Winnie the Pooh* by A.A. Milne, Copyright © The Estate of E.H. Shepard: **93, 94**

Robert Whelan: **166 (a), 169 (a)**

Thinkstock: **263**

Text Credits and Sources

Stories

'**The Bremen Town Musicians**' adapted from *Grimm's Household Tales* by Jakob and Wilheim Grimm, translated from the German and edited by Margret Hunt, London: George Bell and Sons (1884)

'**Chicken Little**' adapted from *The Remarkable Story of Chicken Little,* Boston: Degen, Estes & Co. (1865), author unknown

'*Cinderella*' primarily adapted from the version by Charles Perrault, in *The Blue Fairy Book,* edited by A. Lang, London: Longmans (1889) and incorporating elements of the Brothers Grimm version from, Grimm's Household Tales by Jakob and Wilheim Grimm, translated from the German and edited by Margret Hunt, London: George Bell and Sons (1884)

'**Goldilocks and the Three Bears**' adapted from *Famous Animal Stories* edited by Ernest Thompson Seton, London: John Lane the Bodley Head Ltd. (1933)

'**King Arthur and the Knights of the Round Table**' adapted from *Our Island Story* by H. E. Marshall (1905) republished in 2005 by Galore Park in association with Civitas.

'**King Midas and the Golden Touch**' condensed and adapted from 'The Golden Touch', in *A Wonder-Book for Boys and Girls* by Nathaniel Hawthorne, Boston: Ticknor, Reed & Fields (1852)

'**Little Red Riding Hood**' adapted from *Grimm's Household Tales* translated from the German and edited by Margret Hunt, London: George Bell and Sons (1884)

'**Pooh Goes Visiting and Gets into a Tight Place**' from *Winnie the Pooh* by A.A. Milne, illustrated by E.H. Shepard. Text copyright © The Trustees of the Pooh Properties 1926. Published by Egmont UK Ltd. London and used with permission. Image © The Estate of E.H. Shepard

'**St. George and the Dragon**' adapted from the original story of *The Seven Champions* by Richard Johnson (1596)

'**Snow White**' adapted from *Household Stories from the Brothers Grimm* translated by Lucy Crane, London: Macmillan and Co. (1886)

'**The King with Horse's Ears**' an original retelling based on many versions of this tale, including *Legendary Fictions of the Irish Celts* by Patrick Kennedy, London: Macmillan (1866)

'**The Tiger, The Brahmin and the Jackal**' adapted from *Famous Animal Stories* edited by Ernest Thompson Seton, London: John Lane the Bodley Head Ltd. (1933)

'**The Three Billy Goats Gruff**' adapted from *Popular Tales from the Norse* by Peter Asbjorsen translated by Sir George Webbe Dasent, Edinburgh: David Douglas (1903)

'**The Three Little Pigs**' condensed and adapted from 'The Story of the Three Little Pigs' in *English Fairy Tales*, retold by Joseph Jacobs, London: David Nutt (1892)

Tug-of-War: an original retelling based on many versions of this tale

The Ugly Duckling: adapted from the original story by Hans Christian Andersen and translated Alfred Wehnert, London: Bell and Daldy (1866)

The Velveteen Rabbit by Margery Williams. First published in Great Britain in 1922. Published by Egmont UK Ltd. London and used with permission

The Wolf and the Seven Little Kids: adapted from *Grimm's Household Tales* by Jakob and Wilhelm Grimm, translated from the German and edited by Margret Hunt, London: George Bell and Sons (1884)

Poetry

'**I Do Not Mind You Winter Wind**' from *It's Snowing! It's Snowing!* by Jack Prelutsky © 1984 by Jack Prelutsky. Used with permission of HarperCollins Children's Division.

'**The More It Snows**' from *The House at Pooh Corner* by A.A. Milne. Text copyright © The Trustees of the Pooh Properties 1926. Published by Egmont UK Ltd. London and used with permission. Image © The Estate of E.H. Shepard

'**Boat**' by Michael Rosen from *Mustard, Custard, Grumble Belly and Gravy,* illustrated by Quentin Blake. Text copyright © Michael Rosen 2006, image copyright © Quentin Blake, 2006 reprinted with permission from Bloomsbury Publishing Plc.

While every care has been taken to trace and acknowledge copyright, the editors tender their apologies for any accidental infringement where copyright has proved untraceable. They would be pleased to insert the appropriate acknowledgement in any subsequent edition of this publication.

Index